Escape into War?

German Historical Perspectives Series
General Editors:
Gerhard A. Ritter, Werner Pöls, Anthony J. Nicholls

Volume I
Population, Labour and Migration in 19th- and 20th-Century Germany
Edited by Klaus J. Bade

Volume II
Wealth and Taxation in Central Europe: The History and Sociology of Public Finance
Edited by Peter-Christian Witt

Volume III
Nation-Building in Central Europe
Edited by Hagen Schulze

Volume IV
Elections, Parties and Political Traditions: Social Foundations of German Parties and Party Systems
Edited by Karl Rohe

Volume V
Economic Crisis and Political Collapse: The Weimar Republic, 1924–1933
Edited by Jürgen Baron von Kruedener

German Historical Perspectives/VI

Escape into War?

The Foreign Policy of Imperial Germany

Edited by
GREGOR SCHÖLLGEN

BERG
Oxford / New York / Munich
Distributed exclusively in the US and Canada by
St Martin's Press, New York

First published in 1990 by
Berg Publishers Limited
Editorial Offices
150 Cowley Road, Oxford OX4 1JJ, UK
165 Taber Avenue, Providence R.I., 02906, USA
Westermühlstraße 26, 8000 München 5, FRG

© Gregor Schöllgen 1990

British Library Cataloguing in Publication Data

Escape into war? : the foreign policy of imperial Germany. –
    (German Historical perspectives; vol. 6).
    1. Germany. Foreign relations. Policies of government,
    history
    I. Title   II. Series
    327.43
    ISBN 0–85496–275–1

Library of Congress Cataloging-in-Publication Data

Escape into war? : the foreign policy of imperial Germany / edited by
    Gregor Schöllgen.
        p.   cm. — (German historical perspectives : 4)
    Includes bibliographical references.
    ISBN 0–85496–275–1
        1. Germany—Foreign relations—1871–1918.   I. Schöllgen, Gregor.
    II. Series.
    DD221.5.E8   1990
    327.43—dc20
                                                    90–345
                                                    CIP

Printed in Great Britain by Billing and Sons Ltd Worcester

Contents

Editorial Preface

The purpose of this series of books is to present the results of research by German historians and social scientists to readers in English-speaking countries. Each of the volumes has a particular theme which will be handled from different points of view by specialists. The series is not limited to the problems of Germany but will also involve publications dealing with the history of other countries, with the general problems of political, economic, social and intellectual history as well as international relations and studies in comparative history.

We hope the series will help to help overcome the language barrier which experience has shown obstructs the rapid appreciation of German research in English-speaking countries.

The publication of the series is closely associated with the German Visiting Fellowship at St Antony's College, Oxford, which has existed since 1965, having been originally funded by the Stiftung Volkswagenwerk, later by the British Leverhulme Foundation, by the Ministry of Education and Science in the Federal Republic of Germany, and, starting in 1990, by the Stiftverband für die Deutsche Wissenschaft with special funding from C. & A. Brenninkmeyer Deutschland. Each volume will be based on a series of seminars held in Oxford, which will have been conceived and directed by the Visiting Fellow and organised in collaboration with St Antony's College.

The editors wish to thank the Stiftverband für die Deutsche Wissenschaft for meeting the expenses of the original lecture series and for generous assistance with the publication. They hope that this enterprise will help to overcome national introspection and to further international academic discourse and cooperation.

It is with great sadness that we note the loss of our co-editor, Werner Pöls, who died in Brunswick on 21 February 1989. The series owes much to his enthusiasm and support. We hope it will serve as a memorial to his commitment to Anglo-German academic contacts.

Gerhard A. Ritter   **Werner Pöls**[†]   **Anthony J. Nicholls**

GREGOR SCHÖLLGEN

Foreword

This volume unites the lectures given at a seminar which was organised by the editor in the winter of 1988/9 and held at St Antony's College, Oxford. It includes a contribution by Andreas Hillgruber who provided his paper shortly before his death in May 1989.

The conception of this volume and its place within the framework of recent German research is developed in the editor's introductory essay.

The editor would like to express his gratitude to the authors for their excellent co-operation, to St Antony's College for its hospitality, to the Stiftverband für die Deutsche Wissenschaft for its generous support and, not least, to Anthony Nicholls.

Abbreviations

AA	Auswärtiges Amt
BA	Bundesarchiv (Koblenz)
BD	*British Documents on the Origins of the War 1889–1914*, 11 vols, London, 1926–36
DD	*Die Deutschen Dokumente zum Kriegsausbruch 1914*, 4 vols, Berlin, 1921
FO	Foreign Office
GP	*Die Große Politik der Europäischen Kabinette 1871–1914. Sammlung der Diplomatischen Akten des Auswärtigen Amtes*, 40 vols in 54, Berlin, 1922–27
GWU	*Geschichte in Wissenschaft und Unterricht*
HZ	*Historische Zeitschrift*
MGM	*Militärgeschichtliche Mitteilungen*
NA	National Archives (Washington, D.C.)
ÖU	*Österreich-Ungarns Außenpolitik von der Bosnischen Krise 1908 bis zum Kriegsausbruch 1914. Diplomatische Aktenstücke des Österreichisch-ungarischen Ministeriums des Äußeren*, 9 vols, Vienna, Leipzig, 1930
PA	Politisches Archiv (Bonn)
PRO	Public Record Office (London)
ZfG	*Zeitschrift für Geschichtswissenschaft*
ZStA	Zentrales Staatsarchiv (Potsdam)

GREGOR SCHÖLLGEN

Introduction: The Theme Reflected in Recent German Research

I

Since the first days of August 1914, the debate about the reasons for the outbreak of the First World War – that 'seminal catastrophe' of the twentieth century – has never been silenced. No other outbreak of war has preoccupied historians so persistently and intensively. No other event of modern history has been so extensively and passionately discussed by specialists and the general public alike.[1] Finally, no other international crisis has stimulated such far-reaching historical and political comparisons as that of the summer of 1914. This fact was made particularly clear in 1979–80, against the background of the conflict between China and Vietnam, the crisis in Iran, the Soviet invasion of Afghanistan and the naval operations of the two super-powers in the Indian Ocean. These circumstances led some leading statesmen – including Henry Kissinger and Helmut Schmidt – to draw sombre parallels with the situation of July 1914.[2]

Traditionally, one major issue has been at the centre of debate: what role was played by German foreign policy in the outbreak of the First World War? It has consistently attracted the interest of historians and

1. See most recently R.J.W. Evans and Hartmut Pogge von Strandmann (eds), *The Coming of the First World War*, Oxford, 1988.
2. See also *Der Spiegel*, 10 March 1980, No. 17, pp. 21 ff., which devoted its cover story to the theme: 'Wie im August 1914? Angst vor dem großen Krieg'. One impulse behind the revival of the debate was the relatively wide acceptance of the analysis by Miles Kahler, 'Rumors of War: The 1914 Analogy', *Foreign Affairs*, 58, 1979–80, pp. 374 ff.

1

a historically and politically aware public from the end of the war until the present day. This was the issue which lay behind the unequivocal attribution of guilt made by the allies in Article 231 of the Treaty of Versailles of 28 June 1919, and also behind the controversy which was first stimulated by the work of Fritz Fischer and then revived in the mid-1980s.[3]

Because of the explosive nature of the question, the foreign policy of Imperial Germany has inevitably been the subject of constant reinterpretation over the decades. Foremost amongst these new approaches was the 'powerful initiative'[4] of Fritz Fischer in the 1960s. Fischer then exerted a recognisable influence on the establishment of 'structural history' or the 'history of society', which reached its peak in the Federal Republic during the 1970s and also produced research into various aspects of German foreign policy. These aspects included the imperialism of the Bismarck era as well as the 'armaments policy' and *Weltpolitik* of the Wilhelmine period.

In this introduction, some trends in recent German research will be outlined. The main concern will be with developments in the Federal Republic, because this volume also includes a contribution from Willibald Gutsche, an acknowledged expert on historiographical developments in the GDR.[5]

II

Fischer's great contribution to the debate came in the form of two major works, published in 1961 and 1969: *Griff nach der Weltmacht. Die Kriegszielpolitik des kaiserlichen Deutschland 1914/18* and *Krieg der Illusionen. Die deutsche Politik von 1911 bis 1914*. In these, he advanced the thesis that the German government bore the 'decisive' share of

3. The latest round of this debate concerned the diaries of Bethmann Hollweg's confidante, Kurt Riezler, and the question of whether they were valuable as source material, particularly for the July crisis. See Kurt Riezler, *Tagebücher, Aufsätze, Dokumente*, ed. K.D. Erdmann, Göttingen, 1972; also Fritz Fischer, *Wir sind nicht hineingeschlittert. Das Staatsgeheimnis der Riezler-Tagebücher. Eine Streitschrift*, Reinbek, 1983; Bernd Sösemann, 'Die Tagebücher Kurt Riezlers. Untersuchungen zu ihrer Echtheit und Edition', *HZ*, 236, 1983, pp. 327 ff.; Karl Dietrich Erdmann, 'Zur Echtheit der Tagebücher Kurt Riezlers. Eine Antikritik', ibid., pp. 371 ff.; Agnes Blänsdorf, 'Der Weg der Riezler-Tagebücher. Zur Kontroverse über die Echtheit der Tagebücher Kurt Riezlers', in *GWU*, 35, 1984, pp. 651 ff.; Bernd F. Schulte, *Die Verfälschung der Riezler-Tagebücher. Ein Beitrag zur Wissenschaftsgeschichte der 50iger und 60iger Jahre*, Frankfurt a. M., Bern, New York, 1985.
4. Klaus Hildebrand, *Das Dritte Reich*, 3rd edn, Munich, 1987, p. 225.
5. See also Andreas Dorpalen, *German History in Marxist Perspective. The East German Approach*, London, 1985, esp. pp. 271 ff.

historical responsibility for the fact that the crisis of July 1914 ended in a 'general' European war.[6]

In support of this theory Fischer put forward the following arguments: Germany not only wanted the Austro-Serbian war, but actually made it possible in the first place by issuing the famous 'blank cheque', the guarantee of unconditional loyalty to Austria-Hungary, on 5–6 July. Moreover, that step also demonstrated the willingness of the German Reich in 1914 – gambling on British neutrality – consciously to accept the risk of war with Russia and France. After the experiences of 1905 (first Morocco crisis), 1908–9 (Bosnian annexation crisis) and 1911 (second Morocco crisis), the German government knew that any kind of regional war in Europe which involved a great power would make the danger of a general war draw 'unavoidably close'. Fischer claimed that after the second Morocco crisis, and especially after December 1912, the German leadership and the emperor had actually worked towards this general war. Indeed, they had also entered into it with a prepared catalogue of war aims with the ultimate goal of establishing the 'hegemony of Germany over Europe'.

This is not the place to describe in detail the academic debate which followed the publication of Fischer's thesis, which was sometimes extremely emotional and polemical.[7] Among Fischer's opponents, the argument was led initially by Gerhard Ritter, and later by Karl Dietrich Erdmann, Egmont Zechlin[8] and Andreas Hillgruber. Now that thirty years have passed,[9] it is possible to perceive three main trends and results of that debate.

(1) Firstly, there is increasing support for the view that the events of July and August 1914 do not sustain either the theory of a defensive war by Germany – as was maintained in the inter-war years and then by Gerhard Ritter during the 'Fischer controversy' – or the concept of

---

6. Fritz Fischer, *Griff nach der Weltmacht. Die Kriegszielpolitik des kaiserlichen Deutschland 1914/18*, Düsseldorf, 1961; special edn, 1967; most recently – with an explanation by the author – Kronberg/Ts., 1977; English edn, *Germany's Aims in the First World War*, London, 1967; Fritz Fischer, *Krieg der Illusionen. Die deutsche Politik von 1911 bis 1914*, Düsseldorf, 1969; 2nd edn, 1970; most recently Kronberg/Ts., 1978; English edn, *War of Illusions: German Policies from 1911 to 1914*, London, New York, 1975. See the studies in this tradition by Imanuel Geiss (ed.), *Julikrise und Kriegsausbruch 1914. Eine Dokumentation*, 2 vols, Hanover, 1963–4; *idem, German Foreign Policy, 1871–1914*, London, Boston, 1976; *idem, Das deutsche Reich und die Vorgeschichte des Ersten Weltkriegs*, Munich, Vienna, 1978.
7. In 1977, Fischer himself spoke of over 300 reviews and articles! See recently Gregor Schöllgen, 'Griff nach der Weltmacht? 25 Jahre Fischer-Kontroverse', *Historisches Jahrbuch*, 106, 1986, pp. 386 ff., see n. 33 there for further references to the literature.
8. See most recently the contributions by Karl Dietrich Erdmann and Egmont Zechlin in their *Politik und Geschichte. Europa 1914: Krieg oder Frieden*, Kiel, 1985.
9. Fritz Fischer published the first results of his research in 1959: 'Deutsche Kriegsziele, Revolutionierung und Separatfrieden im Osten', *HZ*, 188, 1959, pp. 249 ff.

a war of aggression, as was assumed by the victorious powers of the First World War and later by Fritz Fischer and his adherents. Instead, it seems possible to accept Hillgruber's summary of prevailing interpretations. According to this analysis, German policy in the July crisis involved an unsuccessful attempt to implement the 'conception of a calculated risk for the achievement of limited power political changes by exploiting situations of international crisis'.[10] The relevant contributions to this volume demonstrate, however, that Fischer and his disciples, as well as historians in the GDR, continue to accept the theory of a war of aggression.

(2) Secondly, the debate on the outbreak of the First World War has turned away from overly emotional discussions of guilt and returned to the sober analysis of events which characterised Fischer's own approach in 1959. The attention of recent researchers has therefore been devoted to the factors that shaped or predetermined the thinking of the leading figures in the crisis and thereby limited their freedom of manoeuvre from the outset.[11] Such factors included developments in the economy, in public opinion and even in culture, as well as imperialist movements and, of course, the planning of the military. As the British historian James Joll has stated: 'The individuals who took those decisions were, often to a greater extent than they realized, limited in their choice of action not only by their own nature but by a multitude of earlier decisions taken by themselves and by their predecessors in office.'[12]

(3) Finally, it is beyond doubt that Fritz Fischer's research, based on intensive study of the sources, has had a profound effect on German historical writing. Whether one accepts his main theses or not, the results of his work now form an integral part of any analysis of the foreign policy of Imperial Germany. The contributions to this volume make the extent of his achievement clear. Fischer's research has also influenced those interpretations which are concerned mainly with the wider framework of the European and world order and attempt to investigate the possibilities and limits placed on German foreign policy from outside.

10. Andreas Hillgruber, 'Riezlers Theorie des kalkulierten Risikos und Bethmann Hollwegs politische Konzeption in der Julikrise 1914' in his *Deutsche Großmacht- und Weltpolitik im 19. and 20. Jahrhundert*, Düsseldorf, 1977, pp. 91 ff., cit. p. 92.
11. See here Gregor Schöllgen, *Das Zeitalter des Imperialismus*, 2nd edn, Munich, 1990, part II, pp. 91 ff.
12. James Joll, *The Origins of the First World War*, London, New York, 1984, p. 201.

III

Other attempts to re-interpret the foreign policy of Imperial Germany never met with a comparable response to that stimulated by Fischer. This was true even of the 'structural' or 'socio-historical' approach, whose representatives based some of their thinking on the work of Fischer and of George W.F. Hallgarten. In his two-volume work *Imperialismus vor 1914*, completed in 1933 but published only after the Second World War, Hallgarten attempted to provide a 'description of the social substratum of the foreign policy of modern states before the war, and especially the foundations of German foreign policy'. It should be noted, however, that his work was intended 'to complement, not replace, political history'.[13]

Greatly influenced by Hallgarten's work, and incorporating some of the theories put forward by Fischer, a 'history of society' school became established within West German historiography at the end of the 1960s. It deviated from the approach of Hallgarten and Fischer, however, in its uncompromising insistence on the inadequacy of political history and the need to replace it with 'structural history', to use the term coined by its adherents. 'Structural' historians directed particular attention towards German policy in the Age of Imperialism.[14] In this case, too, it is impossible to give a detailed account of the subsequent debates of the 1970s. Nevertheless, some general conclusions can be drawn:

(1) Though 'structural' or 'social history' has given new and important impetus to historical research in a number of ways, it seems manifestly to have failed as a theoretical model and methodological concept. In a fundamental critique, Lothar Gall has recently assessed the evidence for this assertion and has referred to the 'banality' of the argumentation, the 'relativity' of the perspective and the 'dependence and historicity' of the approach.[15]

(2) As regards the relationship of the 'history of society' to the history of international relations, Andreas Hillgruber in particular has repeatedly pointed out that the representatives of a 'political' history

13. George W.F. Hallgarten, *Imperialismus vor 1914. Die soziologischen Grundlagen der Außenpolitik europäischer Großmächte vor dem Ersten Weltkrieg*, 2 vols, 2nd edn, Munich, 1963.
14. See esp. Hans-Ulrich Wehler, *Das Deutsche Kaiserreich 1871–1918*, 5th edn, Göttingen, 1983, esp. pp. 11 ff.; English edn, *The German Empire 1871–1918*, trans. K.M. Traynor, Leamington Spa, 1985; *idem*, 'Moderne Politikgeschichte oder "Große Politik der Kabinette"?', *Geschichte und Gesellschaft*, 1, 1975, pp. 344 ff.
15. Lothar Gall, 'Deutsche Gesellschaftsgeschichte', *HZ*, 248, 1989, pp. 365 ff., esp. pp. 371 and 174.

never made any claim to the exclusive validity of their own approach.[16] At the same time, the explicit demand for exclusivity of the 'critical' method led to a narrowing of the outlook of many German historians.

Developments in Great Britain, the USA, the Soviet Union and France thus differed from those in the Federal Republic. In the latter, historians with a particular interest in international relations and especially German foreign policy found themselves subjected to fierce attack. In such circumstances, a concern with the history of the international order (*Staatensystem*) was regarded as reprehensible or even as an apologia; the desire to follow a native tradition associated with names such as Leopold von Ranke, Ludwig Dehio, Friedrich Meinecke and Gerhard Ritter was suspect. It was this situation which the American historian Gordon A. Craig had in mind in 1983, when he commented:

> German historians . . . have for some time been arguing that traditional paradigms like the national state and the concepts of hegemony and balance are no longer satisfactory and that the great movements of modern politics must be regarded as functions of the process of modern industrialism. Works of this sort, and the varied attempts to assert a *Primat der Innenpolitik*, have been less than satisfactory.

Klaus Hildebrand has given an account of the debate of the 1970s and argued that 'the intensive preoccupation with the social and internal political conditions of external and international policy, for so long characteristic of research, has [revealed] more clearly than before precisely their high degree of autonomy'.[17]

(3) There has been another, more fundamental criticism of the structural history approach, and particularly the claim that it can adequately understand, analyse and describe every aspect of political life in Imperial Germany. It has been pointed out that no major work 'professing loyalty to "historical social science"' on 'themes of international relations or the foreign policy of the great powers' has yet gained international attention in the field of academic history.[18]

---

16. Andreas Hillgruber, 'Die Diskussion über den "Primat der Außenpolitik" und die Geschichte der internationalen Beziehungen in der westdeutschen Geschichtswissenschaft seit 1945' in his *Die Zerstörung Europas. Beiträge zur Weltkriegsepoche 1914 bis 1945*, Frankfurt a. M., Berlin, 1988, pp. 32 ff.

17. Gordon A. Craig, 'The Historian and the Study of International Relations', *American Historical Review*, 88, 1983, pp. 1 ff., cit. p. 3; Klaus Hildebrand, *Deutsche Außenpolitik 1871–1918*, Munich, 1989, p. 1.

18. Hillgruber, 'Die Diskussion', p. 39.

During the 1980s, on the other hand, there was a remarkable renaissance in the writing of political history in West Germany. One consequence has been the publication of a significant number of monographs on the foreign policy of Imperial Germany.[19] Furthermore, these works generally incorporate the results of other historical disciplines or research directions whenever these are relevant and useful from a methodological point of view.

Due attention has been paid, for example, to the knowledge made available by modern economic and social history (in the original meaning of the term). Equally, the results of the research of George W.F. Hallgarten and Fritz Fischer are also taken into account; critics and supporters alike have often overlooked the fact that these two historians both began with the study of international relations, and particularly German foreign policy before 1914. Finally, it should also be said that some results of 'structural history' research, where these can assist our understanding of the developments under investigation, have a part to play in the writing of a modern political history. Specifically, studies of the (social) imperialism of the Bismarck era and the armaments policy and *Weltpolitik* of Wilhelmine Germany have to be mentioned.

---

19. See for example Jost Dülffer, *Regeln gegen den Krieg? Die Haager Friedenskonferenzen von 1899 und 1907 in der internationalen Politik*, Frankfurt a. M., Berlin, Vienna, 1981; Ragnhild Fiebig-von Hase, *Lateinamerika als Konfliktherd der deutsch-amerikanischen Beziehungen 1890–1903. Vom Beginn der Panamerikapolitik bis zur Venezuelakrise von 1902/03*, 2 vols, Göttingen, 1986; Klaus Hildebrand, *Deutsche Außenpolitik 1871–1918*; Rainer Lahme, *Deutsche Außenpolitik 1890–1894. Von der Gleichgewichtspolitik Bismarcks zur Allianzstrategie Caprivis*, Göttingen, 1990; Ulrich Lappenküper, *Die Mission Radowitz. Untersuchungen zur Rußlandpolitik Otto von Bismarcks 1871–1875*, Göttingen, 1990; Emily Oncken, *Panthersprung nach Agadir. Die deutsche Politik während der Zweiten Marokkokrise 1911*, Düsseldorf, 1981; Reiner Pommerin, *Der Kaiser und Amerika. Die USA in der Politik der Reichsleitung 1890–1917*, Cologne, Vienna, 1986; Gregor Schöllgen, *Imperialismus und Gleichgewicht. Deutschland, England und die orientalische Frage 1871–1914*, Munich, 1984; Michael Stürmer, *Die Reichsgründung. Deutscher Nationalstaat und europäisches Gleichgewicht im Zeitalter Bismarcks*, Munich, 1984; Rolf-Harald Wippich, *Japan und die deutsche Fernostpolitik 1894–1898. Vom Ausbruch des Chinesisch-Japanischen Krieges bis zur Besetzung der Kiautschou-Bucht. Ein Beitrag zur Wilhelminischen Weltpolitik*, Wiesbaden, 1987; Wilhelm Ernst Winterhager, *Mission für den Frieden. Europäische Mächtepolitik und dänische Friedensvermittlung im Ersten Weltkrieg. Vom August 1914 bis zum italienischen Kriegseintritt Mai 1915*, Wiesbaden, Stuttgart, 1984. During the 1980s, historians from the GDR have also contributed a number of studies on the foreign policy of Imperial Germany. Though they may be controversial in interpretation, these are also valuable additions to our knowledge of the era. See for example Konrad Canis, *Bismarck und Waldersee. Die außenpolitischen Krisenerscheinungen und das Verhalten des Generalstabes 1882 bis 1890*, Berlin (GDR), 1980; Willibald Gutsche, *Monopole, Staat und Expansion vor 1914. Zum Funktionsmechanismus zwischen Industriemonopolen, Großbanken und Staatsorganen in der Außenpolitik des Deutschen Reiches 1897 bis Sommer 1914*, Berlin(GDR), 1986; Heinz Wolter, *Bismarcks Außenpolitik 1871–1881. Außenpolitische Grundlinien von der Reichsgründung bis zum Dreikaiserbündnis*, Berlin (GDR), 1983.

IV

Representatives of the theory of social imperialism, developed by Hans-Ulrich Wehler in particular, saw it as a strategy of ruling elites 'to direct the dynamic force of the economy and the social and political struggles for emancipation into external expansion, to divert attention from the internal inadequacies of the socio-economic and political system and to offset them by means of tangible successes in expansion or at least the increase of national-ideological prestige'.[20] Though the theory was originally developed as an explanatory model for imperialism in the Bismarck era, Wehler subsequently suggested its general applicability to conditions in Europe during the Age of Imperialism.[21] Furthermore, adopting but also radicalising the theories of Fischer, he attempted to define the tactics of the 'defensive with aggressive means', which in his view was perceptible initially in German imperialism, as the basic plan of German foreign policy as a whole. According to this interpretation, the outbreak of war in August 1914 was the logical consequence of a 'Flucht nach vorn' (literally, an escape forwards); it was the attempt to use the July crisis 'as the lever for a spectacular external success with beneficial repercussions at home'.[22]

For a short period, Wehler's interpretation of German foreign policy before 1914 was also the subject of an intensive debate.[23] Criticism was aroused by three main points. (Where this criticism also affects the question of whether the foreign policy of Imperial Germany can be interpreted as an escape into war, the reader is directed to the articles in this volume.)

(1) During a critical debate on the theory of social imperialism, George W.F. Hallgarten concluded in 1971 that Wehler's book on Bismarck and imperialism should be 'judged primarily as a highly interesting collection of material'.[24] As such, it still has value today, not least in the context of a modern historiography of German foreign policy in the sense mentioned above. But in response to Wehler's interpretation of the first Reich Chancellor as a 'social imperialist', the doyen of research into imperialism, using the tools of social history,

---

20. Hans-Ulrich Wehler, 'Sozialimperialismus', in Wehler (ed.), *Imperialismus*, 3rd edn, Cologne, 1976, pp. 83 ff., cit. p. 86.
21. See Hans-Ulrich Wehler, *Bismarck und der Imperialismus*, Cologne/Berlin, 1969.
22. H.-U. Wehler, *Das Deutsche Kaiserreich*, pp. 197–8.
23. See here Gustav Schmidt, *Der europäische Imperialismus*, Munich, 1985, pp. 132 ff.
24. George W.F. Hallgarten, 'War Bismarck ein Imperialist? Die Außenpolitik des Reichsgründers im Lichte der Gegenwart', *GWU*, 22, 1971, pp. 257 ff., cit. p. 264.

accused Wehler of an 'absurd representation of Reich policy'. In particular, he had not given 'proper' consideration to the 'uncommonly important economic and political developments in the east', and therefore to the European dimension and dependence of Bismarckian colonial policy.[25] Similar conclusions were reached by Thomas Nipperdey, who pointed to the autonomy of foreign-policy factors, constellations and decisions in his criticism of Wehler's work:

> All foreign policy considerations and movements were also . . . guided by 'autonomous' power relations, by compulsions inherent in the situation, even, *horribile dictu*, by an irreducible will to power. They are not reducible to internal political strategies. The basic fact of the division of the world (and the challenge for the latecomers) can . . . not . . . be explained monocausally with the model of social imperialism.[26]

(2) The criticism did not end there. In particular, Gilbert Ziebura[27] and Wolfgang J. Mommsen have referred to the 'eclecticism' of a theory which 'of its nature' combines 'completely different explanatory models in a less than precise way'. This allows it 'to place any one of these explanatory models in the foreground at the expense of the others according to the argument at issue'.[28] Instead of the promised theory of social imperialism, the reader receives only an 'agglomeration of the most varied explanatory models, thus producing a higher figure than is consistent with reality'.[29] Such criticisms have led to the rejection of the claim that the theory of social imperialism is valid not merely for the foreign policy of Imperial Germany in particular, but also as a model to explain the imperialism of other European states such as Great Britain, France or Italy.[30]

(3) Finally, much attention within this debate has been devoted to one further question: to what extent was the economy, in the form of the banks and industrial enterprises, the driving force behind German

25. Ibid., pp. 260 and 263. Consideration of these factors instead of the 'relatively less important colonial policy' would, according to Hallgarten, necessarily turn Wehler's 'picture of Bismarck almost upside down'.
26. Thomas Nipperdey, 'Wehler's "Kaiserreich". Eine kritische Auseinandersetzung', *Geschichte und Gesellschaft*, 1, 1975, pp. 539 ff., cit. p. 549.
27. See Gilbert Ziebura, 'Sozialökonomische Grundfragen des deutschen Imperialismus vor 1914', in H.-U. Wehler (ed.), *Sozialgeschichte Heute. Festschrift für Hans Rosenberg zum 70. Geburtstag*, Göttingen, 1974, pp. 495 ff., esp. pp. 501 ff.
28. Wolfgang J. Mommsen, *Imperialismustheorien. Ein Überblick über die neueren Imperialismusinterpretationen*, Göttingen, 1977, p. 79.
29. Wolfgang J. Mommsen, 'Bismarck und der Imperialismus. Zu Hans-Ulrich Wehlers gleichnamigem Buch' in his *Der europäische Imperialismus. Aufsätze und Abhandlungen*, Göttingen, 1979, pp. 77 ff., cit. p. 83.
30. See for example the contributions by Karl Rohe, Wolfgang Schieder and Gilbert Ziebura in W.J. Mommsen (ed.), *Der moderne Imperialismus*, Stuttgart et al., 1971.

foreign policy and especially German imperialism?[31] As part of the theory of social imperialism, it was argued that the primary motive persuading the German elites to join the competition for overseas territories was the prospect of investment possibilities and markets (and thus the chance to 'regain or maintain economic prosperity' at home),[32] combined with the strategy of these same elites to safeguard the established order.

Many of these arguments have been refuted. Firstly, it has been pointed out that colonies had only a second-ranking significance for the German economy: 'Germany's colonial policy had a very narrow economic basis. Its advocates were professors, school-teachers and clergymen rather than businessmen . . .'[33] Secondly, in major undertakings and projects it was generally the politicians who drove the rather hesitant financiers to take part. Even then, the financiers were often ready to agree only if state guarantees were provided. Most strikingly, this was the case in the most important prestige project of German *Weltpolitik* before 1914, the Berlin–Baghdad railway.[34]

V

German *Weltpolitik* has in fact been the chief focus of interest for 'structural' and 'socio-historical' historians. Two of its aspects have been accorded particular attention in this context: armaments policy and the issue of whether there was a rigorous and fully developed concept underlying *Weltpolitik*.

Extending the interpretation first put forward by Eckhart Kehr in 1930,[35] Volker R. Berghahn has referred to the internal political

31. See, for example, Wolfgang Zorn, 'Wirtschaft und Politik im deutschen Imperialismus', in W. Abel et al. (eds), *Wirtschaft, Geschichte und Wirtschaftsgeschichte. Festschrift zum 65. Geburtstag von F. Lütge*, Stuttgart, 1966, pp. 340 ff.; see also Ziebura, 'Sozialökonomische Grundfragen'.

32. Wehler, *Das deutsche Kaiserreich*, p. 173.

33. Wolfram Fischer, *Germany and the World Economy during the Nineteenth Century*, London, 1984, p. 26.

34. See most recently G. Schöllgen, *Imperialismus und Gleichgewicht*. In this context, Winfried Baumgart has claimed that the attempt 'to postulate a primacy of social-economic or domestic policy in Bismarck's formal imperialism . . . for the whole of the Bismarck era of 1862–1890 and to reduce it mainly to the informal variety of foreign trade . . . [appears] grotesquely exaggerated'. See W. Baumgart, *Der Imperialismus. Idee und Wirklichkeit der englischen und französischen Kolonialexpansion 1880–1914*, Wiesbaden, 1975, p. 108.

35. Eckart Kehr, *Schlachtflottenbau und Parteipolitik 1898–1901. Versuch eines Querschnitts durch die innenpolitischen, sozialen und ideologischen Voraussetzungen des deutschen Imperialismus*, Berlin, 1930.

significance of German naval expansion, which did so much to increase tensions with Great Britain. Not least thanks to the work of Berghahn,[36] German naval expansion is now one of the best researched chapters in the history of Imperial Germany. In his studies, Berghahn described a 'naval policy understood in a social-imperialist sense', which had a relatively broad 'basis of integration'. Only on this basis could 'industrial and agrarian-conservative interests' have come together, namely against the 'fourth estate'.[37] Berghahn was thus arguing that the armaments policy and, especially, the naval policy of Imperial Germany were adopted in the first instance because they were 'necessary to the system' (*systemnotwendig*) and assisted the goal of social integration.[38] But these policies were dependent on an artificial 'foe image', that of Britain. Consequently, the international situation after 1904/07 was perceived 'by the emperor and his advisers . . . in a way which turned reality upside down'. With its programme of naval expansion, the Reich thus 'itself engendered' the 'isolation' which became manifest in the Triple Entente.[39]

Closely linked with this analysis of German armaments policy was the thesis that there was a rigorous concept underlying German foreign policy, at least during the era of Bernhard von Bülow, secretary of state for foreign affairs and later Reich Chancellor (1897–1909). In the 1970s this view was taken particularly by Volker R. Berghahn, Peter Winzen and Barbara Vogel.[40] According to it, Bülow possessed a 'world power concept' directed against Britain and even aimed at overpowering the British Empire (Winzen). Moreover, the intention was to accelerate German naval expansion through the uncertain early stages (Berghahn) and was based on the idea of a 'German hegemony in Europe' (Vogel).

Naturally, these theories have also been challenged. Though there is

36. See above all Volker R. Berghahn, *Der Tirpitz-Plan. Genesis und Verfall einer innenpolitischen Krisenstrategie unter Wilhelm II.*, Düsseldorf, 1971. Since 1985 there has also been a corresponding study of German army expansion: Stig Förster, *Der doppelte Militarismus. Die deutsche Heeresrüstungspolitik zwischen Status-Quo-Sicherung und Aggression 1890–1913*, Stuttgart, 1985.
37. Volker R. Berghahn, 'Flottenrüstung und Machtgefüge', in M. Stürmer (ed.), *Das kaiserliche Deutschland. Politik und Gesellschaft 1870–1918*, Düsseldorf, 1970; most recently Kronberg/Ts., 1977, pp. 378 ff., cit. pp. 381, 383.
38. Volker R. Berghahn, *Rüstung und Machtpolitik. Zur Anatomie des 'Kalten Krieges' vor 1914*, Düsseldorf, 1973, p. 79.
39. Ibid., pp. 84–5.
40. V. Berghahn, *Der Tirpitz-Plan*; Barbara Vogel, *Deutsche Rußlandpolitik. Das Scheitern der deutschen Weltpolitik unter Bülow 1900–1906*, Düsseldorf, 1973; Peter Winzen, 'Die Englandpolitik Friedrich von Holsteins 1895–1901', Diss., vol. II, Cologne, 1975; *idem*, *Bülows Weltmachtkonzept. Untersuchungen zur Frühphase seiner Außenpolitik 1897–1901*, Boppard, 1977.

no doubt that the discussion has been greatly enriched by the arguments and evidence assembled by Berghahn and Winzen, they have
been criticised on three main points. To some extent, the debate has
since extended beyond the original points of dispute.

(1) Andreas Hillgruber, Klaus Hildebrand and others have suggested that the 'conception' of German *Weltpolitik* around the turn of
the century may have been no more and no less than a fateful decision
to 'catch up' with the other great powers in the field of imperialist
activity, however and wherever possible. The relative lack of planning
and of an underlying conception was manifested in a 'fumbling on very
different scenes and in widely varying areas of tension'.[41] It was this
lack of planning which distinguished German *Weltpolitik* in the most
glaring way from the foreign policy of the Bismarck era. With the
departure of the first Reich Chancellor, German foreign policy lost the
element of calculability which had, for example, guaranteed something
like a 'bilateral normality' in British–German relations between 1875
and 1890.[42]

Moreover, the thinking of leading German figures of the period –
Bülow, Wilhelm II, Holstein and Tirpitz – was far from identical in all
respects. Winzen himself established that even 'Bülow's world power
concept' was 'never on record' in the form reconstructed by him.[43]
Only after the turn of the century has Hillgruber detected a 'gradual
concentration on the winning of a strong economic, military and
political influence in the Middle East, particularly in the Turkish
empire'.[44] These findings are fully compatible with the research results
of, for example, George W.F. Hallgarten and Fritz Fischer.

In this context, it has been observed that German foreign policy after
1890 was characterised by a peculiar oscillation between two extremes
of political conduct. This tendency, of course, hardly permitted the
adoption of a clear line. Even in 1948, Ludwig Dehio had pointed out
the 'simultaneously noisy and insecure conduct of Germany and the
Germans'.[45] His findings have been developed and combined with the

41. Andreas Hillgruber, *Deutschlands Rolle in der Vorgeschichte der beiden Weltkriege*, 2nd
edn, Göttingen, 1979, pp. 20–1.
42. See Klaus Hildebrand, 'Zwischen Allianz und Antagonismus. Das Problem
bilateraler Normalität in den britisch-deutschen Beziehungen des 19. Jahrhunderts
(1870–1914)' in H. Dollinger et al. (eds), *Weltpolitik, Europagedanke, Regionalismus.
Festschrift für Heinz Gollwitzer zum 65. Geburtstag* (Münster, 1982), pp. 305 ff.; Klaus
Hildebrand, 'Julikrise 1914; Das europäische Sicherheitsdilemma. Betrachtungen über
den Ausbruch des Ersten Weltkrieges', *GWU*, 36, 1985, pp. 469 ff.; G. Schöllgen,
Imperialismus und Gleichgewicht, esp. pp. 177 ff. and 417 ff.
43. P. Winzen, *Bülows Weltmachtkonzept*, pp. 431 ff.
44. A. Hillgruber, *Deutschlands Rolle*, p. 21.
45. Ludwig Dehio, *Gleichgewicht oder Hegemonie. Betrachtungen über ein Grundproblem der*

results of more recent American research to produce a different picture of German foreign policy at the turn of the century, containing an explosive mixture of ignorance and inexperience, of arrogance and anxiety.[46]

(2) Recently, the exposed geostrategic position of the Reich has been seen as one of the reasons why this fluctuation of policy between two poles was so extreme in the case of Germany. Though contemporaries were aware of its significance, this factor was long neglected in academic history. Attention has now been drawn to it by Klaus Hildebrand, himself incorporating American research findings.[47] His work gave the crucial academic stimulus to a wide discussion of the problem in the Federal Republic.[48] Thus, it is argued that the 'constraints' of the international 'system', which could never be independent of the geographical facts, made special demands on the German Reich in its central position on the continent. In particular, it was required to demonstrate a particularly high degree of statecraft.[49]

The change of course in German foreign policy after 1890–7 appeared radical to contemporaries as well as later observers. It was due partly to the fact that Bismarck's successors lacked his 'statesmanlike superiority, springing from the intellect and from long political experience'.[50] The consequence, as the publication of the 'Eulenburg Papers' revealed,[51] was a melting down of political authority in Germany[52] and the simultaneous coexistence of and competition between various political and military agencies and authorities. A major result was the abandonment of an insight which had been of fundamental importance to Bismarck: that *Weltpolitik* was incompatible with the security policy which was the primary requirement of a purely continental power.

Security factors were replaced by the conviction that 'the foundation stone must be laid "now or never"' if Germany was to belong to 'the

neueren Staatengeschichte, Krefeld, 1948, p. 201.

46. L.L. Farrar, Jr, *Arrogance and Anxiety. The Ambivalence of German Power, 1848–1914*, Iowa City, 1981; G. Schöllgen, *Imperialismus und Gleichgewicht*, esp. pp. 177 ff.

47. See in particular David Calleo, *The German Problem Reconsidered. Germany and the World Order, 1870 to the Present*, Cambridge et al., 1978.

48. See in particular Michael Stürmer, *Das ruhelose Reich. Deutschland 1866–1918*, Berlin, 1983; idem, *Die Reichsgründung*.

49. Klaus Hildebrand, 'Staatskunst oder Systemzwang. Die "Deutsche Frage" als Problem der Weltpolitik', *HZ*, 228, 1979, pp. 624 ff.

50. A. Hillgruber, *Deutschlands Rolle*, p. 15.

51. Philipp Eulenburg, *Politische Korrespondenz*, ed. J.C.G. Röhl, 3 vols, Boppard, 1976–83.

52. See Gregor Schöllgen, 'Wer machte im Kaiserreich Politik? Zwischen "persönlichem Regiment" und "polykratischem Chaos"', *Neue Politische Literatur*, 25, 1980, pp. 79 ff.

exclusive club of world powers'.[53] But in adopting a 'worldwide orientation and expansive direction of goals', the German Reich was taking
the crucial step 'from Bismarck's limited spheres of influence policy to
one he had rejected, the power and prestige policy' of his successors.[54]
Historians now debate whether there was any real choice for German
policy after Bismarck in the Age of Imperialism. The alternative to
Weltpolitik appeared to be the loss of that 'equal standing which had
just been achieved in Europe on the world stage which was now the
yardstick'.[55] This issue is also reflected in the relevant contributions to
this volume.[56]

✳Certain features of German *Weltpolitik* – its comparative lack of
success, its 'laughably modest' nature (Max Weber), its failure to
exploit the 'unique advantage of the international constellation' caused
by the weakness of the British Empire in 1897–8, when it 'overplayed
its hand'[57] – may have been the result of the lack of a rigorous concept
binding on all the protagonists and institutions involved.

(3) This quality is also revealed in the attempts to reach agreement
which formed *one* of several strands of German foreign policy and
Weltpolitik after 1898. In recent years, historians have devoted much
attention to an aspect which was generally excluded from 'structural
historical' analyses of German foreign policy.

For example, it is now clear that the German–American relationship, long neglected by research, was characterised by 'friendly co-
operation' after 1890, at least at the governmental level and as a basic
tendency.[58] A similar trend can also be detected during certain short
phases of British–German relations. Both in 1898–1900 and in
1911–14, Germany and Britain concluded a number of agreements on
issues of world politics. Moreover, between 1911 and 1914 the German
Reich reached agreement with Russia and France as well as Britain on
the sensitive eastern question.[59] Developments of this kind clearly

53. G. Schmidt, *Der europäische Imperialismus*, pp. 90–1.
54. Willibald Gutsche, 'Außenpolitische Ziele, Rüstungspolitik und Kriegsdisposition
der deutschen Reichsleitung vor 1914', *ZfG*, 36, 1988, pp. 963 ff., cit. p. 970; see also *idem*,
Monopole, pp. 230 ff.
55. Andreas Hillgruber, *Die gescheiterte Großmacht. Eine Skizze des Deutschen Reiches
1871–1945*, Düsseldorf, 1980, p. 21.
56. See most recently Gregor Schöllgen, 'Die Großmacht als Weltmacht. Idee, Wirklichkeit und Perzeption deutscher Weltpolitik im Zeitalter des Imperialismus', *HZ*, 248,
1989, pp. 79 ff. This is the extended German version of the paper published in this
volume.
57. Gustav Schmidt, 'Der deutsch-englische Gegensatz im Zeitalter des Imperialismus', in H. Köhler (ed.), *Deutschland und der Westen. Vorträge und Diskussionsbeiträge des
Symposions zu Ehren von Gordon A. Craig*, Berlin, 1984, pp. 59 ff., cit. p. 81.
58. R. Pommerin, *Der Kaiser und Amerika*, cit. p. 379.
59. However, the motives for this attempt to reach agreement remain controversial.

reveal how variable were the 'world political concepts' under consideration at various levels of the German military and political leadership.

Obviously, the multiplicity of plans and concepts – naval expansion programme, primacy of army expansion, *Mitteleuropa*, *Mittelafrika*, policy of reaching agreement on 'peripheral' issues – did not help to increase or re-establish the calculability of German foreign policy. When they created the Entente, Russia, France and especially Britain were attempting to provide an element which seemed to be constantly threatened by German policy: stability in the international sphere. To this extent, there is wide agreement among German historians, the German Reich did indeed 'itself engender' its own isolation.

Historians have furnished detailed accounts of the extent to which this isolation was intensified after 1908–9[60] by the internal disintegration of the Triple Alliance.[61] One result was Germany's uncompromising support for its sole remaining reliable ally, Austria–Hungary. The various attempts to end the isolation and to shatter the 'ring' of the Triple Entente, which was perceived as 'encirclement', are among the best-researched chapters of the foreign policy of Imperial Germany. However, any attempt to define the goals of this policy inevitably leads back to the controversy surrounding the theses of Fritz Fischer.

VI

An analysis and summary by Fritz Fischer, whose name has been associated with research into this theme for more than thirty years, is therefore the first contribution to this volume. For the first time, it unites in one study the two focal points of his work: the foreign policy of Imperial Germany since the end of the 1890s and the outbreak of the First World War.

This volume should not, however, be regarded as a contribution to the 'Fischer controversy'. Its framework is deliberately broader than that: the case studies are intended to provide a representative picture

---

Was it an attempt to persuade Britain 'at the last moment to observe restraint in a continental war'? (I. Geiss, *Das Deutsche Reich*, p. 74), or was there a hope that, through initial agreement in 'peripheral' questions, deep mistrust could be reduced and a solution of 'central' issues (naval and political agreements) subsequently reached? (see G. Schöllgen, *Das Zeitalter des Imperialismus*, p. 146).

60. See most recently Michael Behnen, *Rüstung – Bündnis – Sicherheit, Dreibund und informeller Imperialismus 1900–1908*, Tübingen, 1985.

61. See for example Heinz Alfred Gemeinhardt, *Deutsche und österreichische Pressepolitik während der Bosnischen Krise 1908–09*, Hamburg, 1980.

both of German foreign policy in the years between 1871 and 1914 and of its preconditions and consequences. This representative nature is demonstrated on three levels. The first lies in the selection and arrangement of the themes and the second in the choice of authors, who are committed to a variety of approaches and methods. Thirdly, however, the contributions have been selected to reflect the current position of German research. Partly for that reason, the participation of Willibald Gutsche is greatly to be welcomed, since it ensures that the views of a specialist from the GDR are included within the 'German Historical Perspectives' series for the first time. Gutsche analyses the foreign policy of Imperial Germany and the outbreak of war as reflected in the historiography of the GDR.

The essay by Michael Stürmer investigates the starting point and framework of German policy. According to Stürmer, the German national state was confronted by three main dilemmas *ex origine*, which had to be taken into account by any foreign policy: history, geography and the dynamism of mass democracy in the modern state. In Klaus Hildebrand's analysis of the opportunities and limits of German foreign policy in the Bismarckian era, he demonstrates how the first Chancellor of the German Reich dealt with these problems. By pointing to the problem of wide differences in domestic and foreign *raison d'état*, Hildebrand also addresses a central issue for other authors in this volume – whether, under the changing conditions at home and within the European order, Germany was not forced to adopt a different course after the departure of Bismarck, at the latest.

This issue is further investigated by Reiner Pommerin. His contribution analyses Germany's reaction to the new imperialist drive, and particularly to the entry of Japan and the USA into the world system during the 1890s. Pommerin asks whether the Reich leadership had adequately grasped this new dimension of a globalisation of international relations and how it perceived the new relationship between continental and *Weltpolitik*.

Both Imanuel Geiss and the editor are concerned with this German *Weltpolitik*, which is one of the most bitterly disputed chapters in the history of Imperial Germany. Geiss has no doubt that the German variant of imperialism, the *Weltpolitik* of the German Reich, failed in its core of armaments policy, particularly over the construction of the battle fleet and the German refusal to negotiate with Britain for an appropriate agreement. It was this element which did most to give German imperialism its unique and disastrous quality. The editor deals with the issue of whether a great power such as the German

Reich, in the Age of Imperialism and given the attitude of contemporaries, had any real alternative to the adoption of *Weltpolitik* if it were not to lose the status which had just been achieved in Europe.

The two concluding contributions are concerned with the immediate results and long-term consequences of German *Weltpolitik*. In his analysis of the July crisis, Gustav Schmidt concentrates on the factors which prevented the localisation of the conflict. The military leaders on both sides were committed to established plans; as they advanced to become the real actors in the crisis, military preparations concentrated primarily on the fulfilment of obligations towards allies. Inevitably, however, alliance mechanisms and localisation of conflict were mutually exclusive. The long-term results of the 'seminal catastrophe' of the twentieth century are the focus of the concluding essay by Andreas Hillgruber. When American and Soviet forces met in the middle of Germany and the continent on 25 April 1945, they were also symbolically putting an end to the autonomous political role of Europe. It had been this Europe that had taken the decisive step towards its own destruction in August 1914 and had proved unable to take the path of a peaceful and permanent settlement after 1918. Yet a durable and peaceful arrangement remains the most important political requirement, within the overall framework of a world order which incorporates the European system that had been so dominant before 1914.

If there is a common basic trend in the following contributions, it perhaps lies in a globalisation of historical perspective. It is true that all the contributors pay heed to the question of the internal driving forces of foreign policy. But equally clearly this is not, or no longer, the main issue for the majority of authors. Instead, they are concerned with the wider framework of the European and world order, and thus with the externally fixed possibilities and limitations of German foreign policy in the decades before the outbreak of the First World War. At the same time, they also address the vital question of the compatibility of German great- and world-power status with the principle of the balance of power in the European and world order. The following contributions offer some new answers to these questions.

FRITZ FISCHER

The Foreign Policy of Imperial Germany and the Outbreak of the First World War

The situation of the German Reich in the last two decades before the First World War was characterised by the antagonism between Germany and her three great neighbours. This led to an isolation of Germany in the European state system. The first part of this paper traces the origins of Germany's conflicts with Great Britain, France and Russia.

German–British Tensions

The partition of Africa, of the Pacific islands and of China and a series of wars – the Sino-Japanese War of 1894–5, the Spanish-American War of 1898, the Boer War of 1899–1902 and the Russo-Japanese War of 1904–5 – produced an upsurge of 'navalism' (prompted in part by the theories of the American admiral Mahan on the influence of sea power on a nation's global power position), inducing established naval powers to expand their fleets and rising states like Japan, the USA and imperial Germany to embark on naval construction.

Of these new navies, the first two, USA and Japan, although offering unwelcome competition, presented no real threat to the British Empire in view of the Anglo-American accommodation after 1900 and the Anglo-Japanese alliance of 1902. The German naval programme, on the other hand, through geographical proximity (the operational radius of the German fleet did not extend beyond the North Sea) and by virtue of the fact that it assumed the form of a battleship fleet, presented an immediate threat to the British Isles. Britain answered this challenge by strengthening its fleet through accelerated naval construction, including, in 1905, the transition to dreadnought-type building. This led to a naval arms race which only Britain was financially able to sustain: by concentrating its East Asian, West Indian and Mediterranean squadrons in home waters; by concluding *ententes cordiales* with France in 1904 and Russia in 1907 (thereby eliminating colonial and other bones of contention in its relations with traditional rivals); and finally, after 1905, by creating a small but powerful professional army intended for use in the event of war as a British Expeditionary Force in France. Germany, in turn, perceived this response as an 'encirclement' (*Einkreisung*), and German public opinion saw it as a serious diminution in the power of the German Reich in comparison with the international position Germany had occupied under Bismarck.

How had it come to this? Following Bismarck's dismissal in 1890 and the conclusion of the Franco-Russian military alliance in 1894, the German Reich, in case of war, was henceforth threatened on two fronts by two neighbouring Great Powers. Nevertheless, Wilhelm II, who, after 1897, was advised by the new Navy Secretary Tirpitz and the new Foreign Secretary Bülow, inaugurated an era of naval construction and *Weltpolitik*, thereby challenging Great Britain, a third Great Power and the strongest naval power of the age. Tirpitz may have been partly motivated by 'social imperialism'[1] – using the navy as a national symbol to unify Germany against Social Democracy and to weaken the position of the Reichstag in the German government system by the so-called '*Aeternat*' of the navy budget. In fact, despite serious reservations and initial resistance – the Conservative agrarians were bought off by means of high protective tariffs – virtually all non-socialist parties in the Reichstag voted in favour of the naval programme. Such support was generated in part by the direct interests of heavy industry, but its principal success derived above all from the propaganda of the Imperial Navy Office, which argued that the long-term future of Germany as an industrial and commercial power could be secured only through the navy and that only by this means would it

---

1. Volker R. Berghahn, *Der Tirpitz-Plan. Genesis und Verfall einer innenpolitischen Krisen-strategie unter Wilhelm II.*, Düsseldorf, 1971.

be possible to overcome British opposition to Germany's aspirations to further colonial acquisitions.

The most recent book on the armaments policy of Imperial Germany states in one lapidary sentence: 'Here we have the one-sided and veiled armament of the naval forces of the German Reich since 1897, which was not caused by any acute threat.'[2] The authors continue: 'The German battle fleet, after its completion in about 1920, would have consisted of 60 dreadnoughts and was conceived as a power-political and, if necessary, military lever [*Hebel*] able to push Great Britain, the first sea power of the era, out of its maritime and colonial hegemonial position.'

Whatever colonial and commercial interests or fears there may have been, however, the instinctive drive for an anti-British policy came from Kaiser Wilhelm II personally, from his love–hate relationship with Britain, nurtured by his childhood impressions of visits there and by his childish wish to possess a fleet more powerful than the mighty British Navy. As early as 1895 his mother informed her own mother, Queen Victoria, how horrified she was at Wilhelm's anti-British plans.[3] In February 1896, a month after the Kaiser's telegram to Krüger, Korvettenkapitän Müller, later Admiral von Müller, chief of the Kaiser's naval cabinet, made the following statement in a memorandum: 'The war which could break out because of this aggressive attitude and, as many people think, must break out has, as is generally accepted here in Germany, the aim of breaking Britain's domination of the world and thus leaving the way open for us to acquire colonial possessions, as central Europe is becoming too small for us . . .'[4] And in 1903, after the first Navy Law of 1898 and the second of 1900 were passed, Theobald von Bethmann Hollweg, a close friend of the Kaiser, was to state:

The Kaiser's policy is not 'wavering', [on the contrary,] his first and basic idea is to break Britain's leading position in the world in favour of Germany [note the ominous word 'break' again!]. For this a fleet is required, and in order to build it, a lot of money which only a rich country can afford; so Germany should become rich. Hence the priority given to industry, and the fury of the farmers who are opposing this policy in order to save themselves from ruin.[5]

2. Volker R. Berghahn and Wilhelm Deist (eds), *Rüstung im Zeichen der Wilhelminischen Weltpolitik. Grundlegende Dokumente 1890–1914*, Düsseldorf, 1988, p. 11.
3. Information from Professor John Röhl in a public lecture on Wilhelm II in Munich (Historisches Kolleg), June 1987.
4. V. Berghahn and W. Deist (eds), *Rüstung*, pp. 118–22: ch. II, document 9: 'Aufzeichnungen des Korvettenkapitäns Müller aus dem Jahre 1896: Perspektiven einer künftigen deutschen Weltpolitik'.
5. *Das Tagebuch der Baronin Spitzemberg*, ed. Rudolf Vierhaus, Göttingen, 1960, pp.

The Kaiser stuck to his anti-British policy, with three amendments (1906, 1908, 1912) to the two Navy Laws, and neglected the army.[6] For twenty years, from 1893 to 1913, the German army was not expanded, although at least since 1905, following the plans of the General Staff, the so-called Schlieffen Plan, a numerical superiority of the German army in a war with France was necessary. This neglect led in the foreign policy crisis in 1912–13 to the precipitate and very ostentatious enlargement of the German army, which irritated Europe and especially Germany's neighbours, France and Russia, who responded with great expansions of their armies. In July 1914 Grand Admiral Tirpitz declared to Prince Heinrich, the Kaiser's brother: 'the navy is not yet ready, its building up and outfitting [ihr Auf- und Ausbau] has not yet been finished.'[7] For a war expected in a short time the costly navy would only be of very limited value.

The Renewed Hostility Towards France

Meanwhile, the Franco-German antagonism, created by the German annexation of Alsace-Lorraine in 1871, had been revived by Germany's Moroccan policy when, in 1905, the Reich attempted to exploit the weakness of Russia (in the wake of the Russo-Japanese war and the 1905 revolution in Russia) in order to disrupt the *entente cordiale* by menacing France (the Tangiers landing). The Kaiser only very reluctantly followed the advice of Bülow in taking this dramatic action, because it could have led – prematurely – to a war with France and Britain which did indeed support her *entente cordiale* partner. It was at this time that the first military discussions between these two powers began.[8] The German efforts in Morocco were repeated in 1911 with the 'Panther's leap' at Agadir. On both occasions the German Reich went to the brink of war, but the only result was the consolidation of the Anglo-French *entente*, which was now augmented by military discussions.[9] Entering into German calculations here, as in the case of

427 f. (entry of 14.3.1903).

6. V. Berghahn and W. Deist (eds), *Rüstung*, ch. I: Rüstungspolitik der Armee 1891–1909; ch. IX: Die Aufrüstung der Armee 1910–1914.

7. Baldur Kaulisch, *Alfred von Tirpitz und die imperialistische deutsche Flottenrüstung*, Berlin (GDR), 1982, pp. 164 f.: 'Dabei wußte er [Tirpitz] doch, daß sich auf Grund des höheren englischen Bautempos das Kräfteverhältnis weiter zu Ungunsten der deutschen Flotte verschieben würde.'

8. Samuel R. Williamson, Jr, *The Politics of Grand Strategy. Britain and France Prepare for War, 1904–1914*, Cambridge, MA, 1969, pp. 59 ff.

9. Ibid.

German naval policy, were real or alleged economic interests – it was hoped that iron ore would be found in Morocco – prestige and power politics, as well as schemes for territorial exchanges. The German government hoped to acquire a central African empire incorporating parts of the French or Belgian Congo as a quid pro quo for renouncing its disputed claims or rights in Morocco. In 1911 German public opinion,[10] especially the Pan-Germans and the right-wing press, functioned as an aroused participant in these deliberations, expressing its disappointment, even bitterness, at the meagre attainments of German policy. Again, France came to be regarded as the 'hereditary enemy', everywhere standing in the path of a rising Germany. Gradually, German armaments priorities switched from the navy to the army. This animosity increased still further in 1914 when Turkey took the place of Morocco as a field of activity for German economic and political interests.[11] Here they competed with the interests of France, a financially more powerful country, and with those of Britain and Russia.

The New Enmity against Russia

In the interval a third antagonism had become apparent, this time concerning eastern and south-eastern Europe and involving Austria-Hungary, the only remaining certain ally of the German Reich. This was the Russo-German antagonism, the immediate source of the World War. Austria-Hungary's annexation in 1908 of the Serbo-Croatian provinces of Bosnia and Herzegovina – Turkish until 1878 but administered by Vienna since the Congress of Berlin – embittered Serbia, which functioned as a base for Bosnian irredentist movements. As Russia had been induced to recognise the annexation only by Berlin's threat of war in March 1909, Russian popular opinion became increasingly antagonistic towards Germany. Relations between the two powers had been clouded by economic frictions since the late Bismarckian era and especially since the Russo-German commercial treaty of July 1904, which had been forced on Russia largely at the behest of East Elbian grain producers. An even greater irritant to Russia, as

10. Fritz Fischer, *War of Illusions. German policies from 1911 to 1914*, London, New York, 1975, pp. 71 ff., ch. 5: Morocco Crisis 1911. The Breakthrough of the National Opposition.
11. F. Fischer, *War of Illusions*, pp. 298 ff., ch. 14: Growing Difficulties for German Expansion, II. Turkey: The Centre of German Economic and Political Interests in the Near East.

indeed to Britain and France, was Germany's Turkish policy, the construction of the Baghdad railway and the German military links with the Turkish army, as this policy imperilled a vital Russian interest in free access to the Straits while also jeopardising long-term aspirations of Russia in the area.

The unexpected and rapid defeat of the Turkish army in October 1912, extruding Turkey from its last European possessions, unleashed the final significant war scare before the First World War: Austria–Hungary viewed Serbian access to the Adriatic as endangering its vital interests, which it proposed to defend against such a Serbian advance by means of military intervention, even at the risk of war with Russia and hence, in view of existing alliance obligations, at the risk of a world war. War was avoided through the collaboration of Britain and Germany at the London ambassadors' conference, when concessions were made to Vienna, a decision which was accepted by both Serbia and its Russian protector.

Yet Germany was shocked by the (at least momentary) collapse of its presumptive Turkish ally and by the enlargement of Serbia, which in a future major military conflagration would tie down Austro-Hungarian troops that might otherwise be deployed against Russia. Germany was also shocked by Britain's warning that it would side with France, in the event of a German attack on this ally of Russia, rather than face the prospect of standing alone against a continent dominated by a single power: i.e. the German Reich.[12] These shocks resulted in the massive German army expansion of 1913, which in turn produced increases in the French and Russian armies. The extent of the latter, not fully apparent until 1913–14, created expectations of a numerical superiority of Germany's two continental neighbouring powers over Germany and Austria-Hungary by about 1916–17.

During discussions on the scale of the German army the antagonism of the 'Slavs and Teutons' became the latest catchword. Moltke and Wilhelm II spoke of a 'decisive struggle' or 'final struggle' between these peoples.[13] In 1913–14 a profound change came about in the

---

12. Wilhelm II was so shocked (he had hoped for an alliance with England) that he called together his military advisers to a (later) so-called 'War-Council' on 8 December 1912. See F. Fischer, *War of Illusions*, pp. 161 ff.; John C.G. Röhl, 'An der Schwelle zum Weltkrieg', MGM, 1977/1, pp. 77–134; J.C.G. Röhl, 'Die Generalprobe. Zur Geschichte und Bedeutung des "Kriegsrats" vom 8. Dez. 1912' in Dirk Stegmann, B.-J. Wendt, P.-Chr. Witt (eds), *Industrielle Gesellschaft und politisches System (Festschrift für Fritz Fischer z. 70. Geburtstag)*, Bonn, 1978, pp. 357–74, reprinted in *Deutschlands Sonderung von Europa 1862–1945*, ed. W. Alff, Frankfurt a. M., Bern, New York, 1984.
13. F. Fischer, *War of Illusions*, p. 207: 'Slavs and Teutons'; p. 212: Wilhelm II: 'The

German people's conception of and feelings for Russia, which until 1909, during Bülow's chancellorship, had been regarded as a friendly power in spite of the Franco-Russian alliance. Now it was seen as the Russian colossus, dominated by a hate of everything German and by an expansionist Pan-Slavism and Neo-Slavism in which dynastic connections with the German princely houses no longer meant anything, being increasingly replaced by the nationalism of the new Russian industrial bourgeoisie. This change was of epoch-making significance and opened the way for Hitler. Above all, the Baltic Germans, who in the 1880s and 1890s had come to Germany in protest against the Russification of the Baltic provinces, were filled with a deep hatred for Russia and also with a fear of the rising power of Slavism. Among them were such influential men as the professor for Eastern European history at Berlin University, Theodor Schiemann, also a teacher at the War Academy, who exercised a powerful influence on the Prusso-German officers' corps with his ideas about the multi-national state of Russia and its vulnerability.

The Situation in the Year before the War

During the Balkan wars (in November–December 1912 and in February and July 1913) Berlin had firmly restrained Vienna from military intervention against Serbia, as this would unavoidably have entailed the intervention of Russia and thus caused a world war. Bethmann Hollweg therefore urged the Austrian Foreign Minister Berchtold to think carefully about the consequences of an Austrian war against Serbia and Montenegro.[14] The advocates of the peaceful line in Russia, Kokovtsov and Sazonov, would 'be simply swept away by the tide of public opinion if they should try to stem it'. An objective examination of the situation must lead to the view 'that for Russia with its traditional links with the Balkan states it is almost impossible without immense loss of prestige to stand by while Austria-Hungary takes military action against Serbia'. Could Bethmann Hollweg have forgotten this in July 1914? However, from September 1913, after the

---

struggle between the Slavs and the Teutons is unavoidable, it must come. When? We shall see.'

14. F. Fischer, *War of Illusions*, p. 206. Bethmann Hollweg warned against waging the conflict *now* 'at a moment when there is the possibility – if only a remote one – that we may be able to wage the conflict under conditions much more favorable to us' (that is, as the following text shows, with English neutrality); see Fritz Fischer, *Juli 1914. Wir sind nicht hineingeschlittert*, Hamburg, 1983, p. 40.

German army build-up had begun to take effect, a change took place in the thinking of the political leadership of Germany; the help of a disappointed Austria-Hungary was again enlisted. In this the Kaiser was especially active in October 1913, visiting Konopischt to talk to Franz Ferdinand and Vienna to speak with Berchtold.[15] In November 1913 Kaiser Wilhelm and Moltke tried to persuade Albert, King of the Belgians, to allow free passage for German troops through his country in the event of war.[16] For 'war with France is unavoidable and actually impending' said the Kaiser. And Moltke repeated that 'war is unavoidable' and, what is more, added 'much nearer than you think'. The Belgians understood the reason for the warlike attitude of the generals. Like so many of their countrymen, these military leaders were exasperated by the way France 'constantly gets in Germany's way, involves it in rebuffs, opposes its domination and its desire for colonies, in desperation increases its army to maintain the balance of power, which they, the Germans, think has long since ceased to exist'. This was also Chancellor Bethmann Hollweg's opinion.[17] At the Kaiser's birthday celebrations on 27 January 1914, he expressed the same – essentially Darwinian – reasons for Germany's embitterment towards France to Jules Cambon, the French ambassador. Germany needs a field of activity for its perpetually growing economy: 'Every day Germany sees its population growing by leaps and bounds; its navy, its trade and industry are making unparalleled developments . . . it is forced to expand somehow or other; it has not yet found that "place in the sun" which is its due.' Should France dare to oppose its growth, it will find Germany as its enemy, not only in Asia Minor but everywhere. This was the threat of a man who, according to Friedrich Naumann and Theodor Wolff,[18] had considered war with France and Russia as unavoidable since December 1913 or at latest since February 1914 (after the dismissal of the pro-German prime minister Kokovtsov) and who sought the most favourable opportunity when all pre-conditions for a great war – in which Russia should be the aggressor and Britain neutral – would be fulfilled.

In December 1913 the new military mission under General Liman

---

15. F. Fischer, *War of Illusions*, pp. 219 ff.

16. Ibid., pp. 225 ff.

17. Ibid., pp. 444 ff.

18. Theodor Heuss, *Friedrich Naumann*, Berlin 1937, p. 513; 'Gespräch Theodor Wolff mit Bethmann Hollweg nach dessen Entlassung' in Bernd Sösemann, *Die Erforderlichkeit des Unmöglichen. Kritische Bemerkungen zu der Edition* [von K.D. Erdmann]: Kurt Riezler, *Tagebücher* [etc.] in *Blätter für deutsche Landesgeschichte*, 110, 1974, p. 272. Cf. F. Fischer, *Juli 1914, wir sind nicht hineingeschlittert*, p. 109.

von Sanders, later to be commander of the First Turkish Army Corps in Constantinople, caused a direct clash with Russia, a violation of vital Russian interests by German political action.[19] Although the crisis was defused by Germany backing down, it aroused a feeling of deep mistrust and hostility towards Germany in Russian society and government circles. The anti-German trend was intensified by a German press campaign and an anti-Russian article of 2 March 1914 in the *Kölnische Zeitung*, a mouthpiece of the Foreign Office. The article maintained that Russia was preparing for a war planned shortly to take place against Germany. This article caused a sensation in the whole German press and was capped by another article in the liberal *Berliner Tageblatt* (9 March). This article publicly demanded a preventive war against Russia. The climax was reached in a discussion between Moltke and Jagow (at the end of May or beginning of June) in which the former, Germany's highest military officer, demanded that the latter, the head of the Foreign Office, should pursue a policy making a 'preventive war' possible.[20]

Here a digression is necessary to describe Germany's policy to neutralise Britain. In a study entitled 'The Miscalculation of English Neutrality: An Aspect of German Foreign Policy on the Eve of World War I' I have shown how Bülow's successor, Chancellor Bethmann Hollweg, made the neutralisation of Britain in the event of a continental war the central feature of his British policy.[21] He stubbornly abided by this policy until the outbreak of the First World War in spite of the continuing naval armaments race. During the crisis of December 1912, the Kaiser confirmed that it was the task of the two ambassadors he sent to London, Marschall and Lichnowsky, 'to achieve English neutrality in case of open conflict with Russia and France'.[22] At almost the same time the then State Secretary of Foreign Affairs, von Kiderlen-Wächter, said to Helferich, director of the Deutsche Bank: 'I am not afraid of a war [with Russia and France]; but should it occur, it would be a great advantage to keep Britain neutral'.[23] The more the conflict with Russia developed in the years 1913 and 1914, the more persistently did Bethmann Hollweg pursue his aim. This he did mainly

19. F. Fischer, *War of Illusions*, pp. 330 ff.: 'The Liman Sanders Crisis: German-Russian Confrontation in Constantinople and on the Straits'.
20. Ibid., pp. 401 f.
21. In S. Wank et al. (eds), *The Mirror of History. Festschrift for Fritz Fellner, University of Salzburg*, Santa Barbara, CA, Oxford, 1988, pp. 369–93.
22. F. Fischer, *War of Illusions*, p. 165: 12 December 1912, Wilhelm II to Eisendecher.
23. *Kiderlen-Wächter der Staatsmann und Mensch. Briefwechsel und Nachlaß*, ed. Ernst Jäckh, Berlin, Leipzig, 1924, vol. 2, p. 192, n. 1.

by months of patient negotiation with the British government on colonial and Near East questions in order to achieve a Berlin–London *rapprochement* and, through this, Britain's secession from the Triple Entente.

Even the secret report of Anglo-Russian naval negotiations in May and June 1914 did not deter Bethmann Hollweg.[24] He used the negotiations to put pressure on London to adopt a policy of neutrality. On 16 June 1914 he ordered Fürst von Lichnowsky, German ambassador in London, to tell Sir Edward Grey, the British Foreign Minister, that Germany might possibly be compelled to strengthen its army and its fleet. Only if Britain and Germany co-ordinated their policy (as in December 1912), could they avert the danger of a European conflict as could be caused by a new Balkan crisis. There were lots of actual conflicts in the Balkans.

After Sarajevo (28 June 1914), Bethmann Hollweg instructed Lichnowsky on 29 June to say to Grey that the Austro-Hungarian government should not be blamed if it retaliated against this provocation which, it was proved (as he maintained), had been supported by Belgrade.[25] On four occasions in the week after Sarajevo the German Chancellor visited the Kaiser in Potsdam, where discussions between the Chancellor and the generals took place, and on 3 July the Kaiser made his famous marginal comment on a report from Tschirschky: 'Now or never . . . we must make a clean sweep of the Serbs and soon!' (which was understood by the German authorities as an order!).[26] The decision to use Sarajevo as an excuse for a major military conflict was, nevertheless, not primarily motivated by the desire to support Austria-Hungary against Serbia. For the Serbian question, paramount for Vienna, was merely of secondary importance to Berlin, only a vehicle for drawing Russia into the Vienna–Belgrade conflict and thus unleashing the great war with Russia and France (which was exactly what Vienna with Berlin's help hoped to avoid). Bethmann Hollweg was certain of achieving Britain's neutrality by presenting Russia as the 'aggressor' and Germany as the 'offended' party. This scenario had often been discussed before the war in leading German circles as a pre-condition for the unleashing of a general war. It was a renewed attempt to split the Triple Entente and to weaken the two continental neighbours of Germany for the future.

Let us not forget the prevailing mood in Germany in the years

24. Ibid., pp. 432 ff.; Bethmann Hollweg to Lichnowsky, 16 June 1914, p. 438.
25. Ibid., pp. 471 ff.
26. Ibid., p. 475.

1913–14. In a semi-official publication by the representative of Wolff-Telegraphenbüro in London in May 1913, intended to calm European public opinion, 'German "world policy" and no war' (*Deutsche Weltpolitik und kein Krieg*), the author Hans Plehn stated that since the last Moroccan crisis of 1911 the feeling was already 'almost general among the German nation . . . that it is only with a Great European War that we could obtain the freedom needed to be active in world politics'.[27]

German Policy in the July Crisis of 1914

After Sarajevo the government in Vienna was split into two groups, the military and the civilians, and was therefore hesitating and wavering. The determination to act came from the German side. In the week immediately after Sarajevo Vienna began to feel German pressure, menacingly urging the Austrians to use the propitious moment for action against Serbia (so by Viktor Naumann,[28] personal friend of Wilhelm von Stumm, the director of the Political Department of the Foreign Office in Berlin, Hugo Ganz,[29] correspondent of the *Frankfurter Zeitung* in Vienna, and of course at the end of this week during the mission of Count Hoyos to Potsdam and Berlin). At the decisive meeting of the common ministerial council on 8 July in Vienna the Minister President of Austria, Graf Stürgkh, warned his colleagues that, if Austria-Hungary continued to hesitate and did not decide to act, then there was a possibility that Germany would end the alliance between Berlin and Vienna.[30] The Germans would then come to an arrangement with Russia, and Austria-Hungary would be left alone.

27. Ibid., p. 319. Even the most pro-British group – Solf, Rosen, Lichnowsky, Kühlmann – was disappointed in its hopes for a German Central Africa (to be conceded by Great Britain).
28. Imanuel Geiss (ed.), *Julikrise und Kriegsausbruch 1914. Eine Dokumentensammlung*, vol. 1, Hanover, 1963, pp. 60 ff.: 'Aufzeichnung Hoyos über Unterredung mit Viktor Naumann, Wien 1.7.1914', 'Streng geheim!' (*ÖU* 9966). See also F. Fischer, *War of Illusions*, p. 473.
29. I. Geiss (ed.), *Julikrise und Kriegsausbruch 1914*, vol. 1, pp. 77 ff. 'On that day the Vienna correspondent of the *Frankfurter Zeitung*, Ganz, on the instructions of the German ambassador, Tschirschky, said in the Foreign Ministry in Vienna that "Germany would support the Monarchy through thick and thin whatever the latter would decide about Serbia . . . the sooner Austria-Hungary started the better. Yesterday would have been better than today but today was better than tomorrow".' (Memorandum by Forgách, Vienna 4.7.1914, *ÖU* 10038) quoted from F. Fischer, *War of Illusions*, p. 476
30. I. Geiss (ed.), *Julikrise und Kriegsausbruch 1914*, vol. 1, pp. 104 ff.: 'Protokoll des Gemeinsamen Ministerrats unter dem Vorsitz Berchtolds vom 7.7.1914'; pp. 107 f.: Stürgkh (*ÖU* 10118).

On 5 and 6 July 1914 Berlin had given Vienna a 'blank cheque' to
attack Serbia, even pressing Vienna towards such action despite the
danger of Russian intervention and thus of a major war. This may be
interpreted as a 'calculated risk'. At any rate, the then acting German
Foreign Minister, Under-Secretary Zimmermann, in conversation with
the Austrian special emissary Count Hoyos on 5 July described the
'risk' as 90 per cent likely to produce war with Russia,[31] which cannot
be interpreted otherwise than as a certain anticipation of a major war.
As it happened, Count Hoyos was one of the young 'hawks' at the
'Ballhausplatz' and a great admirer of the German army.

On the evening of 6 July the Kaiser, who was preparing to leave at
Kiel for his North Sea cruise, assured Krupp von Bohlen and Halbach,
with whom he was on intimate terms, that: 'We would declare war at
once, if Russia mobilised. This time people would see that he was not
"backing out" [daß er nicht umfallen würde]' – that is, as he had done
in 1905, 1909 and 1911.[32] And for Germany mobilisation would immediately mean war.

On 12 July Szögyéni, Vienna's ambassador in Berlin, wrote that the
'absolute' insistence on war against Serbia by the Emperor and the
Chancellor was based on two considerations: firstly, that Russia and
France 'were not yet ready' and, secondly, that Britain 'will not at this
juncture intervene in a war which breaks out over a Balkan state, *even if
this should lead to a conflict with Russia, possibly also France. . . .*' And he
concludes: 'In general, then, it appears from all this that the political
constellation is as favourable for us as it could possibly be'; therefore,
this moment shall be used by Germany *now.*[33]

What is the meaning of that phrase 'to use the moment now' which
confirms that the Central Powers in no way 'slid into war'? Josef
Baernreither, former Austrian Minister of Commerce, made the following entry on the July crisis in his diary for December 1914:

> The Germans were afraid that *we* would refuse to go with them if the war
> broke out over some question remote from us . . . In the Morocco crisis we
> did not stand by Germany firmly. But war was bound to come, as things had
> developed, through the faults of German and Austro-Hungarian diplomacy.
> Therefore, when the Sarajevo murder happened, Germany seized the oppor-
> tunity and made an *Austrian* grievance her signal for action.

31. Fritz Fellner, 'Die "Mission Hoyos" (nach dem Hoyos-Nachlaß)' in W. Alff (ed.),
Deutschlands Sonderung von Europa 1862–1945, pp. 283–316, cit. p. 296.
32. Fritz Fischer, *Germany's Aims in the First World War*, London, New York, 1967, p.
55.
33. I. Geiss (ed.), *Julikrise und Kriegsdusbruch 1914*, vol. I., pp. 150 ff.: '12.7.14 Szögyéni
to Berchtold' (*ÖU* 10 215).

The entry in Baernreither's diary goes on:

> The Emperor went off to Norway, knowing certainly that war would break out. Germany had arranged all this very cleverly and had shown alertness and judgement in picking the opportunity to act, when she was certain of Austria's support in waging war, the inevitability of which had been becoming apparent for years past.[34]

There can be no question of the 'fatalism' of the German Chancellor. Bethmann Hollweg interrupted his 'leave' at Hohenfinow, his estate, which he had begun on the afternoon of 4 July, not only on 5–6 July for the Austrian emissary but on three more occasions (10, 15 and 18 July) for visits to Berlin where he conferred with the heads of the German government departments (Reichsämter), with the Prussian ministries and with military offices in order to prepare in detail, for a war now considered certain, questions of mobilisation, supplies and future co-operation between civilian and military authorities.[35] All this is officially recorded; the Chancellor was, in fact, a bundle of energy and activity.

After the Austrian ultimatum to Serbia of 23 July the atmosphere in Europe, advantageous to the Central Powers up to that point, shifted drastically. Grey attempted to mediate and made four separate proposals for tempering the crisis, all of which were sabotaged by Berlin, which only *pretended* to co-operate with the British Foreign Office. On 25 July, the day Vienna cut off relations with Belgrade and mobilised, Theodor Wolff (*Berliner Tageblatt*) asked Jagow, Secretary of Foreign Affairs in the Foreign Office: 'Is it not possible that we might end up involved in a world war? What if Russia does not back down?' To which Jagow replied: 'The diplomatic situation is very advantageous. Neither Russia, France nor England want war. And if worst came [smiling] a war is bound to come sooner or later the way things are now, and in two or three years Russia will be even stronger.'[36] This same Jagow was the man to whom Albert Ballin, director of the

34. Josef M. Baernreither, *Dem Weltbrand entgegen*, Berlin, 1928; F. Fischer, *Germany's Aims*, p. 89; *idem, War of Illusions*, p. 260: Baernreither paraphrased the goals of German expansion in the Balkans as follows: 'To safeguard the existence of Turkey, the road to Asia Minor and Mesopotamia, and German expansion in the Near and the Far East' (in competition with Austria-Hungary, its ally).

35. Willibald Gutsche, *Aufstieg und Fall eines kaiserlichen Reichskanzlers. Theobald von Bethmann Hollweg 1856–1921*, Berlin (GDR), 1973, pp. 118 ff. (10.7.), pp. 119 ff. (15.7.), pp. 121 f. (18.7.1914).

36. Theodor Wolff, *Tagebücher 1914–1919*, ed. Bernd Sösemann (Deutsche Geschichtsquellen des 19. und 20. Jahrhunderts, vol. 54/I and II), Boppard a. Rh., 1984, vol. I, p. 64 (25. 7. 1914).

HAPAG shipping line, wrote in 1915, based on his intimate knowledge of what had been done in July 1914: 'I make every allowance for a man who is heavily incriminated, as Your Excellency is, and has to bear the frightful responsibility for having staged this war (für die Inscenierung dieses Kriegs) which is costing Germany generations of splendid men and setting her back 100 years.'[37] On the question of whether Germany really wanted the war, we have Jagow's unequivocal answer: 'Yes, we wanted it.'[38] This is why he could not sleep any more, as he said to Countess Treuberg in November 1918. Under-Secretary Wilhelm von Stumm, chief of the Political Department of the Foreign Office, stated to Theodor Wolff on the same day, 25 July 1914, that: 'In two years war would become inevitable if we don't free ourselves of the present situation.'[39] This was the same 'Herr von Stumm in the Foreign Office' who at the end of August 1914 was named by Arthur von Gwinner, Director of the Deutsche Bank, as 'the power pushing towards the conflict' or perhaps, Gwinner added, it had been a whole group in the Foreign Office.[40] In a later discussion with Theodor Wolff (17 February 1915) Stumm, when asked whether Germany was bluffing in July 1914, replied: 'What do you mean? We weren't bluffing. We were prepared for a war with Russia.'[41] Incidentally, Stumm maintained: 'If the war had not come then, we would have had to face it under much less favourable conditions two years later'[42] – this Wolff did not accept. It is the historical truth: *two or three men decided the fate of Europe* (Bethmann Hollweg, Jagow, Stumm)![43]

After returning to Berlin on Sunday 26 July, the Reich Chancellor defined his policy. Maintenance of peace in Europe now depended on Russia: Germany had to remain 'calm'; Germany could assure English neutrality and domestic support only if it *appeared* to be the victim of aggression. The German emperor returned from Norway the next day,

37. F. Fischer, *Germany's Aims*, p. 91.
38. T. Wolff, *Tagebücher*, vol. II, p. 665.
39. Ibid., vol. I, p. 64. Stumm continued: 'Es handele sich darum, festzustellen, ob Österreich bei uns noch als Bundesgenosse etwas wert sei. Es dürfe nicht zurückweichen.'
40. F. Fischer, *Germany's Aims*, p. 90.
41. T. Wolff, *Tagebücher*, vol. I, pp. 166 f.
42. Chancellor Bethmann Hollweg kept the same conviction even after his dismissal from office in 1917. He remarked to Conrad Haussman: 'Well, yes, in a sense it was a preventive war. But the war was hanging over us anyway. Two years later it would have been even more dangerous and unavoidable, and the soldiers were saying that now it can still be fought without a defeat but not in two years from now. Ah well, the soldiers!' (implying: 'What haven't they promised us!') quoted from Wolfgang Steglich, *Die Friedenspolitik der Mittelmächte 1917/18*, Wiesbaden, 1964, vol. 1, p. 418, n. 3.
43. This was the title the Hamburg weekly *Die Zeit* used for my review of the Wolff diaries on 13 April 1984, pp. 17 f.

Monday 27 July, to Potsdam. Admiral von Müller, chief of the emperor's naval cabinet, wrote in his diary on that occasion: 'Our policy to remain calm, to put Russia in the wrong, and then not to shy away from war'.[44]

On these two days the peace of Europe could have been saved – if Germany had wanted it.

On 27 July Grey addressed his fifth urgent mediation proposal to Berlin, entreating it to appeal to Vienna to accept the Serbian reply, otherwise he would not be able to convince St Petersburg to temper its position. Bethmann Hollweg, who had rejected a British plan (Grey's fourth) the same day, calling for a conference of the four major powers not directly involved in the conflict, realised, as he put it to the Kaiser, that if Germany rejected every role as a mediator *a limine*, they would be seen by Britain and the whole world as responsible for the conflagration and as the real warmongers.[45] This would make it impossible to preserve the momentary good mood of the German population (which was excited over the Austrian mobilisation), and on the other hand, it would also deflect Britain from its neutrality. In his instructions to Tschirschky, the German ambassador in Vienna, the Chancellor emphasised that 'we [Germany] must give the impression of being forced into the war . . .'[46] On 1 August, the day Berlin declared war on Russia, Admiral von Müller wrote in his diary: 'The mood is brilliant. The government has managed to make us appear to be attacked' (Stimmung glänzend. Die Regierung hat eine glückliche Hand gehabt, uns als die Angegriffenen hinzustellen).[47] This convinced the German Social Democrats but not Britain.

Bethmann Hollweg was not concerned with preventing a continental war but with achieving the most advantageous starting position possible for Germany in the major war which was assumed to be at hand. Having pressured Austria from 25 July onwards, he was well aware that Vienna was going to declare war on Serbia the following day, 28 July (although the Austrian mobilisation would not have been finished before 4 August, so that enough time for negotiations would have been left) and to bombard Belgrade the day after, on 29 July.

---

44. For 26 and 27 July, see *The Mirror of History*, p. 380.
45. F. Fischer, *War of Illusions*, pp. 485 f.
46. Ibid., p. 486. After the war Jagow stated that it had been the task of German diplomacy to justify the war in a form, 'die uns als die "Angegriffenen" erscheinen lassen konnte" (which could us let appear as the 'attacked'); see W. Gutsche, *Aufstieg und Fall*, p. 121.
47. 1.8.1914, diary of v. Müller, Fischer, *War of Illusions*, p. 505. See also *The Mirror of History*, pp. 380 ff.

Bethmann Hollweg also realised very clearly what effect these two actions would have on Russian public opinion.

On Tuesday 28 July the Kaiser was beginning to back out again (er 'fiel wieder um') when he stated that the Serbian reply to the Austrian ultimatum was adequate and made his 'halt in Belgrade' proposal. It was on the next day that he was brought back to the pro-war line. On this 29 July at the consultations in Potsdam, the decision was taken for immediate war. The Chancellor now had to make his most important contribution to the continental war, namely, the securing of Britain's neutrality by treaty. He discussed this matter late the same evening with Goschen, the British ambassador. The British government learned from this discussion that the German government had decided on war, intended to start with the attack on France (Schlieffen Plan) and would thereby violate Belgian neutrality. It rejected the demand for a treaty of neutrality on 30 July.

It is known that immediately after Goschen had left the Chancellor late on the night of 29 July, a telegram arrived from Lichnowsky. It repeated the British mediation proposals but also contained the warning that Britain could not remain an onlooker if Germany attacked France. The Chancellor wavered for a moment and then sent off the so-called 'world conflagration' (Weltbrand) telegrams to Vienna. He did this only half-heartedly, for what really concerned him was waiting for Russian general mobilisation: and he had the nerve and the energy to insist on waiting despite urgent pressure by the German military. When, at about noon on 31 July, the news of Russian general mobilisation was officially announced, a 'state of imminent threat of war' was immediately proclaimed in Berlin, which had to be followed by mobilisation within twenty-four hours. On the same afternoon an ultimatum (of twelve hours) was sent to Russia and the same (of eighteen hours) to France. These ultimata made the great war unavoidable.

We are given an even deeper insight into German motives and actions by the Bethmann Hollweg telegram to Berchtold, Moltke's telegram to Conrad ('Will Austria-Hungary leave us in the lurch?' – 'Will Österreich uns im Stiche lassen?') and Kaiser Wilhelm's telegram to Kaiser Franz Josef. Wilhelm telegraphed:

> I am prepared to fulfil the duties of our alliance and immediately go to war against Russia and France. In this difficult struggle it is of utmost importance that Austria throw its main forces against Russia and not dissipate them in an offensive against Serbia . . . *Serbia plays only a minor role in this tremendous struggle* and requires, therefore, only those defensive measures which are absolutely necessary.[48]

Austria, however, was primarily interested in dealing with Serbia and warding off Greater Serbian aspirations through punitive military action. Vienna had not considered the contingency of the conflict spreading into a major war. Austrian hopes of limited military action were nourished by British willingness (in principle) to recognise Vienna's right to demand satisfaction from Serbia. As a report reached Vienna from its ambassador in London (sent 29 July, 16.32, arrived 30 July, 9.00) that Britain would intervene if a war resulted,[49] Austria decided to carry out its action against Serbia only so far that Russia would not become involved. Austria was encouraged by verbal recognition by Sergei Sazonov and the Russian ambassador in Vienna, Nikolai N. Shebekov, of Austria's right to teach Serbia a 'lesson'. The negotiations between Vienna, St Petersburg and Paris on an appropriate 'lesson' for Serbia had begun on 30 July, but they were cut short on 31 July by Berlin's 'lightning-like' decisions. Characteristic of this situation is the fact that, although the Germans declared war on Russia on 1 August, the Austrians only did so as late as 6 August and only after severe German warnings. This delay greatly disturbed Berlin, as Tirpitz later recalled.[50] If Austria had left Germany in the lurch or had backed out, Germany would not have been able to conduct the war. For the attack on France would have been impossible if the Austro-Hungarian army had not engaged five out of seven Russian armies for four to six weeks until the German army from France could be thrown against the east. At any rate, from 6 August onwards the apparently sovereign state of Austria-Hungary had become a helpmate of Germany in a major war which it had hoped to avoid and which overtaxed its powers.

We need not to go into closer detail about the alleged and completely fictitious 'facts' of French bombs on railway lines near Karlsruhe and Nuremberg, which were required to justify the German declaration of

---

48. Wilhelm II to Kaiser Franz Josef, 31 July 1914, in I. Geiss (ed.), *Julikrise und Kriegsausbruch 1914*, vol. II, Doc. No. 896, pp. 467 f. See also F. Fischer, *Germany's Aims*, p. 83.

49. Graf Mensdorf to Berchtold 29.7.1914, sent 29.7., 16.32, arrived 30.7., 9.00, I. Geiss (ed.), *July 1914. The Outbreak of the First World War: Selected Documents*, London, 1967, p. 277: 'Sir E. Grey was very anxious and continually endeavouring to find a way to prevent a conflagration . . . Russian interests leave England cool; but should it affect *a vital interest of France's or, what is more, a question of the position of France as a Power*, no English Government would be capable of preventing the participation of Great Britain on the side of France' (italics mine).

50. Alfred von Tirpitz, *Erinnerungen*, Leipzig, 1920, p. 243, n. 1: 'I was horrified to hear from Moltke that if Austria had shied away we would have needed to search for peace at any price.' Hartmut Pogge von Strandmann, 'Germany and the Coming of the War', in R.J.W. Evans and Harmut Pogge von Strandmann (eds), *The Coming of the First World War*, Oxford, 1988, p. 116.

war on France on 3 August. Nor will we deal with Chancellor Bethmann Hollweg's last attempt in his speech at midday on 4 August in
the Reichstag to gain, by concessions in the war at sea, Britain's
neutrality in Germany's war against France, which by now had already
begun, while castigating Russia as responsible for the war: 'Russia has
hurled a firebrand into our house. A war with Russia and France has
been forced upon us!' The British government did not accept the
renewed German proposal of a neutrality treaty. It declared through its
ambassador, Goschen, that it would be in a state of war with Germany
unless Germany withdrew its troops from Belgium before midnight
4 August. This Germany did not do.

Did Bethmann Hollweg actually believe that, even after violating
Belgian neutrality, he could enforce British neutrality by offering
German restraint in a naval war against France coupled with vocifer-
ous verbal attacks on Russia as the sole aggressor? If so, he was
suffering from the greatest delusion, and this was the greatest miscalculation of his entire career. Some even called it his *idée fixe*. In this he
completely misunderstood the logic behind British foreign policy
(aimed at upholding French independence and the *entente cordiale* with
Russia and perhaps also in consideration of the defence of India) and
the moral effect of Germany's violation of Belgian neutrality (which
Grey was waiting for). This violation enabled Grey to rally cabinet,
parliament and population against Germany and to win the sympathy
of international public opinion for the Triple Entente. Benthmann
Hollweg's policies had, in his own words, collapsed 'like a house of
cards'.[51]

Conclusions

Out of a continental war against France and Russia, envisaged in July–August 1914, there developed a world war. In place of
the 'short war', it developed from November 1914 into a war of
stopgaps, of exhaustion, an economic war, a war of resources, which
was to last another four years, and a war for which Germany was not
prepared. The German government had staked everything on one card
(the civilians had subjected themselves to the military concept) and

---

51. *British Blue Book*, Doc. No. 160 (1914), Sir E. Goschen to Sir Edward Grey,
London, 8 August 1914, referring to a conversation of Goschen with Reich Chancellor
Bethmann Hollweg on 4 August 1914 at about 19.30, on a desperate exclamation of the
Chancellor during this farewell discussion.

had lost first the battle of the Marne in September and then again the battle of Ypres and Langemark in November 1914 with dreadful losses of men. Falkenhayn, Moltke's successor, called the German army 'a broken tool'.[52] The Prusso-German Empire had passed the zenith of its power.

Was this a preventive war, as Egmont Zechlin and Karl Dietrich Erdmann today maintain?[53] Or a preventive war, as Hillgruber maintains, in accordance with the German military doctrine which considered it as the right or even the duty of a statesman to prevent the threatened formation of a more powerful hostile coalition in two or three years' time, and this regardless of any political or diplomatic development that may have occurred during this period? Was there such a threat in the expansion of the Russian army (and fleet) to an enormous peacetime strength by the year 1917, together with the building of fortifications and railways? Was there a real danger that Russia and France together would attack Germany in 1917? Would Britain, the strongest partner in the Triple Entente, have given its approval and support to an offensive war by Russia and France against Germany?

But what is a defensive war? Who threatened or attacked Germany? It was at any rate clear to the German government under Bethmann Hollweg even before the war that France must be eliminated as a great power for the foreseeable future and should exist as an ally or vassal-state of Germany. The reasons for this were France's alliance with Russia and its continual clashes with Germany in Turkey and in the Balkans, mainly with the help of its 'arme financière'. No French territory was to be annexed (with the exception of Longwy-Briey and a few important military strongpoints). But France would have to disarm, to pay a high sum of war reparations and be integrated into 'Central Europe', an economic block dominated by Germany. Here all French resources would be put at the disposal of Germany, which lacked capital, and the whole of France would be a market for German goods, unrestricted by import duties.

As far as Russia was concerned, the German Chancellor, two days after his speech in the Reichstag on 4 August, already had a clear

52. F. Fischer, *War of Illusions*, p. 545.
53. Karl Dietrich Erdmann, 'Hat Deutschland auch den Ersten Weltkrieg entfesselt? Kontroversen zur Politik der Mächte im Juli 1914'; Egmont Zechlin, 'Julikrise und Kriegsausbruch 1914' both in their *Politik und Geschichte. Europa 1914 – Krieg oder Frieden*, Kiel, 1985, pp. 19–48, 51 and pp. 90 ff. respectively, for the German tradition of preventive war. For a refutation of Erdmann's and Zechlin's views, see H. Pogge von Strandmann, 'Germany and the coming of the War', pp. 92–6, 107–14.

objective for the war on the eastern front. He described his aims as the liberation and securing of the races subjugated by Russia, the pushing back of the Russian frontier to Moscow and the establishment of a number of buffer states (Finland, Poland, Ukraine, Georgia) between Germany or Austria-Hungary and Russia.[54] This was over a month earlier than the much discussed 'September programme', which stated 'that Russia must be thrust back as far as possible from Germany's eastern frontier, and its domination over the non-Russian peoples broken'.[55]

Britain was expected to accept these changes on the continent and also to permit the acquisition of Portuguese, Belgian and French colonies for the creation of a defensible German Central Africa (this in an era when the idea of colonies was already disputed for economic as well as moral reasons). However one may judge these plans for the expansion of the German sphere of influence westwards and eastwards, disguised as it was by the Central European Economic Union (which was to be composed in the West of France and Belgium, the Netherlands and Denmark and eventually Norway and Italy; in the East of Austria-Hungary and Poland, but which should extend over Romania and Bulgaria as far as Turkey and the Hamburg-Baghdad line),[56] one thing is certain, namely, that this aim did not first originate in the war and that, intentionally or not, it amounted to a German hegemony on the continent.

Was it not the greatest of delusions that Germany believed it had to fight this war and that this was necessary for its own security? Bethmann Hollweg, the Russophobe, still claimed after the war in his memoirs that the war against Russia was necessary to maintain the independence of the German Reich and of Austria-Hungary.[57] Yet Russia was still lagging far behind in its development and, furthermore, was threatened with internal revolution. Germany was rich, flourishing and industrially the most progressive country in Europe, having already overtaken France and even Britain in many sectors. This Germany, with its 67 million inhabitants, led the way in science, particularly in the natural sciences; it led the way with its technical

---

54. Fritz Fischer, *Der Erste Weltkrieg und das deutsche Geschichtsbild*, Düsseldorf, 1977, esp. pp. 151–206: 'Deutsche Kriegsziele, Revolutionierung und Separatfrieden im Osten 1914–1918', cit. p. 158.
55. 'Septemberprogramm' in F. Fischer, *Germany's Aims*, pp. 103 ff.
56. 'Central European Economic Union' in ibid., p. 104, Program No. 4.
57. Theobald von Bethmann Hollweg, *Betrachtungen zum Weltkriege*, vol. I: *Vor dem Kriege*, Berlin, 1919, and vol. II: *Während des Krieges*, Berlin, 1921, ed. F. Bethmann Hollweg; See vol. 1, pp. 188, 189; vol. II, pp. 65 f., 67 f.

universities and with its applied research. Germany had a rising share of world trade, flourishing shipping interests, a highly developed banking system which was dovetailed with industry, and at a time when industry and research were already of decisive importance for the standing of a country in the world.

The 'War-Guilt' Question

It is not legitimate to approach the issue of the origins of the First World War and the July crisis of 1914 in terms of the 'war-guilt' thesis of 1919 and the related reparations question. As the Swiss historian Adolf Gasser has observed, in 1914 war was still, from the standpoint of *international law*, a recognised means of policy, and so regarded by all the Great Powers of the era.[58] The British scholars Zara Steiner[59] and James Joll[60] share this judgement. Considered in *moral* terms, it is undeniable that all the Great Powers practised expansionist and power politics, even if some did so more with the intent of preserving rather than modifying the status quo. Viewed *politically*, however, the question arises as to whether in the case of Prussia-Germany it was clever, wise or practicable to aspire, in such a short time, with such impatience and vehemence, and by means of such a 'hothouse' naval and military armaments policy, to effect an alteration in the international political system; in short, to practise a policy which must more or less inevitably lead to war.

The Germans after 1914 and after 1919 – even among the educated classes – did not realise and did not recognise that the German government in 1914 bore a decisive part of the responsibility for unleashing the World War but instead fought a twenty-year apologia against the 'Kriegsschuldlüge' (the lie of German war-guilt). Neither did the Germans realise or recognise the defeat of 1918 (through the brave resistance of French and British soldiers and the aid of fresh American troops) but instead took refuge in the so-called 'stab-in-the-back-legend' (Dolchstoßlegende, that is, treachery by Jews, defeatists,

---

58. Adolf Gasser, 'Der deutsche Hegemonialkrieg von 1914' in *Deutschland in der Weltpolitik des 19. und 20. Jahrhunderts. Festschrift für Fritz Fischer zum 65. Geburtstag*, ed. Imanuel Geiss and Bernd Jürgen Wendt, Düsseldorf, 1973, pp. 307–39, esp. p. 338; reprinted in Adolf Gasser, *Ausgewählte historische Schriften*, Basel, Frankfurt a. M., 1983, pp. 47–82.
59. Zara S. Steiner, *Britain and the Origins of the First World War*, London, 1977, pp. 213–41.
60. James Joll, *The Origins of the First World War*, London, New York, 1984; German ed: *Die Ursprünge des Ersten Weltkrieges*, Munich, 1988, *passim*.

pacifists, socialists, communists). And it was this twofold refusal by the German nation to see the truth that made it possible to lead this population to a new rearmament, to new expansionist policies and finally into a Second World War.

WILLIBALD GUTSCHE

The Foreign Policy of Imperial Germany and the Outbreak of the War in the Historiography of the GDR

Ever since history established itself as a science in the German Democratic Republic, it has devoted special attention to the causes of the First World War and, in this context, to the foreign policy of Imperial Germany and the role it played in the genesis of that war.[1]

Research based on Lenin's fundamental analysis of imperialism and on contemporary findings of Marxist historians and politicians in the 1950s and 1960s led to the publication in 1961 of Fritz Klein's comprehensive account entitled *Deutschland von 1897–98 bis 1917* (Germany from 1897–98 to 1917)[2] and to the three-volume edition of *Deutschland*

Abbreviations: *IHH* = *Illustrierte Historische Hefte*; *JbfG* = *Jahrbuch für Geschichte*; *JbfWg* = *Jahrbuch für Wirtschaftsgeschichte*; *Jahrb. Gesch. sozial. Länder Eur.* = *Jahrbuch für Geschichte der sozialistischen Länder Europas*; *Wiss.Z.* = *Wissenschaftliche Zeitschrift der Humboldt-Universität zu Berlin*; *ZfG* = *Zeitschrift für Geschichtswissenschaft*; ZStA = Zentrales Staatsarchiv.

1. Hans Joachim Bernhard and Dieter Fricke, 'Forschungen zur Geschichte Deutschlands und der deutschen Arbeiterbewegung von 1900–1917/18' in *Historische Forschungen in der DDR. Analysen und Berichte. Zum XI. Internationalen Historikerkongreß in Stockholm, August 1960*, Berlin (GDR), 1960, pp. 300 ff.; Willibald Gutsche and Annelies Laschitza, 'Forschungen zur deutschen Geschichte von der Jahrhundertwende bis 1917' in *Historische Forschungen in der DDR 1960–1970. Analysen und Berichte. Zum XIII. Internationalen Historikerkongreß in Moskau 1970*, Berlin, 1970, pp. 476 ff., 491 ff.; Willibald Gutsche and Helmut Otto, 'Der Erste Weltkrieg in der DDR-Geschichtswissenschaft' in Jürgen Rohwer (ed.), *Neue Forschungen zum Ersten Weltkrieg. Literaturberichte und Bibliographien von 30 Mitgliedstaaten der 'Commission Internationale d' Histoire Militaire Comparée'*, Koblenz, 1985, pp. 91 ff.

2. Fritz Klein, *Deutschland von 1897–98 bis 1917*, 5th edn, Berlin (GDR), 1986 (1st edn, 1961).

im ersten Weltkrieg (Germany in the First World War),[3] which came out in 1968. They offered a point of departure for further specialised studies. Those works already focussed particularly on the role of German foreign policy in the emergence of the First World War, as well as on the causes of its outbreak. Through an in-depth analysis of economic, social, political, military, cultural and ideological developments, the authors succeeded in demonstrating that the war of conquest, which all major imperialist powers fought, resulted primarily from conflicts of interest among the Great Powers, notably the one pitting the German Reich against Great Britain. What is more, they proved that those conflicts had begun to emerge with the transition to imperialism that started at the turn of the century in the wake of growing expansionist ambitions by monopoly capitalism. The authors made it clear that German imperialism and militarism played a specific part in the aggravation of international tensions by exhibiting a particularly unbridled hunger for expansion. Thus, these two factors not only bore the main responsibility for the actual eruption of the First World War but also for everything that led up to it, a phenomenon which is attributable to the militarist, semi-absolutist nature of the German Reich, to the uneven development of capitalist countries and, especially, to the rapid process of monopolisation.

In the 1970s and 1980s, GDR historians scrutinised the causes of the First World War in an even more elaborate and comprehensive fashion. The findings of that research have recently been compiled by a team of authors as Volume 6 of *Deutsche Geschichte in zwölf Bänden* (German History in Twelve Volumes). Volume 6, due to be published in 1990, will treat, again in an integrated manner, German history from 1897 to 1917.[4] Volume 5 of *Deutsche Geschichte*, depicting German history from 1871 to 1897, was published in 1988.[5]

The dispute over the causes of the war and Germany's responsibility, which since the 1960s has occupied non-Marxist historiographers, notably in the FRG, not least in what became known as the Fischer controversy, has entailed an intensification of relevant research work.

3. *Deutschland im ersten Weltkrieg. Von einem Autorenkollektiv unter Leitung von Fritz Klein*, Vol. 1: *Vorbereitung, Entfesselung und Verlauf des Krieges bis Ende 1914. Von einem Autorenkollektiv unter Leitung von Fritz Klein*, 2nd edn, Berlin (GDR), 1970 (1st edn, 1968).
4. *Deutsche Geschichte in zwölf Bänden*, ed. by the Zentralinstitut für Geschichte der AdW der DDR, Herausgeberkollegium, under the direction of Walter Schmidt, vol. 6: *Imperialismus im Kaiserreich und erster Weltkrieg von 1897 bis 1917*, by an author collective under the direction of Willibald Gutsche, in press 1990.
5. *Deutsche Geschichte in zwölf Bänden*, vol. 5: *Der Kapitalismus der freien Konkurrenz und der Übergang zum Monopolkapitalismus von 1871 bis 1897*, by an author collective under the direction of Gustav Seeber, Berlin (GDR), 1988.

As a result of that controversy, non-Marxist historiography no longer generally denied that German foreign policy displayed particular aggressiveness and that it had a considerable share in the developments leading up to the outbreak of the First World War. At the outset, Fritz Fischer's theory was resolutely rebuffed. According to him, the 'interaction of economics and politics' had been a factor 'which had made an appreciable impact both on diplomatic actions and domestic policy trends'. He was also convinced that the imperial government's policies aimed at translating its world-power plans into reality 'had been driven by quite palpable interests on the part of German industrial groups'.[6] Thereupon, numerous non-Marxist historians conceded that imperialism and the First World War had their roots in the emergence of 'industrial society' and that 'economic motives'[7] and 'economic antagonisms'[8] had played a major role, as well. They acknowledged that the German Reich had actively encouraged 'imperial competition' and finally and fatalistically[9] seen in war a 'certainty of the future'.[10] On the whole, however, the view prevailed that German foreign policy had been 'defensive in nature'.[11] According to Andreas Hillgruber, for example, it had merely followed the concept of a 'calculable risk for the purpose of achieving limited changes in the structure of political power by taking advantage of international crises'.[12] The resultant limited 'share of responsibility' for the German Reich, the extent of which has remained a matter of considerable debate,[13] continues to be perceived primarily in terms of political conditions and those related to the social structure, as well as in terms of ideological phenomena. In most cases, it is interpreted, and I quote, as 'an extreme deterioration of the competitive relationship which has always existed between sovereign nations', as 'a worsening of traditional government-to-government conflicts', brought about by nationalism – this is, for instance, the view of Gottfried Niedhardt[14] – and as 'a continuation of the old struggle

---

6. Fritz Fischer, *Griff nach der Weltmacht. Die Kriegszielpolitik des kaiserlichen Deutschland 1914–18*, Düsseldorf, 1961, p. 11; 3rd edn, 1964, p. 25; *idem, Krieg der Illusionen. Die deutsche Politik von 1911 bis 1914*, Düsseldorf, 1969, p. 13.
    7. See, for example, Wolfgang J. Mommsen, 'Der moderne Imperialismus als innergesellschaftliches Phänomen. Versuch einer universalgeschichtlichen Einordnung' in his *Der europäische Imperialismus. Aufsätze und Abhandlungen*, Göttingen, 1979, p. 61.
    8. Ploetz, 'Geschichte der Weltkriege' in Andreas Hillgruber and Jost Dülffer (eds), *Mächte Ereignisse, Entwicklungen 1900–1945*, Freiburg, Würzburg, 1981, p. 58.
    9. Ploetz, 'Das deutsche Kaiserreich 1870/71 bis 1918' in Dieter Langewiesche (ed.), *Bilanz einer Epoche*, Freiburg, Würzburg, 1984, p. 55.
    10. Ibid., p. 60.
    11. Gregor Schöllgen, *Das Zeitalter des Imperialismus*, Munich, 1986, p. 144.
    12. Cited in ibid., pp. 154 f.
    13. Ploetz, 'Geschichte der Weltkriege', p. 10.
    14. Ibid., p. 53.

within the existing system of states in Europe', as expressed by Hillgruber.[15]

Despite differences in the evaluation of the various driving forces of foreign policy, all these models boil down to one common denominator, namely, that German *Weltpolitik*, like the very conflict among the Great European Powers – which, for the first time ever in history, culminated in a world-wide war – must be viewed merely as a continuation of past international power rivalry, which had hardly anything to do with the transition from the capitalism of free competition to monopoly capitalism. That is why non-Marxist historiography in the FRG regards superstructural phenomena such as nationalist ideology, a semi-absolutist constitution and militaristic traditions of Prussian origin, or phenomena of a subjective nature such as lack of diplomatic experience, lack of understanding concerning the policies pursued by the other Great Powers, hunger for prestige and misinterpretation of international developments as the main causes prompting a German foreign policy that led to the isolation of the German Reich, to the establishment of the Triple Entente and eventually to armed confrontation.

It is our belief that such an interpretation may help to shed light on important facets of the causes of war, but it falls short of an answer to the question of what crucial driving forces had been at work in a foreign policy which, more than that of any other Great Power, had contributed to the aggravation of international tensions and prevented imperialist compromises.

The question must be asked as to whether lack of experience, shortage of able leaders and ignorance about enemy threats are really sufficient to explain a foreign policy consistently pursued by different political figures for more than two decades. Can one arrive at a comprehensive verdict if one interprets this foreign policy primarily in its own terms? Does it suffice to judge the policy decisions taken by the Reich's leadership mainly by the criteria of whether it could have acted with greater wisdom, more vision and more readiness for compromise and whether it could have refrained from its far-reaching expansionist plans? Of course, these are quite legitimate questions. An answer to them would be of benefit. Still, they remain largely academic, for the feelings, thoughts and actions of those responsible for foreign policy in the years preceding 1914 cannot, in the final analysis, be attributed merely to illusions or misconceptions. They must ultimately be attri-

15. Ibid., p. 59.

buted to a *Zeitgeist* inspired by the 'signs of the times', namely, a craving for power and expansion on the part of the classes which dominated society and on whose behalf politicians acted, or even had to act if they wanted to hold their own under the prevailing conditions. Examples of diplomats, like Lichnowsky, sounding a note of caution demonstrate that it was next to impossible to go against the tide, as long as the rule of Junker and bourgeois imperialism persisted.

This is precisely why GDR historians view it as their prime task, in studying the foreign policy of imperial Germany and the developments that triggered the First World War, to examine the driving forces and mechanisms which instigated a foreign policy that led to war. And why did it arise even though there were warning voices from the working-class movement and leading political figures like Bethmann Hollweg who also expressed qualms about the implications of such an adventurous foreign policy, about a world war and its unforeseeable consequences? In order to answer these crucial questions, it is not sufficient just to analyse the connection between foreign policy and the outbreak of war. Rather, any satisfactory answer would require a close examination of the interactions and relationships between economic, social, military and ideological developments, on the one hand, and the foreign policy course which Germany steered in its international relations, on the other.

Since the facts about German foreign policy between 1897 and 1914 are largely known, I will concentrate on elucidating the methodological aspects under which historians in the GDR have, with the above-mentioned objectives in mind, been pursuing their research during the last two decades. I will also draw attention to their main findings.

In preparing the book *Deutschland im ersten Weltkrieg*, research had focussed on how the war had been engineered politically and militarily, what influence big business had upon the war objectives of the imperial government, how a state-monopoly war economy was organised and how the war was conducted. Later, GDR historians devoted greater attention to the link between pre-war expansion and war policy and to the forces which had pressed for military expansion and the imperial government decisions which had led to the outbreak of war.[16]

Expansionist endeavours particularly affected the plans regarding Central Europe.[17] Those plans were identical to those at the turn of the

---

16. See here *JbfG*, vol. 15: *Studien zur Geschichte deu deutschen Imperialismus von der Jahrhundertwende bis 1917*, ed. by the Abteilung 1900–1917 des Zentralinstituts für Geschichte der AdW der DDR under the direction of Willibald Gutsche, Berlin (GDR), 1977.

17. In this context see Willibald Gutsche, 'Mitteleuropaplanungen in der Außenpoli-

century, as far as the goal of establishing a large German-dominated area was concerned. They differed, however, in terms of contents and approaches, due to the special economic and political interests pursued by influential groupings of the monopoly bourgeoisie and Junkers. The contradictions inherent in those plans[18] apply equally to the 'Central Europe' concept devised by the imperial government, [19] to expansion in south-east Europe, which had a major bearing on the decision to risk war and which was linked with Middle-East expansion,[20] to the policy of colonial expansion whose aim had been, from as far back as the turn of the century, to set up a large German colonial empire in Central Africa,[21] and to the 'cold invasion' of France.[22]

From a methodological point of view, specialised studies on the principal directions and objects of expansion have been increasingly combined with questions about the relationship between economics and politics in general and monopoly capital and the state apparatus in particular. One of the results of those studies has been that the weight and forms of these relationships have taken on clearer contours. Special attention was devoted to the development of the mechanisms underlying the interrelationships between economics and politics in the period from the close of the nineteenth century until 1914. In this context, it was asked if, previously, too static a view – i.e. the assumption of enduring monopoly dominance in the economy as it had evolved at the turn of the century – had not made it almost impossible to gain deeper

tik des deutschen Imperialismus vor 1918', *ZfG*, 20, 1972, pp. 533 ff.; Herbert Gottwald, 'Gemeinsamkeiten und Unterschiede in der Mitteleuropapolitik der herrschenden Klassen in Deutschland von der Jahrhundertwende bis 1918', *JbfG*, vol. 15, pp. 145 ff.; Ursula Mader, 'Europapläne und Kriegsziele Walther Rathenaus (1912–1916), *JbfG*, vol. 15, pp. 191 ff.; Jörg Villain, 'Zur Genesis der Mitteleuropakonzeption Friedrich Naumanns bis zum Jahre 1915', *JbfG*, vol. 15, pp. 207 ff.

18. In this context see Alfred Schröter, 'Die objektiven Triebkräfte und Hemmnisse der deutschen imperialistischen Mitteleuropapläne', *JbfG*, vol. 15, pp. 19 ff.; Helga Nussbaum, 'Außenhandelsverflechtung und imperialistische deutsche Mitteleuropapläne 1899 bis 1914', *JbfG*, vol. 15, pp. 31 ff.

19. Willibald Gutsche, 'Zur Mitteleuropapolitik der deutschen Reichsleitung von der Jahrhundertwende bis zum Ende des ersten Weltkrieges', *JbfG*, vol. 15, pp. 85 ff.

20. In this context see W. Gutsche, 'Zur Südosteuropaexpansion des deutschen Imperialismus vom Ende des 19. Jahrhunderts bis zum Ende des ersten Weltkrieges', *JbfG*, vol. 15, pp. 235 ff.; *idem*, 'Serbien in den Mitteleuropaplänen des deutschen Imperialismus am Vorabend des ersten Weltkrieges', *ZfG*, 23, 1975, pp. 35 ff.

21. In this context see Helmut Stoecker (ed.), *Drang nach Afrika. Die koloniale Expansionspolitik und Herrschaft des deutschen Imperialismus in Afrika von den Anfängen bis zum Ende des zweiten Weltkrieges*, Berlin (GDR), 1977; Willibald Gutsche, 'Zu Hintergründen und Zielen des "Panthersprungs" nach Marokko von 1911', *ZfG*, 2, 1980, pp. 134 ff.

22. See in this context Willibald Gutsche, 'Die deutschen Montanmonopole und Großbanken und die französischen Erzfelder vor dem ersten Weltkrieg', *ZfG*, 24, 1976, pp. 681 ff.

insights into the changes that had taken place in the run-up to the First World War.

These studies reveal that, especially in the last decade before the beginning of the war, profound changes were taking place with respect to the objective and subjective influence monopoly capital was having on the state apparatus. As a result, it is now more widely recognised that, first and foremost, the interaction of those base-level processes with political, social and ideological phenomena occasioned a growing inclination on the part of the political and military leadership towards an aggressive foreign policy, which eventually came to regard war as the only possible way of realising their ambitious claims to economic and political supremacy.

But an even more exact analysis of the mechanisms governing the relationship between monopoly capital and the state apparatus, and of the ways it reflected upon the process by which the leadership of the German Reich became more and more willing to wage war, was still desirable. In order to achieve this, empirical research to explain the phenomenon of growing expansionism resumed in the 1980s, on the basis of fresh methodological considerations. This research has focussed on the following general issues:

(1) The processes and new quality characterising the relationship between economics and foreign policy in the early stages of German imperialism.[23]

(2) The results of the expansionist pressures which monopoly capitalist relations of production exerted on the foreign policy conducted by the government.[24]

(3) Changes in the subjective attitudes of government leaders towards the pursuit of economic expansion interests as a priority of the government's foreign policy.[25]

(4) The role played by emerging elements of state-monopoly capi-

---

23. Willibald Gutsche, 'Zur Erforschung des Verhältnisses von Ökonomie und Politik im deutschen Imperialismus vor 1917', *Zfg*, 25, 1977, pp. 711 ff.

24. Willibald Gutsche, *Monopole, Staat und Expansion vor 1914. Zum Funktionsmechanismus zwischen Industriemonopolen, Großbanken und Staatsorganen in der Außenpolitik des Deutschen Reiches 1897 bis Sommer 1914*, Berlin (GDR), 1986; 'Fritz Klein, Politische und wirtschaftliche Interessen in der Balkanpolitik Deutschlands und Österreich-Ungarns 1912' in Fritz Klein (ed.), *Neue Studien zum Imperialismus vor 1914*, Berlin (GDR), 1980, pp. 109 ff.; Heinz Lemke, 'Politik und Ökonomie in den deutsch-russischen Beziehungen vor dem ersten Weltkrieg: Bestrebungen, Rußland den deutschen Geldmarkt zu sperren' in ibid., pp. 51 ff.; idem, *Finanztransaktionen und Außenpolitik. Deutsche Banken und Rußland im Jahrzehnt vor dem ersten Weltkrieg*, Berlin (GDR), 1985.

25. W. Gutsche, *Monopole, Staat und Expansion vor 1914*, pp. 120 ff.

talism in the growing aggressiveness of German imperialism.[26]

(5) The *rapprochement* between the monopoly bourgeoisie and Junkerdom and the emergence of a bloc of exploiters, whose views concurred in the basic issues of the class struggle but who remained divided over the motives and ways in which joint class interests should be secured.[27]

(6) The interaction of historical and systemic driving forces and their impact on the growing aggressiveness of German imperialism.[28]

(7) Changes in the disposition of the ruling classes and the imperial government towards war during the period from 1871 to 1914 and their impact on foreign policy.[29]

(8) Principal reasons why direct willingness to wage war prevailed among the ruling classes on the eve of the war.[30]

(9) The interconnection of foreign policy, militarism and the arms race.[31]

(10) The responsibility of the imperialist system in general and German imperialism in particular for the aggravation of the contradictions and the unleashing of war in the summer of 1914.[32]

26. Helga Nussbaum, 'Zur Imperialismustheorie W.I. Lenins und zur Entwicklung staatsmonopolistischer Züge des deutschen Imperialismus bis 1914', *JbfWg*, 4, 1970, pp. 25 ff.; Dieter Baudis and Helga Nussbaum, *Wirtschaft und Staat in Deutschland vom Ende des 19. Jahrhunderts bis 1918–19* (vol. 1 of Helga Nussbaum and Lotte Zumpe (eds), *Wirtschaft und Staat in Deutschland. Eine Wirtschaftsgeschichte des staatsmonopolistischen Kapitalismus in Deutschland vom Ende des 19. Jahrhunderts bis 1945 in drei Bänden*), Berlin (GDR), 1978.

27. Horst Handke, 'Einige Probleme der Sozialstruktur im imperialistischen Deutschland vor 1914', *JbfG*, vol. 15, pp. 261 ff.; idem, 'Einige Probleme der inneren Struktur der herrschenden Klassen in Deutschland vom Ende des 19. Jahrhunderts bis zum ersten Weltkrieg' in Fritz Klein (ed.), *Studien zum deutschen Imperialismus vor 1914*, Berlin (GDR), 1976, pp. 85 ff.; Wolfgang Küttler, 'Zu den Kriterien einer sozialen Typologie des Junkertums im System des deutschen Imperialismus vor 1917', *ZfG*, 8, 1979, pp. 722 ff.; Willibald Gutsche, 'Monopolbourgeoisie, Staat und Außenpolitik vor dem ersten Weltkrieg. Zu einige Forschungsproblemen der Geschichte der deutschen Bourgeoisie bis zum ersten Weltkrieg', *ZfG*, 29, 1981, pp. 239 ff.

28. Willibald Gutsche, 'Der gewollte Krieg. Zur deutschen Verantwortung für die Entstehung des Ersten Weltkrieges', *Blätter für deutsche und internationale Politik* (Cologne), 6, 1984, pp. 732 ff.

29. *Idem*, 'Außenpolitische Ziele, Rüstungspolitik und Kriegsdisposition der deutschen Reichsleitung vor 1914', *ZfG*, 36, 1988, pp. 963 ff.

30. *Idem*, 'Die Herausbildung der unmittelbaren Kriegsdisposition des deutschen Imperialismus im Sommer 1914', *Militärgeschichte* (Berlin), 2, 1984, pp. 107 ff.; idem, 'Zur Entfesselung des ersten Weltkrieges. Aktuelle Probleme der Forschung', *ZfG*, 33, 1985, pp. 779 ff.

31. Peter Bachmann and Kurt Zeisler, *Der deutsche Militarismus*, vol. 1: *Vom brandenburg-preußischen zum deutschen Militarismus. Illustrierte Geschichte*, 2nd edn, Berlin (GDR), 1986, pp. 312 ff.; Karl Nuss (ed.), *Der deutsche Militarismus in Geschichte und Gegenwart. Studien, Probleme, Analysen*, Berlin (GDR), 1980.

32. Willibald Gutsche, 'Historische Erfahrungen und aktuelle Lehren des ersten imperialistischen Weltkrieges', *Militärgeschichte* (Berlin), 4, 1985, pp. 291 ff.

Such general analyses have been accompanied by empirical studies on numerous facets of foreign policy and expansion: German policy towards South Africa, expansion in China, the Moroccan Crises, German expansion in Brazil, the policy towards the Ukraine, oil policies, German-Russian relations, the relationship between Germany and the United States, expansion in the Middle East and German colonial policy in Africa.[33] A monograph entitled *Monopole, Staat und Expansion vor 1914* (Monopolies, State and Expansion Prior to 1914) sums up the latest research findings on the mechanisms linking big industrial corporations, large banks and government bodies with respect to the foreign policy of the German Reich from 1897 to 1914.[34]

A favourable environment for particular aggressiveness was indeed created by the historical development of capitalism in Germany, particularly by its belated emergence, the failure of the bourgeois-democratic revolution in 1848–9, the Prussian-led unification from above which established Germany as a single-state nation and the early formation of relatively sizeable state property, notably in Prussia. However, the prime movers that escalated that aggressiveness were, in fact, systemic driving forces, i.e. the driving forces inherent in the monopolistic stage of capitalism and not pre-industrial, pre-capitalist or pre-bourgeois elements in the social and political structure of the empire.[35] These systemic forces resulted in a foreign policy that had initially set its sights on a militaristic arms build-up and then went on to accept the risk of war.[36]

From the 1890s, a marked turnaround took place in the foreign-policy calculations of the leadership of the German Reich, to which Gregor Schöllgen has drawn attention in *Imperialismus und Gleichgewicht* (Imperialism and Equilibrium).[37] In the period immediately following 1871, Bismarck was still conducting a relatively peaceful foreign policy. He based his approach on the German Reich's saturation and still viewed economic expansion interests as being primarily a private matter of the parties concerned. This contrasted with the *Weltpolitik* proclaimed by Bernhard von Bülow in 1897, which was aimed at expansion. This policy went through different stages. In the beginning,

33. See the Appendix to this chapter.
34. See note 24.
35. In this context, see Helmut Böhme, 'Thesen zur Beurteilung der gesellschaftlichen, wirtschaftlichen und politischen Ursachen des deutschen Imperialismus' in Wolfgang J. Mommsen (ed.), *Der moderne Imperialismus*, Stuttgart, Berlin (FRG), Cologne, Mainz, 1971, p. 54.
36. W. Gutsche, 'Der gewollte Krieg', pp. 736 ff.
37. Gregor Schöllgen, *Imperialismus und Gleichgewicht. Deutschland, England und die orientalische Frage 1871–1914*, Munich, 1984, p. 87.

'purely economic' expansion interests were still set apart from political ones. However, they were increasingly referred to as 'national interests'. Eventually, in 1910, Theobald von Bethmann Hollweg started to call them 'one of the most important tasks of our foreign policy'. In this context, he regarded England 'as the decisive rival of Germany when it comes to the policy of economic expansion'.[38]

In this process of change, which went hand in hand with an escalated arms race, notably in the navy, German foreign policy abandoned the course of compromise and opted instead for one of confrontation with other imperialist Powers. Committed to the catchword '*Weltpolitik*', Germany's foreign policy at that point was not aimed at attaining more political power as such. The arguments presented as rationale and justification demonstrate that a concrete physical expansion of economic might was sought in the form of colonies and semi-colonies, markets and outlets, raw material resources, spheres of capital investment and influence.[39] Foreign policy was increasingly expected to effect such acquisitions or secure them politically.

Expansionist strivings, which were coupled with the claim to economic and political supremacy, were not primarily brought about by subjective factors, such as wrong political decisions or unrealistic assessments of the international situation, but by the new quality of the relationship between economics and foreign policy. This was a phenomenon that objectively came into being in all developed capitalist countries with their transition to imperialism. Monopoly capitalism produced new dimensions of external economic expansion interests, and the fact that the distribution of the world had been concluded led to a growing rivalry among the Great Powers. Thus, neither economic expansion without political support from the state nor strategic geopolitical expansion of power without economic support from finance capital were possible any more.[40] Incidentally, even prominent bourgeois figures of that period like the historian Karl Lamprecht realised this interrelationship. He wrote, for example, at the beginning of the new century: 'The signature of the times reads expansion: expansion of an economic nature and then, for the purpose of backing it up and increasing it, political expansion. The instinct of economic power has

38. See W. Gutsche, *Monopole, Staat und Expansion vor 1914*, p. 126.
39. In this context, see Willibald Gutsche, Fritz Klein, Joachim Petzold, *Von Sarajevo nach Versailles. Deutschland im ersten Weltkrieg*, Berlin, 1985, pp. 11 ff.; Helmut Otto and Karl Schmiedel, *Der erste Weltkrieg. Militärhistorischer Abriß*, 3rd rev. edn, Berlin (GDR), 1977, pp. 9 ff.
40. W. Gutsche, *Monopole, Staat und Expansion vor 1914*, pp. 93 ff.

turned into a political one, and the movement of unity has been succeeded by the era of *Weltpolitik*.'[41]

This motive force underlying the foreign policy of all imperialist nations made itself particularly felt in the German Reich. German imperialism had got a raw deal when the world had been distributed but, from an economic point of view, was now growing more rapidly and in a more organised manner. It was now bent at all costs on overcoming the deteriorating 'discrepancy between the development of productive forces and the accumulation of capital on the one hand and the distribution of colonies and spheres of influence for finance capital on the other',[42] at the expense of the already 'replete' rivals.

Factors such as the preservation of strong feudal remnants in the class structure, militaristic traditions of the Prussian type and the semi-absolutist nature of the ruling system had an additional impact on the manifestations of the aggressiveness thus generated.

In fact, it is impossible to comprehend the increasing aggressiveness of German foreign policy if the interconnection between imperialism and militarism is not taken into account. All foreign-policy activities were more or less based on a military strategy which anticipated an eventual military confrontation with France and Russia. German diplomacy perceived one of its main tasks to be the creation of favourable conditions for such a war. It continually resorted to military threats and blackmail. As the Hague Peace Conferences bear out, of all the Great Powers Germany was least prepared to accept arms limitations or the commitment to seek peaceful solutions to serious international conflicts.

The results of German foreign policy, inspired by hunger for economic expansion, were by no means insignificant. In terms of the overall objective, however, they remained minimal. This produced growing dissatisfaction among the ruling classes, who turned it into 'public opinion' by means of the chauvinist and militarist propaganda fomented by them. Public opinion lent its own weight, in so far as it brought additional – ideological – pressure to bear on the imperial government from bourgeois parties and other organisations defending the interests of the bourgeoisie and Junkerdom.

In that process, the government of the Reich did not necessarily aim at a European war right from the start. Initially, it had still hoped to

41. Karl Lamprecht, *Deutsche Geschichte*, 2nd supplementary vol., 2nd part, Berlin, 1902–4, pp. 11 f.

42. W.I. Lenin, 'Der Imperialismus als höchstes Stadium des Kapitalismus' in his *Werke*, vol. 22, Berlin (GDR), 1960, p. 280.

reach its geopolitical ends without a war. The attempts undertaken within the framework of Germany's foreign policy to persuade England and Russia into a *rapprochement* with the Triple Alliance served this very purpose. On the assumption that differences among England, France and Russia were irreconcilable and Germany was thus free in its decisions, it conducted an expansionist foreign policy which threatened vital expansionist interests of those countries. As a consequence, the international balance of power changed fundamentally and the German Reich became isolated. Many at the time sounded warnings against that policy; Franz Mehring, for example, foresaw in 1904 that, as a result of German foreign policy, an *entente cordiale* would be formed by England, France and Russia, for German imperialism was the most dangerous rival of all three nations.

When the Triple Entente was set up, chiefly motivated by the German ambition to become a world power, the government of the German Reich considered its destruction a decisive prerequisite for a major breakthrough. It initially tried to accomplish this by relatively 'peaceful' means, especially by prying Britain away from the alliance. The chief reasons for the failure of these attempts were not only its rivals' policies, equally marked by a striving for expansion. As well, the German government's lack of willingness to search for alternatives, in the form of imperialist compromises, and the sustained policy of strength and military threats by which it hoped to get the other Great Powers to acquiesce to its goals in reality only helped to solidify the enemy coalition.

Aggressive foreign politics, accompanied by constant sabre-rattling, was also constantly aimed at strengthening the class compromise between the bourgeoisie and Junkers and alleviating social tensions through success in the area of foreign policy. Even so, motives of political union and social imperialism, on which non-Marxist historians in particular have laid so much stress, remained of secondary importance. Compared with the striving for economic expansion, they were merely supplementary driving forces. This was just as true of the naval arms race as of the construction of the Baghdad Railway and the Moroccan policy.

Not even the war plans devised by the general staff were the ultimate explanation of why Germany conducted a foreign policy that eventually led it to opt for war. Rather, it was the economic movement characteristic of the transition to monopoly capitalism and the increasingly close relationship between the economy and foreign policy that brought about a marked change in the imperial government's war disposition. This change meant that the concept which Bismarck had once propounded, namely, that war was a means to assert power, had lost its foundation. Instead, war was perceived as an instrument to enlarge power and conquer foreign territories and spheres of influence. Of course, this perception was still influenced by obsolete views considering war as a legitimate tool of politics, and it was consistent with the militaristic traditions of Prussia, which fused with the militaristic trends inherent in imperialism.[43] It was thus possible for pre-emptive war plans, which had long ago been worked out by the military, to exert increasing influence on foreign policy considerations.

Even before 1897, the general staff had been preparing for a war on two fronts against France and Russia. On several occasions prior to 1914 it believed the stage had been set, in terms of armaments, for such a war and that an all-out attack could and should be launched. However, the most crucial factor allowing such plans to acquire political relevance was the disposition and preparedness on the part of the civilian leadership of the Reich to make war. Under the influence of the growing expansionist pressure exerted by the ruling classes and as a consequence of the changes in the international balance of power, war plans underwent considerable modification in the period from 1897 to 1914.

With the transition to *Weltpolitik*, the first view to gain currency was that war was inevitable as a tool to enlarge power *vis-à-vis* imperialist rivals but that it would have to be put off until the naval armaments programme begun in 1897 was completed. Still, from the very outset, armament and readiness to wage war had been been regarded as necessary means of pressure in order to obtain a relatively 'peaceful' expansion through predominantly diplomatic efforts. This approach was meant to yield partial successes, some even to be reached in concert with other Great Powers, which were trying to do the same.

This disposition was occasioned, on the one hand, by a level of armament not yet sufficient for any higher risk and, on the other, by the still strong hope of obtaining an appropriate piece of the cake through a 'free hand' policy. It was rooted not only in illusions about the intentions of the other Powers, notably England and Russia, but also in the resolve, fuelled by hunger for power and expansion, not to put up

---

43. See Heinz Wolter, *Bismarcks Außenpolitik 1871–1881. Außenpolitische Grundlinien von der Reichsgründung bis zum Dreikaiserbündnis*, Berlin (GDR), 1983, pp. 81 ff.; Willibald Gutsche, 'Außenpolitische Ziele, Rüstungspolitik und Kriegsdisposition der deutschen Reichsleitung vor 1914', *ZfG*, 36, 1988, pp. 963 ff.

with minor concessions. Hopes that world-power politics might be attainable through peaceful, diplomatic activities dwindled, however. Proof of that is a statement by Bethmann Hollweg, who said at the end of the year 1910 that 'acquisitions are hardly conceivable in any other way than by conquest through war or as a consequence of a nation falling apart'.[44]

The failure of attempts to make progress by relatively 'peaceful' means led to a policy of war threats, coupled with actual readiness to make war. Bethmann Hollweg later on described this concept quite unambiguously as a 'policy of extreme risk, where every repetition' increased the danger of armed conflict.[45] If at all possible, the government of the Reich did not yet want to cross the threshold of war. Increasingly, though, it considered war a possibility, during the second Moroccan Crisis, for example. With respect to that incident, Alfred von Tirpitz characterised this stage of war readiness by the not entirely inappropriate comment: 'In actual fact, one did not want war. But one acted in such a way that things had to move towards it or to a Fashoda.'[46]

When the 'Panthersprung' to Agadir failed in 1911 and diplomatic efforts to make England give a binding promise to remain neutral in the event of a war between Germany, France and Russia did not come to fruition, the ruling classes saw their hopes evaporate. They had pinned their hopes of breaking up the Entente – as a prerequisite for attaining a sweeping expansion – solely on the demonstration of readiness to make war. The conviction that war was inescapable grew further as a result of mounting anxiety that the spheres of influence already conquered in the Near East and in the Balkans might be lost and that, in view of domestic disintegration, one could soon no longer be assured of the Austro-Hungarian monarchy as a reliable ally in a European war. These fears became stronger in the wake of the Balkan wars of 1912–13 and with free capital for foreign loans becoming increasingly scarce.

While the conduct of a war had, up to this point, been regarded as a possible consequence of the policy of war threats, the relationship between politics and war was now turned completely upside down. The notion of the 'extreme risk' took on a new dimension. Germany was

44. Cited by W. Gutsche, *Monopole, Staat und Expansion vor 1914*, p. 226.
45. ZStA, Historische Abteilung I, Potsdam, Nachlaß Otto Hammann, No. 4, Bl. 13, Bethmann Hollweg to Bernhard von Bülow, 10.6.1915.
46. Dieter Fricke and Annelies Laschitza (eds), *Dokumente zur deutschen Geschichte 1910–1914*, Berlin (GDR), 1976, No. 35, p. 54, Alfred von Tirpitz to Eduard von Capelle, 12.8.1911.

now willing to provoke war proper and hoped to be able to blackmail the other Powers into a compromise, which would break up the Entente. This, however, made the risk of a world-wide war incalculable. As a result, war was consciously envisaged in the foreseeable future as a continuation of politics.

Proof of this new stage in a disposition towards war was the reinforcement of the army in 1912 and 1913 for which there was no parallel since 1871. From that time, the aim of the accelerated arms build-up was to obtain a military edge at any cost in order to be able, at the earliest convenience, to start the *Blitzkrieg* against France and Russia, as laid down in the Schlieffen Plan. The general staff cited as reason for increasing the strength of the army the need 'to create the balance of forces required for a westward offensive and, at the same time, to provide sufficient protection to our eastern regions'[47] with a view to preparing the 'great war', which 'will be decided on land and whose outcome will have to be determined by the army'.[48]

But why did German foreign policy not take advantage of the possibilities existing for a German-British accommodation of interests, which arose when England gave up its 'splendid isolation' in 1898, and why did it repeatedly ignore relevant British advances or torpedo them by raising unacceptable conditions? These much discussed questions, in fact, bring us to a key issue of German foreign policy and international relations in the period preceding 1914. The responsibility for the failure of all those contacts did not lie exclusively with the government of the German Reich. British imperialism sought to uphold its domination. British Foreign Secretary Grey, for instance, went as far as conceding in 1911 that Germany had been put at a disadvantage in Africa,[49] but when the German ambassador demanded 'more',[50] Grey was only prepared to make concessions at the expense of other Powers or in the form of insignificant compensation. Most of all, however, the German side thwarted any understanding by its refusal to pay the price for it. That price would have included forgoing the naval arms race, giving up its claim to the dominating position in the construction of the Baghdad railway and refraining from supporting the Austrian Balkans policy. In view of the expansionist strivings of the German ruling circles, such concessions were hardly conceivable. What is more, the

47. Helmut Otto and Karl Schmiedel (eds), *Der erste Weltkrieg. Dokumente*, Berlin (GDR), 1977, Doc. 7, p. 57, memorandum of Helmuth von Moltke of 21.12.1912.
48. Ibid., Doc. 5, p. 51, memorandum of Helmuth von Moltke of 2.12.1911.
49. The Private Papers of Sir Francis Bertie, PRO/FO 800/165, Bl. 104 ff., Grey to Bertie, 20.7.1911.
50. PRO/FO 800/186, Bl. 245, Grey to Goschen, 17.7.1911.

German proposals did not aim at *détente* in Europe. Their only purpose
was to obtain the pledge of British neutrality in the continental war
with France and Russia, which was expected sooner or later. Thus, a
German-British understanding would not have ruled out such a war.
Presumably, it might even have promoted it. The consequence could
well have been that England would have had to face an appreciable
increase of German power on the continent. As Paul M. Kennedy has
pointed out, German-British antagonism was based mainly on economic differences.[51]

It may seem to be a contradiction that the government of the
German Reich was largely responsible for unleashing the war at a time
when it had just opted for a number of compromises with England,
relating to the building of the Baghdad railway and to crude oil fields
in Mesopotamia, compromises which were tantamount to major German concessions. It must be asked, however, whether we are really
talking, as Gregor Schöllgen maintains, about 'considerable' readiness
to seek a compromise and understanding meant to 'prevent' the
catastrophe of war or about the tacit acceptance of Germany's 'role as a
junior partner' *vis-à-vis* England.[52] The circumstances under which
these compromises were initialled and the statements made by those
who took part in the negotiations rather suggest something Fritz
Fischer underlined, namely, that the concessions were economically
necessary in order to save as much as possible at one of the main axes of
German expansion policy and that those compromises constituted the
last attempt to buy British neutrality in the impending war.[53]

These defeats – since this is what all this boils down to – must have
made the leaders in Berlin all the more determined to resort to force.
That conclusion can be drawn from a fake interview with an anony-
mous Entente diplomat. The interview, which has gone unnoticed so
far, was arranged by the German Foreign Office and published in the
Berliner Lokal-Anzeiger on 20 June 1914, in other words, a week before
the assassination incident in Sarajevo. It caused quite a stir among the
governments of the Entente Powers. It referred to the political situation
in south-east Europe, to the future of Austria-Hungary, to adequate
markets and outlets for powerfully and rapidly advancing German
industries and to the growing discrepancy between the German desire
for expansion and borders that were increasingly becoming too narrow

51. Paul M. Kennedy, *The Rise of the Anglo-German Antagonism 1860–1914*, London,
Boston, Sydney, 1980, pp. 320, 464.
52. G. Schöllgen, *Imperialismus und Gleichgewicht*, pp. 433, 430.
53. F. Fischer, *Krieg der Illusionen*, pp. 435 ff., 438 f.

for that desire to be realised. And combined with these issues, the following threat was launched against the Entente countries: 'All these issues will sooner or later produce problems which cannot be resolved by mere love of peace.'[54] This thinly veiled threat did not exactly hint at readiness for compromise. The pan-German newspaper *Die Post*, which endorsed the views of heavy industry, had this comment to offer on the very same evening: 'If . . . our natural and necessary striving for expansion is denied any possibility of being realised, one day the sword will inexorably be laid into our hands. Then however, "vae victis"!'[55]

It is especially in connection with the antagonism between Germany and England that the role which calculable Great-Power policies play in preventing war has frequently been discussed of late. Answers in this regard are of great importance as lessons of history for our own time. Obviously, the conditions allowing relevant insights and conclusions about the need for a balance of power did not exist before 1914. Prevailing notions of security and equilibrium were subordinated to the striving for power and expansion. This resulted in conflicting opinions dictated by the pursuit of one's own advantage. Thus, England interpreted equilibrium as the preservation of the status quo on the continent. Germany saw in its *Weltpolitik* a legitimate attempt to 'emulate other Powers' in conquering 'a place in the sun'. And Russia regarded the equilibrium as being upset if Austria established its hegemony in the Balkans. A common denominator could only have been found if all the sides had subordinated power and expansionist interests to the resolve to maintain peace and to make meaningful concessions. Such a willingness was lacking, however, as the counterforces were still too weak, and the dimensions and implications of a modern world war had not yet been experienced.

The historical and systemic trends outlined above are not sufficient by themselves to specify what motive eventually caused the government of the German Reich in the summer of 1914 to resort to a policy of incalculable risk, which resulted in the outbreak of the First World War. In fact, we have identified six major contributing factors:

Firstly, the German Reich had isolated itself through its aggressive policy. It had also allied itself with the Habsburg Empire, a partner it could no longer count on in the foreseeable future, due to the processes

---

54. *Berliner Lokal-Anzeiger*, No. 307, 20.6.1914 (morning edn); Willibald Gutsche, '"Mitten im Frieden überfällt uns der Feind". Zur Friedensdemagogie des deutschen Imperialismus vor 1914 und ihren Auswirkungen' in Reinhard Kühnl, Karen Schönwälder (eds.), *Sie reden vom Frieden und rüsten zum Krieg. Friedensdemagogie und Kriegsvorbereitung in Geschichte und Gegenwart*, Cologne, 1986, pp. 58 ff.
55. *Die Post*, No. 284, 20.6.1914 (evening edn).

of disintegration taking place inside that state. With Austria-Hungary's power waning, the economic interests of German imperialism were being endangered, too. Support for the Austrian Balkans policy became a vital concern in an effort to maintain and expand pivotal spheres of influence in the Balkans and the Near East.

Secondly, influential quarters of the monopoly bourgeoisie had, since the Second Balkan War, been confronted with growing economic expansion by the Entente, in particular in the Balkans and the Near East. It became very hard for them to counteract that trend by 'peaceful' means. Financial opportunities diminished. This development was further compounded by a fresh cyclical crisis. The capacity of the German capital market was nearing exhaustion. The contradiction between domestic and external capital needs worsened, and Germany was no longer able to withstand the capital superiority of England and France. As a result, its political influence in those areas was in danger of becoming weaker. Those spheres of influence that had already been conquered appeared to be threatened.

Thirdly, in view of this situation, readiness among the ruling classes to start war gained the upper hand. Apart from mining and steel monopolists, influential representatives of large banks, electrical engineering and shipping corporations, which in the past had mostly been opposed to the risk of war because of special universal interests, were now inclined to pursue a non-peaceful option. For they were particularly hit by the difficulties expansion was encountering in the southeast. The following argument first formulated by Krupp's President, Alfred Hugenberg, on 25 April 1914, represents the common denominator: a 'liberating test of strength' could make it possible for us 'to apply much higher standards to our entire economic and political future'.[56]

Fourthly, the very readiness to make war also spread to the state apparatus, since foreign policy was now dominated by monopolistic interests. The Junker element lent an added stimulus to the belligerent striving for expansion, due to the emperor's high-handed methods of rule and the influence of militarism. In particular, it affected the ways in which the war was unleashed and the timing of the war.

Fifthly, the increasing calls for violent action, which was now regarded as the *ultima ratio* of unimpeded expansion, coincided with the conviction of the general staff – which was also that of the emperor and the government of the Reich – that the military edge achieved *vis-à-vis*

---

56. Alfred Hugenberg, *Streiflichter aus Vergangenheit und Gegenwart*, Berlin, 1927, p. 205.

Russia and France was seriously endangered. For what was considered to be an inevitable war, the present opportunity was believed to be the most propitious one, perhaps even the last one there would be.

Sixthly, from as far back as 1908, an Austro-Serbian conflict serving as a pretext of war had been regarded as an optimum situation for a hegemonical war. The assassination incident in Sarajevo offered just that opportunity. This conflict made an Austro-Hungarian partnership possible. It permitted a show of force in what, at that time, was a critical region for German expansionist interests. If the conflict spread, it offered a chance of provoking Russia, thus causing France to step in, creating, in turn, an opportunity to apply the Schlieffen Plan. Over and above that, Russia could then be presented as the culprit of the war. A war of conquest could be camouflaged as a defensive war. That way, the Social Democrats could be induced to 'go along'. Since they were under the influence of opportunism, no opposition was to be expected from them, anyway.

All these factors interacted with each other. The main responsibility of German imperialism had economic, socio-economic, political, military and ideological causes. Seen from a long-term perspective, that responsibility had its roots in historical developments. In the medium term, the origins lay in systemic conditions and judged from a short-term perspective, the responsibility has to be explained by the domestic and external situation existing in the summer of 1914. It does not matter whether economic or non-economic motives prevailed at the different levels at which readiness to wage war evolved; that readiness was deeply and objectively rooted in the economic movement, in the monopolist stage of capitalism.

While differing on details, GDR historiography has arrived at the conclusion that German foreign and armaments policies in the period preceding 1914 did not, in every respect, follow the concept of a 'calculated risk for the purpose of achieving limited changes in power politics'.[57] Rather, they were aimed from the very outset at attaining modifications in the international balance of power and, during that process, had moved from what was initially a 'calculated risk' – a strategy that was preferred out of consideration for the insufficient level of armaments – to an incalculable one. Furthermore, they were not defensive but aggressive policies. Reich Chancellor Bülow himself once conceded this when he stated that the root causes of the changes that

57. Andreas Hillgruber, *Deutsche Großmacht- und Weltpolitik im 19. und 20. Jahrhundert*, Düsseldorf, 1977, p. 92; *idem, Die gescheiterte Großmacht. Eine Skizze des Deutschen Reiches 1871–1945*, Düsseldorf, 1980, pp. 44 ff.

had taken place in the international situation in 1907 were the creation of the Triple Entente and 'the sustained growth of Germany's economic power'. He added that fear of Germany's increasing economic and political strength had driven other nations to form alliances, which had been primarily defensive in nature when they were set up.[58]

As well, Germany's policy during the 1914 July crisis was not a 'defensive' one, either to 'preserve power' or to 'arrive at a balance of power', as it was conducted with 'offensive political means'.[59] It was not a 'calculated risk' which went out of control because of the 'rigidity of military planning'.[60] Nor was it a 'necessary measure of defence' against Russia.[61] This policy was not the main product of social constraints, nationalistic ideologies or a power rivalry as such. It was first and foremost an adventurous offensive entailing an incalculable risk, rooted in the striving of big business for expansion and designed to enlarge economic and political power, an offensive which consciously accepted the use of armed force and the possibility of a world war.

The so-called localisation tactic, which the government of the Reich pursued during the July crisis, involved the risk of a world war. It did not represent an effort to prevent the 'great war' at the last minute. On the contrary, it was meant to secure as favourable a starting position for Germany as possible in the event of war. The decisions adopted in Potsdam on 5 and 6 July 1914, the attitude of the German government towards the Austrian ultimatum to Serbia, the German response to the attempts by Britain and Russia to mediate are all clear indications of Germany's attitude towards endeavours to manage the conflict, which Germany itself had instigated. They were only aimed at keeping England neutral, if only for a short time, in order to be able to carry out the German war plan without British involvement and – in view of widespread popular readiness, notably among Social Democrats, to fight a war – to disguise the war as a German defensive war. None of the other Great Powers exhibited such a prevalent disposition to resort to pre-emptive, offensive, armed action, in the wake of which a 'European war' was considered a possibility. This aggressive disposition, therefore, can be seen to have acted as a catalyst for the large variety of factors pressing for a transition from peaceful to armed expansion and

58. Cited by W. Gutsche, *Monopole, Staat und Expansion vor 1914*, p. 128.
59. Egmont Zechlin, *Krieg und Kriegsrisiko. Zur deutschen Politik im Ersten Weltkrieg. Aufsätze*, Düsseldorf, 1979, pp. 162, 190.
60. A. Hillgruber, *Die gescheiterte Großmacht*, pp. 44 f., 49 f.
61. Gordon A. Craig, *Deutsche Geschichte 1866–1945*, Munich, 1980, pp. 295, 297.

constituted the decisive impulse for the outbreak of the First World War.[62]

Even though Marxist and realistically minded non-Marxist historians may adhere to different concepts, they do see eye to eye when it comes to denouncing the policy responsible for the First World War. They agree that conclusions promoting peace need to be drawn for the present and for the future. Two fundamental historical lessons can be drawn from the experience of the First World War, namely, 'that Great Power wars can no longer be a rational tool of politics' and that 'forgoing the option of war . . . would presuppose mutual agreement.'[63] These can only be constructive, however, if they combine with a full and frank answer as to what objective driving forces, especially systemic ones, brought forth the two catastrophic wars in the first half of this century, and then only if inferences are drawn from them in an effort to safeguard peace in our times. Contributions of this kind will continue to be regarded by the science of history in the GDR as one of its first and foremost tasks.

Appendix: Recent GDR Literature on German Foreign Policy and Expansion before 1914

Jürgen Hell, 'Deutsche Expansion und interimperialistische Rivalität in Brasilien vor 1914' in F. Klein (ed.), *Neue Studien zum Imperialismus vor 1914*; H.-C. Stichler, 'Die Orte Gaomi und Jisozhou während der deutschen Kolonialherrschaft in China', *Wiss. Z.*, 2, 1988; Heinz Lemke, 'Die Erdölinteressen der Deutschen Bank in Mesopotamien in den Jahren 1903–1911', *JbfG*, 24, 1981; idem, 'Verbindungen der Petersburger Internationalen Handelsbank zu deutschen Banken Ende des 19. Jahrhunderts', *Jahrb. Gesch. sozial. Länder Eur.*, 28, 1984; idem, *Finanztransaktionen und Außenpolitik. Deutsche Banken und Rußland im Jahrzehnt vor dem ersten Weltkrieg*, Berlin (GDR), 1985; idem, 'Das Scheitern der Verhandlungen über die offizielle Beteiligung Frankreichs am Bagdadbahnunternehmen 1903', *JbfG*, 29, 1984; idem, 'Deutschland und Rußland während der Krisen im Jahrzehnt vor dem

---

62. Willibald Gutsche, *Sarajevo 1914. Vom Attentat zum Weltkrieg*, Berlin (GDR), 1984, pp. 50 ff.
63. Ploetz, 'Geschichte der Weltkriege', p. 24.

ersten Weltkrieg' in Fritz Klein (ed.), *Kriegsgefahren und Friedenschancen im 20.
Jahrhundert*, Berlin, 1985; idem, 'Politik und Ökonomie in den deutsch-
russischen Beziehungen vor dem ersten Weltkrieg: Bestrebungen, Rußland den
deutschen Geldmarkt zu sperren' in F. Klein (ed.), *Neue Studien zum Imperialismus vor 1914*; idem, 'Der Abschluß des Urheberrechtsvertrages zwischen Rußland und Deutschland im Jahre 1913', *Jahrb. Gesch. sozial. Länder Eur.*, 26/1,
1982; Claus Remer, 'Voraussetzungen und Bedingungen der Ukrainepolitik
des deutschen Imperialismus von der Jahrhundertwende bis zur Großen
Sozialistischen Oktoberrevolution', unpub. dissertation, [Diss. B], Jena, 1985;
idem, 'Einige Voraussetzungen und Aspekte der Ukrainepolitik des deutschen
Imperialismus zu Beginn des 20. Jahrhunderts', *Jahrb. Gesch. sozial. Länder Eur.*,
27, 1983; idem, 'Zur Wirtschaftsentwicklung und insbesondere zur Anlage
deutschen Kapitals in der Ukraine von der Jahrhundertwende bis 1914',
JbfWg, 2, 1985; idem, 'Zur Rolle der Rußlanddeutschen im Kalkül des deutschen Imperialismus', *Jenaer Beiträge zür Parteiengeschichte*, 48, 1986; Ludmilla
Thomas, 'Rivalitäten deutscher und russischer Schiffahrtsgessellschaften im
Transatlantikgeschäft', *JbfG*, 29, 1984; Siegrid Wegner-Korfes, 'Politische und
ökonomische Aspekte des deutschen Kapitalexports in den privaten russischen
Eisenbahnbau in den 80er und 90er Jahren des 19. Jahrhunderts', *JbfG*, 29,
1984; Dietmar Wulff, 'Handel und Politik in den russisch-deutschen Bezie-
hungen 1894–1904. Zu den Auseinandersetzungen um den russischen
Agrarexport', unpub. dissertation [Diss. A], Berlin, 1986; Inge Baumgart and
Horst Benneckenstein, 'Die Erdölpolitik des deutschen Imperialismus vom
Ausgang des 19. Jahrhunderts bis zum ersten Weltkrieg. Eine Studie zum
Wechselverhältnis von Ökonomie und Politik', unpub. dissertation [Diss. B],
Jena, 1986; Bernd Schmiale, 'Zur Tätigkeit der Philipp Holzmann AG im
Rahmen der Nahostexpansion der Deutschen Bank AG – eine wirtschaftshis-
torische Betrachtung unter besonderer Berücksichtigung des Zeitraumes zwi-
schen 1888 und 1918', unpub. dissertation [Diss. A], Berlin (GDR), 1986;
Jochen Laufer, 'Die deutsche Südafrikapolitik 1890–1898 im Spannungsfeld
zwischen deutsch-englischen Beziehungen, Wirtschaftsinteressen und Expan-
sionsforderungen in der bürgerlichen Öffentlichkeit', unpub. dissertation, Ber-
lin (GDR), 1987; Rudolf Felber and Horst Rostek, *Der 'Hunnenkrieg' Kaiser
Wilhelms II.*, Berlin (GDR), 1987 (*IHH*, No. 45); Willibald Gutsche, 'Zu
Hintergründen und Zielen des "Panthersprungs" nach Marokko von 1911',
ZfG, 28/1980, idem, *'Panthersprung' nach Agadir 1911*, Berlin, 1988 (*IHH*, No. 48);
Helmut Otto, 'Der "Panthersprung" nach Agadir. Zum 75. Jahrestag der
zweiten Marokkokrise 1911' *Militärgeschichte* (Berlin), 3, 1986; Dieter Schulte,
'Die Monopolpolitik des Reichskolonialamtes in der "Ära Dernburg"
1906–1910. Zu frühen Formen des Funktionsmechanismus zwischen Mono-
polkapital und Staat', *JbfG*, 24, 1981; Peter Sebald, *Togo 1884–1914. Eine
Geschichte der deutschen 'Musterkolonie' auf der Grundlage amtlicher Quellen*, Berlin
(GDR), 1988; Horst Drechsler, *Aufstände in Südwestafrika. Der Kampf der Herero
und Nama gegen die Kolonialherrschaft*, Berlin (GDR), 1984; Klaus Büttner and
Heinrich Loth (eds), *Philosophie der Eroberer und koloniale Wirklichkeit. Ostafrika
1884–1918*, Berlin (GDR), 1981; Klaus Brade, 'Die Entstehung eines kolonialen
Siedlertums während der deutschen Kolonialherrschaft über Südwestafrika',
in *Die koloniale Aufteilung Afrikas und ihre Folgen, Berichte der Humboldt-Universität
Berlin*, no. 7, Berlin (GDR), 1985.

MICHAEL STÜRMER

A Nation State against History and Geography: The German Dilemma

It has often been said in the past that by following Bismarck the Germans committed themselves to a *Sonderweg*, and this theory of deviant behaviour has conveniently covered assorted chapters of central European history from the rise of Prussia to the horrors of Hitler. It also set apart the good guys from the bad guys, with the Rhine obviously providing a neat dividing line. More recently, this fashionable assumption has fallen into disrepute partly because it has ceased to be intellectually stimulating, partly as a result of the discovery that Germans, after more than forty years of the Federal Republic, can be well behaved, and partly as a by-product of a more thorough study of the real problems involved.

This debate on the *Sonderweg* is largely a matter of the past, and if the term *Sonderweg* is mentioned in today's political rhetoric, it does not warn against authoritarian temptations of the past but against pacifist or neutralist ones of the present, a new alienation from Atlantic virtues and a rebellion against the configuration which called the Federal Republic into being forty years ago. Thus, all Bonn governments have said time and again that integration into the West is one of the pillars on which the Federal Republic has been built.

No more *Sonderweg* – or so it is hoped. Meanwhile, for the historian it is tempting to look at the nineteenth-century nation state not in terms of the pressures to which it promised an answer but rather in terms of the inescapable dilemmas it produced. In doing so, the concepts developed by, among others, Sebastian Haffner, Lothar Gall and Andreas Hillgruber, are helpful.[1]

There are three chief dilemmas that stand out. Firstly, situated in the strategic heartland of Europe, from where a fair number of Paris metro stations take their names, the Germans were faced with the impossible task of squaring the circle. Faced with the energies of the French Revolution they began to see their past as a mere shadow, worthless and without any positive meaning for the future: the Holy Roman Empire proved to be the first among many pasts not to be built upon and to be forgotten as quickly and as thoroughly as possible. Subjected to the pressures of Napoleon's Empire and drawn into his wars in Spain, Russia and elsewhere, the Germans collectively seemed to have come to the conclusion, in Haffner's words: 'Das soll uns nie wieder passieren. Und das können wir auch!' (This shall never happen again, and we had better do the same.) The means to hedge against the return of that past, in fact any past, seemed to be the nation state: powerful, enlightened, western.

The second dilemma posed itself through the very nature of the concept of self-determination. The promise of modernity and the pursuit of happiness, the combined message of America's revolution and Britain's evolution, were essentially linked to the political dynamism of the nation state, and readers of Tocqueville's *De la démocratie en Amérique* were allowed to conclude that mass democracy coupled with industrial civilisation was the way of the future. If, for once, the Germans wanted to get rid of the past and walk tall, like other self-respecting nations, the nation state promised the only answer to all the political deficiencies and moral weaknesses of the past: no more foreign invasions, no more *Duodezfürsten*, but reason, public opinion, the rule of law and a powerful, well-ordered state. This was not an unreasonable assumption at a time when Poles dreamt of their independence, when Italians rebelled against foreign domination and when the Irish found British rule increasingly intolerable. The Germans, after all, were the most populous nation on the European continent after the Russians, and all over Germany monuments of the past reminded them that, at some stage, the Holy Roman Empire had been theirs. In their innocence, the pilgrims at the Hambach festival in 1832 believed that democracy, the nation state and human brotherhood were all part of the same future scenario and that nothing but the

---

1. S. Haffner, *Von Bismarck zu Hitler: ein Rückblick*, Munich, 1987; L. Gall, *Bismarck, der weiße Revolutionär*, Frankfurt a. M., 1980; A. Hillgruber, *Die Last der Nation. fünf Beiträge über Deutschland und die Deutschen*, Düsseldorf, 1984.

wickedness of their many rulers and Metternich's police stood between them and the promised land. 'Deutschland, Deutschland über alles', as Hoffmann von Fallersleben wrote in youthful enthusiasm, was not a declaration of war on the West but rather a declaration of love – but the message was not well understood, let alone fully appreciated.[2]

Most of the 48ers were shocked and surprised to realise – and most of their followers still refuse to accept – that the rest of Europe, while at best sympathising in theory with the German liberals and German democrats, in practice found their activities rather alarming. In spite of all the re-education in the world, it cannot be said that in 1848 'the West' was in favour of German liberalism, let alone democracy. Most of the disappointments experienced by the German nationalists in 1848, when only the United States formally recognised the Frankfurt parliament's sovereignty and all other powers kept their distance, had long been foreshadowed.[3] Indeed, the misgivings about German nationhood went back to the Vienna Congress and beyond. Goethe contributed a number of lines which reflect the pre-national, cosmopolitan spirit of Germany's ruling classes, what Friedrich Meinecke called *Weltbürgertum* and what, in more political terms, amounted to the analysis that the Germans had better forget their national destiny. 'Deutschland? aber wo liegt es?' (Germany? Where is that?), Goethe and Schiller had asked in 1797, when the French revolutionary army flooded Europe; the two Weimar demigods had found 'Deutschland' on the maps of literature and intellectual life but could not see the country as part of the real world. Their scepticism prevailed for many decades, and in his last years Goethe, in one of his letters to Zelter in Berlin, commented upon the weird ideas that made up the nationalist creed of his age: 'It contracts time and expands space. It seems to dwell only in the realm of the impossible while treating with utter contempt the possible.'[4]

The third dilemma to be mentioned here was of a geostrategic nature, and it is still with us. Germany, unlike Britain, does not enjoy the advantage of being an island, as described by William Shakespeare in verses that have formed much of British identity.[5] And, unlike the

2. V. Valentin, *Geschichte der deutschen Revolution von 1848–1849*, 2 vols, Berlin, 1930 and 1931. For a more sceptical account, see R. Stadelmann, *Soziale und politische Geschichte der Revolution von 1848*, 2nd end, Munich, 1970.
3. M. Stürmer, 'Die Geburt eines Dilemmas: Nationalstaat und Massendemokratie im Mächtesystem, 1848', *Merkur*, 403, 1982, pp. 1–12; idem, *Die Reichsgründung: Deutscher Nationalstaat und europäisches Gleichgewicht im Zeitalter Bismarcks*, Munich, 1984.
4. *Xenien* (1797); J.W. von Goethe, 'Briefe an Zelter', in *Goethes Briefe*, ed. Klaus F. Gille, 2nd edn, Hamburg, 1976, vol. 4.
5. Cf. Shakespeare's *Richard II*, II, i:

United States, Germany is not a continental nation. Germany and the Germans have always found themselves sandwiched in a situation not of their choosing. The insular concept of history shared by the English-speaking nations tends to apply its own unspoken assumptions to the continent, failing to understand the nightmares and traumas prevailing among the lesser breeds. Britain has not experienced a successful invasion since 1066, and the United States was invulnerable until the Soviet Union mastered the technology of nuclear inter-continental ballistic missiles, ICBMs, in the 1960s. The 'frontier' in American history is a positive myth, a promise, a challenge to be overcome. But in French, Polish, Swiss, Austrian and Hungarian history, the frontier has never ceased to be a threat.

And while frontiers have moved, they have not always expanded; they have contracted, as well. The Germans, whatever their history lessons at school, have always found it difficult to forget that being in the centre has its price. In Luther's time Germany was almost crushed between the onslaught of the Turks from the south-east and western pressure from François I, who in his turn fought Charles V and Habsburg encirclement, Madrid and Vienna. Compared to the Thirty Years' War in Germany, the British Civil War of the seventeenth century was child's play, and so were the wars of the Fronde in France. The German Civil War, beginning in Bohemia in 1618, soon spread to the whole of southern Germany and, after a terrible decade, dragged in most of Europe's armies and conflicts, greed and manoeuvring for power, until between one-half and two-thirds of the population were slain. In 1681 Strasbourg, the second largest city of Germany after Cologne, was lost to the Most Christian King, and two years later the Ottoman armies converged on Vienna. These were events the Germans were slow to forget.

The Thirty Years' War in Germany changed the faith and face of Germany for centuries, and perhaps to this present day made *Angst* the prevailing mood in Europe's heartland. Most of the country was in ruins, the proud city republics declining and bankrupt, the patrician elites weakened in their political ambition, the territorial states legit-imised through the Hobbesian notion of the Leviathan state, keeping the peace and holding a check over the state of nature. After 1648 the constitution of Germany became part of European public law, the Holy

---

'This fortress built by Nature for herself/Against infection and the hand of war,/This happy breed of men, this little world,/This precious stone set in the silver sea,/Which serves it in the office of a wall,/Or as a moat defensive to a house,/Against the envy of less happier lands;/This blessed plot, this earth, this realm, this England . . .'

Roman Empire resting in itself and in the rising balance of power. The settlement of 1648 was ingenious, but it sentenced the Germans and the Germanies to 150 years of immobility.[6]

The European concert of the eighteenth century was built on a balance that was anchored somewhere between Maas and Memel, Etsch and Belt: the *iustium potentiae equilibrium*, as the formula of the peace of Utrecht has it, gave Britain and France, Sweden and the Netherlands, every chance to develop independently, to build their pre-national states and to set up overseas empires, while keeping the dynamics of Central Europe stable through a maximum of balance at a minimum of power. In the Seven Years' War, when the colonial empires of France and Britain were redistributed, Russia gained a *droit de regard* in Central Europe, in fact, a veto over any change. Thus, the political constitution of Germany in the eighteenth century remained the heart of the European system. Inside this constitution, political life and social evolution took place within the major territorial states. The city republics never recovered from the Thirty Years' War. The emperor presided over a museum of medieval estates, religious armistice and geostrategic expediency. Thus the setting was prepared for the slow breakdown of state and society at the time of the French Revolution and Napoleon.

Nevertheless, it should not be forgotten, and this has been highlighted in recent years by a number of historians like Gerhard Oestreich, Mack Walker and, above all, Freiherr von Aretin and Hans Boldt, that in the eighteenth century the Holy Roman Empire, in spite of its shadowy existence, contributed decisively to European peace.[7] It was in itself a system of balances, set into a larger European balance, so that changes, while not altogether impossible, were difficult to justify and to maintain, as Frederick the Great and his Bavarian colleague had to learn the hard way.

The French Revolution posed two challenges, one old, one new. The challenge of hegemony, although couched in ideological language, was old, and it was at the heart of the Franco-British antagonism, from the beginning to the bitter end in the mud of Waterloo, as French hegemony was incompatible with British interests. The challenge of revol-

---

6. M. Walker, *German Home Towns: Community, State, and General Estate, 1648–1971*, Ithaca, NY, 1971; O. von Aretin, *Heiliges Römisches Reich, 1776–1806 – Reichsverfassung und Staatssouveränität*, Wiesbaden, 1967.

7. G. Oestreich, *Geist und Gestalt des frühmodernen Staates: Ausgewählte Aufsätze*, Berlin, 1969; idem, *Strukturprobleme der Frühen Neuzeit: Ausgewählte Aufsätze von Gerhard Oestreich*, ed. Brigitta Oestreich, Berlin, 1980; Hans Boldt *Deutsche Verfassungsgeschichte*, vol. 1: *Von den Anfängen bis zum Ende des älteren deutschen Reiches, 1806*, Munich, 1984.

ution from above, of the role of reason and of *la nation une et indivisible* was new. The net result of this ambiguity was change and upheaval on the continent.

It can be said that the first challenge was met by the concept of a balance of power, most forcefully expressed in William Pitt's plan for European peace after Napoleon, designed in 1805 and reactivated in 1813.[8] In 1805, before Austerlitz and Jena, Europe had been in a situation not unlike the one that recurred after the Spanish *guerilla* and the Beresina. The idea was to reconstruct a balance weighted against Napoleon's dominance, but in 1805 Pitt failed to convince Vienna and Berlin that they could only save their existences through their alliance with London: France was to give up all of her conquests beyond the borders of 1792; new states were to contain the powerful ambitions of France; and the creation of a peaceful co-existence was to rest on the balance of power and mutual guarantees. What sounded very abstract was in fact the formula for a revived and more reliable European concert, immune from both hegemony and revolutionary nationalism. It resumed, as Henry Kissinger has shown, all the statecraft of the eighteenth century and aimed at pacifying the international dynamism of nation states while not interfering with their internal dynamics. If this was an ambitious attempt to square the circle, it was, nevertheless, the formula that guided the Vienna Congress and its idea of a general European order, and at the same time it set the scene not only for the rise of the Vienna system but also for its crisis and decline in and after 1848.

The double challenge of the French Revolution, hegemony and revolutionary nationalism, not only changed the framework of Germany in Europe. It also deeply affected the domestic setting, in fact the very foundations of every regime across the Germanies: in 1802 the first great simplification of the political map of Central Europe had taken place, and hundreds of formerly sovereign cities, abbeys and small fiefdoms were wiped out and sucked up by the larger territorial entities. The new territorial states in their turn had every desire not to be swept aside by the rush of German nationalism. Therefore, they consolidated their system not only through bureaucratic revolution from above but also through constitutional compromise with the middle classes. That is why in the time of Napoleon all of the south German states, members of the *Fédération du Rhin*, acquired a handsome written constitution.

8. See also H. Kissinger, *A World Restored – Europe after Napoleon*, Gloucester, Mass., 1957; reprinted 1973.

What gave them the guarantee of their existence, however, was not internal strength but the fact that at the Vienna Congress the thirty-eight or so Germanies were needed to balance each other, to contain France, to put up a dam against Russia and to spare the world the agonies of another hegemony, Russian or German. That is why the related issues of Poland and Saxony could play such a decisive role around the turn of 1814–15, bringing the powers to the verge of war against each other.

In the end William Pitt's concept of five great powers with an array of secondary states around them became the model of European diplomacy for one or two generations. Between Britain, Russia and France, the two German powers were to balance each other, and inside Germany the Prusso-Austrian alliance was designed as a firm foundation on which everything was to rest. While Russian force and German nationalism had been indispensable to conquer Napoleon's armies, in Vienna Metternich, Castlereagh and Talleyrand were united in trying to persuade the Russians to go back to where they had come from and to make the Germans forget what Europe owed them.[9]

While Metternich never had the slightest doubt that revolutionary nationalism was too dangerous a means to save Austria's empire, the Prussian concept was different: the military reformers were deeply affected by the French Revolution and the outburst of military and political energy it had produced. 'Ein Griff ins Zeughaus der Revolution' – mobilising the arsenal of revolution – is how they described their endeavor. But when in March 1813 the volunteer troops passed under his window, the Prussian monarch remarked sombrely: 'Down there, the revolution is marching.' He was aware that the cure for Napoleon might in the end be worse than the disease.

The prophets of nationalism were not present at the Vienna peace conference, with one exception, Freiherr vom Stein, who rumbled against the German princes and their happy survival; as a baron of the old Empire and as a standard-bearer of the new nationalism, he had nowhere to go and withdrew into a kind of splendid isolation.[10] It was not Freiherr vom Stein but Baron von Humboldt, the founder of the Prussian universities and the country's ablest diplomat, who gave expression to the compromise that carried the day: German dualism between Prussia and Austria was to be not only the linchpin of the German balance – it was embodied in the idea of a Germanic confed-

9. H. Kissinger, *A World Restored*; H. Nicolson, *The Congress of Vienna: A Study in Allied Unity, 1812–1822*, London, 1946.
10. G. Ritter, *Stein, eine politische Biographie*, Stuttgart, 1958.

eration emerging at the end of the congress – but also the heart of the
renewed 'Repose of Europe' (Castlereagh). In December 1813 Humboldt wrote a memorandum 'On the German constitution'.[11] He demanded that the Germans should and must advance from cultural
community to political nation. At the same time Humboldt was only
too aware of the dynamism of nationalism and of the German temptation to form a bloc in the heart of Europe incompatible with peace
and balance. Humboldt the diplomat warned Stein and his followers
against a German nation state after the French mode. What he
suggested instead was both old and new: a confederation of German
states that would spare Prussia the ambitions of national identity,
preserve the old bonds of culture, language and history among the
Germans and make Germany a peacekeeping system in the centre of
Europe, resting in itself and in the wider balance of power. Humboldt's
plan was a compromise. He tried to combine the European experience
of the Holy Roman Empire and the modern promise of nationhood,
and in doing so provided a formula under which both Prussia and the
Austrian empire could exist and, in fact, coexist.

Humboldt's concept also fitted neatly into William Pitt's and Castlereagh's European order. It made provisions against the challenge of
hegemony, but it failed to identify, let alone pacify, the social forces
that were to ally themselves with modern nationalism. Humboldt and
his contemporaries thought in terms of peaceful political change: the
idea of industrial revolution and social upheaval and the way in which
the combined facts of both would undermine, in fact explode, the
'Repose of Europe' was beyond their understanding and even beyond
their imagination. And there is no doubt among present-day historians,
from Golo Mann to Gordon Craig,[12] that the politicians assembled in
Vienna may, in the name of peace, be forgiven for their inability to
solve problems that had not yet fully arrived on the social and economic agenda of nineteenth-century Europe.

To conclude, it might be said that in the footsteps of Sybel and
Treitschke[13] historians, left and right, have invariably investigated the
rise of modern nationalism, and the social historians of our time have

---

11. W. von Humboldt, 'Denkschrift über die deutsche Verfassung (Dezember 1813)'
in *Wilhelm von Humboldts Gesammelte Schriften*, ed Königlich Preußische Akademie der
Wissenschaften, Berlin, 1908, vol. 11, pp. 95 ff.
12. G. Mann, *Friedrich von Gentz, Geschichte eines europäischen Staatsmannes*, Zurich, 1947;
G. Craig, *Europe since 1815*, New York, 1961.
13. H. von Sybel, *Begründung des deutschen Reiches durch Wilhelm I*, 7 vols, Munich,
Leipzig, 1889–94; H. Treitschke, *Deutsche Geschichte im 19. Jahrhundert*, 5 vols, Leipzig,
1879–94.

added their irrefutable arguments. History, in various guises, tends to find itself in the victor's camp. Despite Treitschke's verdicts against the dreamers of the pre-national order of Europe and latter-day verdicts against geostrategic interpretations of politics, very rarely has anyone attempted to listen to those voices in the wilderness that had warned against the inheritance of the French Revolution. Such caveats were voiced throughout the nineteenth century, until Bismarck's triumph made them sound hollow and obsolete.

One case in point was the prominent Göttingen historian Adolf Ludwig Heeren, a great writer and editor of books and a powerful *praeceptor Germaniae* in his day – but not powerful enough. In 1816 he wrote the following lines:

> The German Federation finds itself in harmony with the essence of the general political system in Europe only to the extent that it helps to maintain its freedom. The German Federation is, in geographic terms, the centre of the system. It borders wholly or in part on the chief states of East and West, and hardly anything can happen one way or another that would leave it indifferent. The truth is that the foreign powers in their turn as well cannot be indifferent to how the central state of Europe is formed. If this state were a great monarchy with strong political unity, furnished with all the material strength that Germany possesses – how could any safe existence be left for Germany's neighbours? Would such a state for any length of time resist the temptation to make a bid for hegemony over Europe, in keeping with its position and power? The rise of a single and unrestricted monarchy in Germany would before long be the grave of freedom in Europe.[14]

One could say, in qualifying Heeren's sombre warning, that it reflected no less than the collective wisdom of European diplomats since the Thirty Years' War. But with equal justification one could also say that it foreshadowed the trials and tribulations to come.

To add one final dilemma to the ones presented at the beginning: the dualism of Prussia and Austria kept the two German powers apart, and it also kept them together. Any bid for a German nation state would either have to forge a unity between the two or cut the old bonds. But German unity – in the Frankfurt parliament no small group dreamt of an Empire between the four seas – would have been too much for the rest of Europe to bear. This lesson was learnt in 1848 and afterwards by the German Liberals and by Bismarck, and it led to what became known as the *Kleindeutsche Lösung* (small German solution). But

---

14. A.L. Heeren: *Der Deutsche Bund in seinen Verhältnissen zu dem Europäischen Staatensystem*, Göttingen, 1816, pp. 10 f.

this unity would also end in disaster, as Freiherr von der Pfordten, Bavaria's prime minister in 1848, remarked at the end of the revolutionary period: 'Once Austria and Prussia have parted ways, they will hardly, if ever, reunite, In that case, within Austria the German element will decline. In Germany, however, centralisation will triumph, and it is likely that in the not too distant future this great and exclusively German state will exert a powerful attraction towards those German elements defeated in Austria.' The decline and decay of the Habsburg monarchy would follow suit, Russia would grab the Slavonic parts of the Austrian Empire, and the Germans would find themselves in a fight against both the Slavs and the French. Therefore, the two German powers should form a confederation. If they succeeded in doing so, they would keep Europe in balance. If not, in a hundred year's time, Germany would be nothing but a geographic term.[15]

Not a bad prophecy to be made in 1849, if one remembers that 96 years later, at Potsdam, the protocol noted Stalin's remarks that, indeed, Germany was nothing but a geographic term. But between 1848 and 1945 much has happened, and not a few things could have taken a different course.

What remains, however, is the fact that the German nation state, whether in the promise of 1848 or in Bismarckian reality, emerged against the odds of three powerful dilemmas, to be described in terms of history, geography and, last but not least, the dynamism of mass democracy and the modern state.

15. Quoted from M. Stürmer, '1848 in der deutschen Geschichte' in H.-U. Wehler (ed.), *Sozialgeschicte Heute – Festschrift für Hans Rosenberg zum 70. Geburtsag*, Göttingen, 1974.

KLAUS HILDEBRAND

Opportunities and Limits of German Foreign Policy in the Bismarckian Era, 1871–1890: 'A System of Stopgaps'?

In 1928, Ulrich Noack, in his controversial book on Bismarck's peace policy and the problem of the decline in Germany's power, characterised the foreign policy of the Reich Chancellor as a 'system of stopgaps'.[1] After the bold act of founding the Reich, a 'changed mood' had, he argued, governed 'the complacent and ageing statesman'; 'a more tightly proportioned *raison d'état*' was purportedly promoted to 'the norm for the determination of the interests and tasks of his state'.[2] In a state of passivity bereft of ideas, Bismarck, no longer willing to take action, had – Noack argued – neglected to use his creative energies in an active, even bellicose manner, in order to bring about a '*political reshaping of the continent* . . . through which a new ring, so to speak, of buffer states thrown further out'[3] was to be created 'around the German fortress', especially in the shape of an eastern *Mitteleuropa* cut off or liberated from Russia. The upshot was that: 'peace', for the time being, had just managed 'to stay artificially alive' and could now only be 'maintained for a while' by having 'pursued ruinous exploitation with the chance of victory in the coming war'.[4] In

1. Ulrich Noack, *Bismarcks Friedenspolitik und das Problem des deutschen Machtverfalls*, Leipzig, 1928, p. 275.
2. Ibid., p. 132.
3. Ibid., p. 165.
4. Ibid., pp. 463 f.

73

other words Noack emphasises the then supposedly existing opportunity and right of a young nation to power political expansion, an
opportunity which Bismarck, imprisoned within the bounds of existing
conditions, had lost.

We will not go further into the technical and factual dubiousness of
Noack's argument here. It ought merely to be stated that such a judgement obviously corresponds to a critical attitude towards the Reich
Chancellor predominant above all during the latter years of the 1880s.
It represents an exception in German historiography of the inter-war
period, which, marked by a Bismarckian orthodoxy, was virtually
absorbed in admiration of the inspired statesman. A high point of this
inter-war interpretation, which appears outmoded to us today, was
provided by Wolfgang Windelband in his proposition on 'The Unity of
Bismarck's Foreign Policy since 1871'.[5] Assuming the man and his
works to have been identical, he speaks of a 'homogeneous system' to
which Bismarck, as he had put it in the Kissinger *Diktat* on 15 June
1877, had 'unalterably adhered throughout the years 1871 to 1890'.[6]

Diametrically opposed to that and contrasting just as much in
principle to Ulrich Noack's position, Lothar Gall in his biography of
Bismarck – which was published in 1980 and which will certainly
remain definitive for a fairly long time – also diagnosed the domestic
and foreign policy of the Reich Chancellor as a 'system of stopgaps'.[7]
From the end of the 1870s at the latest this system had, according to
Gall, been 'erected for the preservation of the status quo . . . at ever
greater cost and with ever decreasing success'.[8] In the sphere of foreign
policy, it is represented above all by the conclusion of the so-called
Re-insurance Treaty with its 'completely secret supplementary agreement' which appears to Gall to have 'contradicted that minimum of
good faith . . . without which durable relations between peoples and
states are impossible. It also led into a cul-de-sac, laid the Reich
vulnerable to blackmail and opened up no real perspectives of any
kind'.[9] The upshot is that Gall accentuates 'the brittleness and precarious character of the whole'[10] and outlines 'the tendency to the mere

5. Wolfgang Windelband, 'Die Einheitlichkeit von Bismarcks Außenpolitik seit 1871'
in his *Gestalten und Probleme der Außenpolitik. Reden und Aufsätze zu vier Jahrhunderten*, Berlin,
Essen, Leipzig, 1937, pp. 129 ff.
6. Ibid., p. 133.
7. Lothar Gall, *Bismarck. Der weiße Revolutionär*, Frankfurt a. M., Berlin, Vienna,
1980, p. 642.
8. Ibid., p. 597.
9. Ibid., p. 634.
10. Ibid., p. 636.

conservation of what had already been achieved . . . to the rejection of more fundamental changes' and to the 'freezing of a constellation which had once so very much worked to the advantage of himself and his immediate goals'.[11] Indeed, he raises the question of whether this entire system, which appears to him to have had no future, had not been 'in truth only the more or less chance result of immediate crisis management' but, as he repeatedly remarks, had possessed 'no real perspectives whatever'.[12] In other words, Gall acknowledges the historical significance of the statesman and at the same time draws our attention to his limitations. These simply corresponded, however, to the limitations of a political system which, in the author's estimation, was devoid of any real chance of developing in the future.

Let us evaluate these judgements by investigating the opportunities and limits of German foreign policy in the Bismarckian era between 1871 and 1890. Are we justified in excessively elevating Bismarck's foreign policy into a practically perfect system, damning its pilot on the ground of purported failure, or regarding its existence, seen against a background of internationally and socially determined change – or even upheaval – as being antiquated? In this connection there are above all four basic elements determining Bismarck's foreign policy from the outset, burdening it more than advancing it, erecting limits to it rather than opening up opportunities.

Firstly, there was the fact, brought about by the annexation of Alsace-Lorraine, that 'we . . . really are immobilised by France'.[13] The Reich Chancellor himself attributed this continuing antagonism to Germany on the part of her western neighbour less to the German incorporation of the two territories than to France's injured pride respecting her lost hegemony. In any event, France regarded the loss of Alsace and Lorraine as a symbol of French defeat. This meant that Bismarck could not plan the 'general political situation'[14] most advantageous to Germany, which the Kissinger *Diktat* states would have included France, but had to draw up all policy in opposition to France.

Secondly, a dangerously expanding prominence of the military in Europe was developing against Bismarck's will as a consequence of the wars victoriously fought by Prussian Germany between 1864 and 1870–1. A mistaken conclusion was drawn from the successes of these

11. Ibid., p. 727.
12. Ibid., p. 636.
13. Gerhard Ebel (ed.), *Botschafter Paul Graf von Hatzfeldt. Nachgelassene Papiere 1838–1901*, vol. 1, Bopppard a. Rh., 1976, p. 513: Holstein to Graf Hatzfeldt, 26.7.1886.
14. *GP*, vol. 2, No. 294, p. 154.

passages of arms by various continental European powers. The Austro-Hungarian Foreign Minister, Andrássy, acknowledged, for instance, that: 'The consequence of the recent wars is that "might dominates over right" . . . that foreign policy is only correct, when it is also strategically correct.'[15]

Thirdly, a defect which became ever more damagingly apparent was that the German Reich lacked an 'obvious mission'.[16] In contrast to Western and to Eastern Europe, in contrast to the 'Gladstonianism' and 'Pan-Slavism' feared by Bismarck, there was a want of a civilising idea capable of ennobling pure power and focussing attention. In the newly approaching age of the masses, the traditional Prusso-German concept of the state seemed strangely archaic by comparison with the ideologies of societies which were increasingly triumphing over the 'necessities of states'.[17]

And fourthly, another fundamental dilemma of the German Reich lay in the fact that Germany, if it did not wish to provoke unpleasant reactions on the part of Europe, was not allowed to expand. The period of imperialist 'craving for living space'[18] was soon to set in, and while other states would increase in strength, the country in the middle could only grow comparatively weaker. That provoked accusations against Bismarck, soon made in public, that he paid homage to a decrepit and bloodless, a despondent and feeble policy, to a policy, in short, of hopeless stagnation.

Overall, however, the tide of the age had turned fundamentally. Heretofore – from 1862 until 1871 – it had carried Bismarck's policy along so advantageously, from both an international and a social perspective, steering, as it were, along the boundaries between tradition and revolution. After the foundation of the Reich, the predominant historical trend veered against the Reich Chancellor, partly in connection with the turning-point represented by the year 1871, but in large part independently of it and determined by Europe's 'road into modernity'.[19] Bismarck, from being the 'White revolutionary', turned himself into a Metternichian traditionalist who was now only at pains

15. Cited in Heinrich Lutz, *Österreich-Ungarn und die Gründung des Deutschen Reiches. Europäische Entscheidungen 1867–1871*, Frankfurt a. M., Berlin, Vienna, 1979, pp. 488 ff.
16. Ludwig Dehio, 'Gedanken über die deutsche Sendung 1900–1918' in his *Deutschland und die Weltpolitik im 20. Jahrhundert*, Munich, 1955, p. 94.
17. Siegfried A. Kaehler, 'Bemerkungen zu einem Marginal Bismarcks von 1887' in his *Studien zur deutschen Geschichte des 19. und 20. Jahrhunderts. Aufsätze und Vorträge*, Göttingen, 1961, p. 182.
18. Theodor Schieder, *Staatensystem als Vormacht der Welt 1848–1918*, Frankfurt a. M., Berlin, Vienna, 1977, p. 253.
19. Lothar Gall, *Europa auf dem Weg in die Moderne 1850–1890*, Munich, Vienna, 1984.

to stem the current of an age which, henceforth, was noxious to him. But this entailed the increasingly difficult development of the 'community of interest between German security in the centre and the European peace'.[20] Indeed, the question was threateningly raised as to how long the German 'dead weight' on Europe's 'man who always bounces back' would still find the equilibrium necessary to maintain that balance of forces on which the independence of its existence was so elementally dependent. In fact, from 1871 onwards the Reich Chancellor was 'tormented by premonitions of a terrible future', and the rationale of his foreign policy was to defer a looming 'age of the wars' 'for a generation by the painstaking exertions of an elaborate but traditional diplomacy'.[21]

Immediately after the foundation of the German Reich, all these problems drew together into the question of whether, or under what circumstances, the 'predominant Power on the Continent[22] would fit into the geographical and 'spiritual map'[23] of the old world. It is true that, at first, Bismarck did not hesitate to make use of the continuing feeling of terror inspired by the Paris Commune and pursued a conservative foreign policy in collaboration with Austria-Hungary and Russia, bringing the three monarchies together in the League of the Three Emperors of 1873. But even in these first years after the foundation of the Reich developments threatening to Germany began to appear, not only in the public feuds of the international press but also – far more seriously – in the political disputes of the European Cabinets and Chancelleries. The Tsarist Empire, for instance, wished to win back the leading role it had once had with regard to Prussia and accordingly treated Germany as a 'second rate power'.[24] In addition, the Russians and French unmistakably drew closer together so that, especially after the premature evacuation of the French *département* of the East by the German occupation forces in 1873, there emerged what

20. Hermann Oncken, *Das Deutsche Reich und die Vorgeschichte des Weltkriegs*, vol. 1, Berlin, 1933, p. 215.

21. Theodor Schieder, 'Nietzsche und Bismarck', *HZ*, 196, 1963, p. 342; reprinted in *idem, Einsichten in die Geschichte. Essays*, Frankfurt a. M., Berlin, Vienna, 1980, p. 83.

22. Otto Hintze, *Die Hohenzollern und ihr Werk. Fünfhundert Jahre vaterländischer Geschichte*, Berlin, 1915, p. 651.

23. To this formulation of Siegfried A. Kaehler, compare Walter Bußmann, 'Europa und das Bismarckreich' in Lothar Gall (ed.), *Das Bismarck-Problem in der Geschichtsschreibung nach 1945*, Cologne, Berlin, 1971, p. 311.

24. Ulrich Lappenküper, 'Die Mission Radowitz. Das deutsche Reich und die europäischen Mächte in Bismarcks Außenpolitik im Zeitraum zwischen der Reichsgründung und der "Krieg-in-Sicht"-Krise (1871–1875)', unpublished Thesis, Bonn, 1988, p. 238.

appeared to Germany as a dangerous foreign policy situation. Men as different as Dostoevsky and Gladstone saw Germany as 'exposée par sa position centrale à des perils permanents dont leur seule situation géographique préserve la plupart de ses voisins'.[25] Finally, tensions with Austria-Hungary, then entering into closer contact with Russia than had previously been the case, were also increasing, so that in 1874 Bismarck saw a Kaunitzian coalition approaching in spite of all his political and diplomatic counter-attacks.

These tensions burst forth in the 'war-in-sight' crisis of 1875, which offered Bismarck the opportunity of exploring the dimensions of the German Reich's room for manoeuvre. The attempt at finding a settlement of the Great Powers' interests in a conventional fashion through territorial compensation had foundered, culminating in the 'Radowitz Mission' of winter and spring 1875, to Germany's vitally important neighbour, Russia. In contrast to leading military and diplomatic figures, the Chancellor did not think in terms of war to effect the security of the Reich. England and Russia, however, the two world powers flanking Germany, henceforth imperiously demonstrated to Germany the limits of its capacity and, as a precaution, protected the existence of France. Bismarck noted the threatening signals of the British and Russians. It may be, however, that, while immediately recognising the limits set down for Germany, he underestimated the possibility that the Anglo-Russian maintenance of the European status quo could also, at least in principle, guarantee the existence of the new Reich.

In any event, the days were past when Bismarck could almost boisterously state that the fate of Europe could 'always be made ready, combed and brushed in ten to fifteen minutes over breakfast' by him.[26] When, in high spirits, he expressed himself thus in 1872, economic prosperity, which was so markedly to decline a year later, was only just about to falter. From 1873 it gave way to that 'Great Depression' which even if the details of its existence are disputed, certainly extended far beyond the turning-point of 1890. It was a burdensome accompaniment to the 'Bismarck Era'. Irrespective of all the achievements and successes in the field of domestic and above all of foreign policy, not least the maintenance of external peace, this contributed to the absolutely unmistakable mood of dissatisfaction that permeated Otto von Bismarck's period in government. With the policy of 'satiation' he

25. Ibid., p. 188; Jarnac, the French Ambassador to London, to Foreign Minister Decazes, 2.11.1874.
26. *Bismarck, Die gesammelten Werke*, vol. 14, p. 834: to his daughter Marie, 23.6.1872.

chose for reasons of survival, he was at pains to ward off the threatening consequences of three victorious wars and a coalition of the powers against the Reich. Naturally, for more and more of his contemporaries, who regarded the successes at the foundation of the Reich as virtually a matter of course, this policy signified unendurable stagnation. The burden of immobility had an increasingly depressing effect, especially in an age of rapid international and industrial change. Bismarck was constantly aware of the facts that frugality and self-imposed moderation alone were capable of guaranteeing the survival of the Reich and that change and territorial acquisition could be synonymous with downfall, but with the passage of time, he could scarcely make this clear to a new generation.

From the summer of 1875, a superficial but none the less welcome opportunity of relief was once more offered to the German Reich by the reappearance of the south-east European question. In this context, too, however, the limits which Germany had to respect in its course – winding between Austria-Hungary and Russia – became immediately apparent. That course finally led to the turning-point of the years 1878–9 when the external and internal politics of the Reich altered so unmistakably. At the Berlin Congress of summer 1878, Bismarck had saved Europe from the whirlpool of the Turko-Russian and Anglo-Russian conflagrations, and he stood at the height of his reputation and influence, even in France, although his relations with the Tsarist Empire worsened. Domestically, the climate veered to an instability which could only be controlled with difficulty and which continued until the very end of the 'Bismarckian Era' and the transition from the Liberal to the protectionist period. The Reich Chancellor's ever more strongly criticised adherence to temperance in foreign policy corresponded to his tendency toward perseverance in domestic policy.

From this perspective and with certain preconditions, one can already glimpse the prelude to a system of stopgaps in Bismarck's decision on the Austro-German alliance, that is on the limited option in favour of Vienna effected on 7 October 1879. This observation appears all the more plausible if one takes into account the fact that, in connection with the conclusion of this alliance, Bismarck sought the opportunity of fundamentally expanding the narrowing limitations of German power. To anchor the alliance between Vienna and Berlin both publicly and parliamentarily through 'pragmatic arrangements'[27] and in particular to develop a customs union between them, Bismarck

27. Walter Bußmann, *Das Zeitalter Bismarcks*, 4th edn, Frankfurt a. M., 1968, p. 140.

aimed at a renaissance of the German Union as a 'kind of mutual association for peace'[28] In this, the Reich Chancellor attempted to overcome the paralysis affecting the Reich by countering self-imposed immobility and decline relative to expanding world powers with an indirect expansion of its Central European basis. Not least in doing so, he also faced the growing, domestically articulated criticism, primarily from the Liberal camp, of his regime of domestic and foreign political consistency.

But for obvious reasons, Foreign Minister Andrassy rejected this project immediately and unequivocally. He insisted instead on the conclusion of a military defensive alliance, whose defensive thrust was directed against Russia. Since the 'great solution' could not be realised, Bismarck was thus thrown back on 'great power diplomacy'.[29] In this spirit, however, his first intention was to win back Russia, which was turning away from Germany. At this exact time Russia felt its agricultural export interests hard hit by German protectionist policy determined by domestic politics – even though Bismarck consistently tried to keep economic and political interests separate. And it was precisely through the Dual Alliance concluded with Austria-Hungary on 7 October 1879 that St Petersburg's attention was drawn to the necessity of dependency on Germany. The Tsarist Empire thus joined in the Three Emperors' League on 18 June 1881.

The defective power base of the German Reich had not been improved; the art of diplomacy had, by contrast, proved its worth. In those years, then, the opportunities and limits of German foreign policy lay very close together. For the conclusion of the Dual Alliance and the Three Emperors' League – which scarcely remedied the disadvantages of the German position in principle – marked the point of departure for the erection of the Bismarckian alliance system which presented the German Reich with a 'five year term of comparative relief'[30] between 1879 and 1884–5. Accordingly, at that time, Bismarck could remark that his foreign policy was running like clockwork.

But, in the Age of Imperialism which was now dawning, the life-or-death problem of the German Reich – for the moment still covert, yet dangerous in the long term – was unmistakably coming to a head. For, accompanying the general tendency toward the comprehensive

28. *GP*, vol. 3, No. 455. p. 33: Bismarck to Kaiser Wilhelm I, 31.8.1879.

29. Henry A. Kissinger, *Großmacht Diplomatie. Von der Staatskunst Castlereaghs und Metternichs*, Frankfurt a. M., 1962.

30. Gerhard Ritter, *Bismarcks Verhältnis zu England und die Politik des 'Neuen Kurses'*, Berlin, 1924, p. 543.

removal of boundaries between the spheres of state and society on the political mass market of a new era, the traditional European order was also expanding uncontrollably into a world system. This was linked to the revolutionary overturning of all that had hitherto been valid in science and in art through the discovery of unexplored regions in biology and philosophy, in psychology and literature, in music and painting. The tempting challenge – simultaneously promising and destructive – of the onset of revolutionary changes in the international system and the world of ideas did not by any means escape Bismarck. The hidden connection between these changes was illuminated by Hermann von Keyserling in the paradox according to which from hence forward 'the shortest path to oneself' would lead 'all around the world'.[31]

This challenge brought with it a threatening and insidious loss of significance for Bismarck's past accomplishments. Thus, beyond the characteristic instruments of his ingeniously artificial diplomacy, he again seized an opportunity which seemed suitable for a basic resolution of the German dilemma. For the 'five ball game . . . presented engagements with every European great power without, however, being bound to any one of them' from the early 1880s.[32] Thus, we must not underemphasise that Bismarck was constantly on the look-out for fundamental alternatives 'which held more promise of durability and of a future'.[33]

In this sense his colonialist stride toward Africa and into the South Seas, undertaken in 1884–5, did not signify any long-planned strategy of social imperialism to stabilise a purportedly decrepit system of rule, nor is it to be ascribed only to the short-term requirements of electoral tactics or of economics. What was at issue here was rather a tentative attempt to set the Reich in Europe and in the world on a more advantageous basis through a settlement with France effected on an overseas terrain over British opposition. *Uno actu*, so to speak, Germany was carefully trying in the final analysis, to connect itself to the powerful historical tendencies of the imperialist age, and beyond that to improve decisively conditions of its continental existence. For now, in the 1880s, the identity of the virtually leaden burden on the existence

---

31. Count Hermann Keyserling, *Das Reisetagebuch eines Philosophen*, 2 vols, 3rd Edn, Darmstadt, 1920, motto.
32. Jost Dülffer, 'Deutschland als Kaiserreich (1871–1918)' in Martin Vogt (ed.), *Deutsche Geschichte. Begründet von Peter Rassow. Vollständig neu bearbeitete und illustrierte Ausgabe*, Stuttgart, 1987, p. 486.
33. L. Gall, *Bismarck*, p. 619.

of this 'semi-hegemonic'[34] power was emerging wth increasing clarity. The German Reich was at bottom not allowed – or, at least, only with great restraint – to do what all other Great Powers did as a matter of course and with impetuous ruthlessness, namely, to expand. Consequently, Germany was obliged to be satisfied with what it had in order to survive for the present, and in the long run it came to lag behind so significantly as to raise the question of its very existence, since the other Powers were increasing so much in power. The law of 'satiation' which circumscribed the opportunities and limits of Germany as a Great Power produced consequences which tended simultaneously to the preservation and to the endangering of its existence. Uneventfulness in domestic politics, as untimely as its occurrence might be, defined the precondition of such a foreign policy. For internal movement would necessarily pull external impetus along in its wake. The challenges of foreign policy were, however, far riskier still: a vague desire for power for its own sake. That is, the pursuit of the politics of prestige beyond an extent already impermissible for Great Powers, which only *seemed* enlivening and certainly ended up posing a threat to Germany's very existence.

After a short phase of Franco-German co-operation, not least at the Berlin Congo Conference between 15 December 1884 and 26 February 1885, which isolated Britain, Bismarck's attempt at reaching an agreement with France via colonial policy failed. For, irrespective of all the expectations of overseas expansion so temptingly put in prospect for the French, their gaze was not continuously to be diverted from the 'blue ridges of the Vosges'. The domestic political basis of Prime Minister Ferry's government was too insecure for that, even though, as a protagonist of France's world policy orientation, he had served for a time as a useful partner for Bismarck's great experiment. In view of his already apparent failure to find Germany sound foreign-policy alternatives to the mechanism of 'stopgaps' via the African detour, the Reich Chancellor immediately returned to the normality of expediency. The latter found expression in Bismarck's words three years after the end of this Franco-German colonial Entente, this 'passing affair',[35] in conversation with the colonialist proponent Eugen Wolf: 'Your map of Africa is indeed very pretty, but my map of Africa lies in Europe. Here is where Russia lies, and there lies France, and we are in the middle; that

---

34. Ludwig Dehio, 'Deutschland und die Epoche der Weltkriege' in his *Deutschland und die Weltpolitik*, p. 15.
35. Hajo Holborn, *The Political Collapse of Europe*, New York, 1951, p. 53.

is my map of Africa.'[36]

Thus, war and expansion were excluded as options of German foreign policy according to Bismarck's evaluation of the situation. Besides, it became increasingly clear within what curtailed dimensions the German Reich was the real pilot of its own destiny or for that matter the referee of Europe. What was also becoming clear was the extent to which Germany appeared to be influenced by, even dependent upon, the autonomous developments of an international system which was expanding into a world-political one. Bismarck had to face lasting domestic political worries about permanently insecure parliamentary majorities and the condition of a society deeply divided into two camps, first through the *Kulturkampf*, then through the persecution of the Socialists, worries which were scarcely removed even through the model reforms of the German social security policy of the 1880s. Alongside of these concerns, which Theodor Schieder once called the 'cauchemar des révolutions',[37] that 'chauchemar des coalitions'[38] about which he himself so eloquently complained plagued the Reich Chancellor throughout. This was just as much a part of normal German foreign policy as the self-evident dependence of the latter on the method of diplomatic stopgaps. This method seemed to show itself more clearly with respect to Germany than it did in the case of other states in the system, whose invulnerability to wounds or whose invincibility allowed them to exist as great or world powers by virtue of their own strength.

In the great dual crisis of the years of 1885–7 which threatened from both west and east, Bismarck's foreign policy was subjected to a hard test. On the one hand , traditional Austro-Russian friction continued to exist in this constellation. To make use of this undoubtedly offered the Reich foreign policy opportunities which, however, immediately showed up the limits of its scope for action. To glean profit from the Balkan rivalry between Vienna and St Petersburg, Germany might have had to become unduly dependent on one or other of the two powers and above all else would have been drawn dangerously into oriental quarrels in return for nothing more than well-intentioned protestations.

On the other hand, and in the final analysis more importantly, the

36. Eugen Wolf, *Vom Fürsten Bismarck und seinem Haus*, Berlin, 1904, p. 16.
37. Theodor Schieder 'Das Problem der Revolution im 19. Jahrhundert' in his *Staat und Gesellschaft im Wandel unserer Zeit. Studien zur Geschichte des 19. und 20. Jahrhunderts*, Munich, 1958, p. 40.
38. *GP*, vol. 2, No. 294, p. 154.

Anglo-Russian antagonism came to light in this connection, as well. Bismarck had already opined in the Kissinger *Diktat* that it was important both to stimulate this antagonism and to calm it. This would utilise it to German advantage, yet always keep it below the threshold of war which, once it had broken out, would certainly also take hold of the centre of Europe and might all too easily engulf Germany. At the beginning of the great east-west crisis, Herbert von Bismarck sharply, but more coarsely than his father would have, defined the German position with respect to the revival of the Bulgarian question: 'The whole situation has to be handled in such a manner as to lead England and Russia to stand opposed to each other in stark antagonism.'[39] But in the event matters were – if at all possible – not to be allowed to end in a Russo-British war, and so too the Russo-Austrian antagonism which was linked to it was on no account to explode militarily. As early as the end of September 1885, according to Herbert von Bismarck's interpretation of the central calculation of Germany's Bulgarian policy, 'any other result is acceptable to us'.[40]

A really contradictory collection of treaties was concluded in the course of the year 1887, the 'eastern' Re-insurance Treaty, the 'western' Mediterranean agreement and the oriental Triple Alliance, respectively. Their aim was to lure England and Austria-Hungary, on the one hand (together at all costs, and the Austrians in absolutely no case without the British), and Russia, on the other, into the Turkish cul-de-sac and to draw their energies away from the centre of Europe through this peripheral commitment. After all, taken as a whole, these treaties were not geared to the optimal preparation for a future war but to the tolerable securing of a continued peace. This foreign policy had long since virtually ceased to convince the majority of the political and military representatives of the time, but above all the Liberal public, which was overwhelmingly anti-Russian in orientation and which pleaded with growing conviction for war against the Tsarist Empire. But it was precisely this which Bismarck resisted with all his might because, in respect of domestic and foreign policy alike, he expected nothing but disadvantages and could not perceive what advantage was supposed to accrue to Germany even in the event of a victory over

---

39. Walter Bußmann (ed.), *Graf Herbert von Bismarck. Aus seiner politischen Privatkorrespondenz, herausgegeben und eingeleitet von Walter Bußmann unter Mitwirkung von Klaus Peter Hoepke*, Göttingen, 1964, p. 332: Herbert von Bismarck to Bülow, 31.10.1885.
40. BA, Bülow Papers, No. 65, vol. 1, p. 297: cit. in Konrad Canis, *Bismarck und Waldersee. Die außenpolitischen krisenerscheinungen und das Verhalten des Generalstabes 1882 bis 1890*, Berlin, 1980, p. 146.

Russia. To that extent, he held fast to the fragile provisional nature of his alliance system.

Of course, in his estimation this presupposed a tranquil domestic situation which was the price to be paid for peace in foreign policy. Diagnosis of this state of affairs affords yet another description of the opportunities and limits of German foreign policy. This conservative domestic and foreign policy found characteristic expression in the Chancellor's famous Reichstag speech of 11 January 1887 concerning the question of a deferred seven-year increase in the army. The fact was that, after all, military strength appeared to Bismarck to be the unalterable precondition of his foreign policy just as, in a completely Friederician spirit, negotiations without weapons seemed to him to be like a concert without music. The *raison d'état* he prescribed for the German Reich was both necessary to its existence and a curb on the expansionist drive of the young Great Power: 'We have no bellicose desires; we are, as old Prince Metternich put it, among the satiated states; we have no wants which we could satisfy by main force.'[41] Although he was not in principle a man of peace, war was to be avoided if at all possible. After all, one campaign taking an unfortunate course could possibly even lead to the collapse of the Reich, as he put it at the end of 1886, in darkly realistic terms, in his 'Christmas letter' to the Prussian Minister of War von Bronsart.

Yet the 'system of stopgaps', the sole remaining option open to the foreign policy of the Reich, was taking an increasingly questionable shape. For in order temporarily to stop up the now leaky treaty system, the Reich Chancellor had to make problematic concessions to his partners. These caused particular difficulties, for instance, in connection with the renewal of the Triple Alliance – which had developed only with the greatest difficulty before it finally came about on 20 February 1887 – in respect of Italy's North African and Balkan ambitions. Through them, as the price, so to speak, of its existence and maintenance, offensively functioning elements crept into the defensively conceived alliance policy, causing it to degenerate. Thus, the contradiction between peaceful intention and preparation for war rose stealthily and threateningly to displace the Bismarckian alliance network.

The existence of this complicated system notwithstanding, however, Bismarck constantly kept before him the danger – sometimes more, sometimes less pressing – of a war on two fronts. Nevertheless, to the

41. Lothar Gall (ed.), *Bismarck. Die großen Reden*, Berlin, 1981, p. 273.

end of his period in government, he persevered in saving Germany from having to choose an option favouring one of the two Powers on the wings of the state system, the Russians or the British. For according to the received wisdom of the time, to choose in that way meant only 'to step down a rung and altogether to forfeit the precious freedom of movement'[42] which was seen as the noblest characteristic of national sovereignty. It is true that he gave thought to making such a choice as an *ultima ratio*: in case of extreme need, with war on two fronts immediately imminent, he would rescue Germany by 'purchasing Russian neutrality at the last moment . . . letting Austria fall and so delivering the orient to Russia',[43] as the Ambassador to London and for many years Secretary of State, Count Hatzfeldt, retrospectively reported. He was, indeed, only capable of considering a decision in favour of the Tsarist Empire, which was ideologically closer and politically more threatening to him, in a foreign-policy situation of the most extreme danger, in view of the anti-Russian sentiment dominant in the Reich. For otherwise only the British option had domestic political chances of realisation. With the inclusion of Austria-Hungary, this was, in the spirit of Holstein and Ambassador Hatzfeldt, to offer the opportunity of taking up a clear position against the Tsarist Empire. Furthermore, in the judgement of Under-Secretary of State Berchem, it was to put an end to the era of 'make shift' which only contributed to 'allowing the postponement of the moment for an operation'[44] and was finally to render possible a preventive war against Russia envisaged in the military calculations of the Deputy Chief of the General Staff, Waldersee.

Bismarck himself had, in fact again sounded England out in January 1889 and let a proposal through parliament for a ratified defensive agreement 'for collective defence against a French attack'[45] on Great Britain or Germany – an eventuality which hardly seemed acute for the British. The *modus* of this arrangement was unusual. A secret pact, according to Bismarck's line of reasoning, offered both powers security regarding the outcome of a war; a public one would – by contrast – guarantee its prevention. The object of sounding out England was to put a check on France, but it may also have contained a basic option in

42. Ludwig Dehio, *Gleichgewicht oder Hegemonie. Betrachtungen über ein Grundproblem der neueren Staatengeschichte*, Krefeld, 1948, p. 197.
43. *GP*, vol. 9, p. 353: Hatzfeldt to Holstein, 18.6.1895.
44. Hajo Holborn (ed.), *Aufzeichnungen und Erinnerungen aus dem Leben des Botschafters Joseph Maria von Radowitz*, vol. 2, Stuttgart, Berlin, Leipzig, 1925, p. 275: Under-Secretary of State Berchem to Radowitz, 4.12.1887.
45. *GP*, vol. 4, p. 400: Bismarck to Ambassador Hatzfeldt in London, 11.1.1889.

favour of the British in the event of a further deterioration of Russo-German relations. This would have pertained above all if, as Bismarck can scarcely have expected, Great Britain had accepted the parliamentary ratification of a treaty. But things being as they were, Bismarck's British castling move, less fundamentally orientated and rather more concretely calculated, delivered to the Russians a threatening reminder of how much room for manoeuvre German foreign policy still possessed. Once again it was a matter of inducing back the Russians and, in the light of certain 'dissensions'[46] then making themselves noticeable in the Alliance, while simultaneously keeping the Habsburg monarchy from a unilateral approach to Russia.

In the final analysis, however, the Reich Chancellor felt that 'the Russian shirt [was] preferable to the English jacket',[47] in spite of all the pleading for co-operation with Great Britain, which from time to time not even Herbert von Bismarck could ignore – 'if only the English were not quite so very untrustworthy and democratised'.[48] His offer, in a sense, anticipated a British rejection; the extraordinarily smooth way in which he facilitated Prime Minister Salisbury's negative response speaks for itself. Thus, Bismarck had shown the opposition within Germany – which was so strongly critical of his foreign policy – that it was not possible to conclude an alliance with the British. So it was necessary to opt neither for one side nor the other but to continue to hold fast to the policy of a free hand.

He emphasised this necessity with regard to the relationship with the Habsburg monarchy, the Power most closely allied to the Reich. For 'the security of our relations with the Austro-Hungarian state rests in large part on the possibility that, if Austria makes unreasonable demands of us, we can also reach an understanding with Russia'.[49] All in all, after the failure of the British rapport, only one option remained if Bismarck's free-hand policy had to be sacrificed in circumstances of an immediately imminent war on two fronts. Bismarck considered the Tsarist Empire exclusively as German foreign policy's only chance – if a large-scale military conflagration were to be avoided.

Right up to his dismissal in March 1890, the Reich Chancellor succeeded in circumventing a definitive arrangement of that kind,

46. Wolfgang Fritz Horsch 'Unstimmigkeiten im deutsch-österreichischem Bündnis Ende 1888 und Anfang 1889', unpublished thesis, Tübingen, 1931.
47. Karl Messerschmidt, *Bismarcks russische Politik vom Berliner Kongress bis zu seiner Entlassung*, thesis, Hamburg, 1936; published Würzburg, 1936, p. 87.
48. W. Bußmann (ed.), *Graf Herbert von Bismarck*, p. 379: Herbert von Bismarck to Rantzau, 24.9.1886.
49. *GP*, vol. 6, p. 305: Bismarck to the Crown Prince, 9.5.1988.

avoiding the admission of being able to exist only as a junior partner of
one or other of the World Powers. Balancing between Great Britain
and Russia on a progressively narrowing beam, he preserved the
delicate freedom of Germany as a Great Power. This does not imply
that the Reich's unmistakable exposure to peril should be underestimated. The 'system of stopgaps', after all, characterises all diplomacy
to a certain extent, and undoubtedly, its extreme development in
Bismarck's contradictorily harmonious power-game with 'five balls'
met with more rejection than agreement from the mid-1880s on. The
internally contradictory character of a complicated alliance system,
logically bound to collapse in war and constructed primarily for the
preservation of peace, was, in spite or perhaps precisely because of its
superficial artifice, increasingly rejected. The thought of war as a
possibility in international politics entered the consciousness of the
generation succeeding Bismarck with gathering force. A new emotion
was raging, an emotion which perceived the status quo as inadequate
and sought by means of final solutions what was adjudged inevitable.

With his sensitivity to the dangers threatening the Reich, Otto von
Bismarck quite obviously fell, from left to right so to speak, back onto
the defensive in domestic politics. 'All the world is really pro-war here',
his colleague and adversary Holstein stated in January 1888: 'With the
almost exclusive exception of His Excellency, who exerts himself to the
utmost for the maintenance of peace.'[50] For, as has already been said,
the Reich Chancellor was incapable, even in the event of a victorious
war against the Tsarist Empire, of recognising the benefit such a
success against invulnerable Russia would actually bring in its wake.
In the light of its elemental force, there was nothing to do but trust in
the hopeful uncertainty of the refining-mill of history and wait for the
relief which the internal decomposition of the giant empire would
bring. One has to bear in mind, however, that Bismarck's pragmatic
peace policy was anything but popular in contemporary Germany. By
contrast, Wilhelm II's soon proclaimed *Weltpolitik*, whatever it may
have been in detail and in general, met with the enthusiastic approval
of rulers and ruled alike.

By the 1880s at the latest, it had become obvious that the trend of the
fundamentally changing system of states, extending to a world scale,
was increasingly bypassing Bismarck's Germany. For a long while, the
European expansion of the remaining states certainly maintained and
encouraged the German Reich's freedom of movement in Europe.

50. G. Ebel (ed.), *Botschafter Paul Graf von Hatzfeldt*, vol. 1, p. 657.

Ultimately, however, it was precisely this secular development in world history that led the rival Powers, France, Russia and Britain respectively, to arrive at *ententes* or conventions with each other via regulation of overseas conflicts. The inclination to *détente* among the World Powers, which accompanied at least the Russo-British antagonism, triumphed: it was more expensive to engage in military duels than in diplomatic agreements. The disinterest on the part of the British and Russians for the centre of Europe, which had set in after the end of the Crimean War, had opened up the Reich's room for manoeuvre quite advantageously to German interests, but with *détente* options became considerably more restricted. On top of this, the domestic political perspective made matters more difficult still. For the public had changed substantially with the formation of a political mass-market, which virtually constituted its existence, and the press, interest groups and parties impaired – indeed, absorbed and altered – the sphere of *raison d'état* and diplomacy which had hitherto enjoyed near autonomy and subjected it to new conditions of life.

Having at least cursorily discussed the opportunities and limits of German foreign policy in the age of Bismarck between 1871 and 1890, let us now finally consider judgements on the so-called 'system of stopgaps' referred to in the introduction.

Firstly, Bismarck's seemingly artificial power game was certainly anything but a long-term solution, yet neither was it evidence of a foreign policy which had already failed. Assuredly, as Hermann Oncken stated, one must 'remain conscious' of the fact 'that it [Bismarck's foreign policy] was not subjected to the ultimate test'.[51] But leaving aside how difficult it is to specify what is meant by such finality, it is centrally important to bear in mind that the evasion of that 'test' was made possible precisely by Germany's foreign policy as directed by Bismarck.

Secondly, in view of its hallmarks of improvisation, fragility and the provisional, which no one recognised more clearly than Bismarck himself, the thesis of a system of German foreign policy unitarily drawn up and realised by the Chancellor and characterised, without substantial qualifications, by planning, stability and success, can scarcely be

---

51. Hermann Oncken, 'Ziele und Grundlagen der auswärtigen Politik des Deutschen Reiches von 1871 bis 1914' in Bernhard Harms (ed.), *Volk und Reich der Deutschen . . .*, vol. 1, Berlin, 1929, p. 154.

sustained any longer. In this sense, the controversial Re-insurance Treaty with Russia, too, represented 'neither the crowning nor the keystone of a self-contained system' but 'merely a further stopgap'.[52]

Thirdly, there is no basis in the evidence for speaking pejoratively of a 'system of stopgaps' because the supposedly real alternative to it was the opportunity of a preventive war, missed through shilly-shallying. For one thing, the possibility suggested by Ulrich Noack of an Anglo-German alliance offensively directed against Russia did not exist. For another, the consciousness of the horror of the Napoleonic Wars was still just about alive in his generation, and as well, the Crimean War, the American war of secession and the Franco-Prussian War had given evidence of the new destructive quality of military conflicts in the modern era. Bismarck was simply one of the few to expect more damage than profit to accrue to the German Reich from an armed conflagration.

Fourthly, we would concur with Lothar Gall that Bismarck's foreign policy represented a 'system of stopgaps' whose limits were finally more striking than its opportunities. But one ought to ask what foreign policy alternative to this system existed and with what implications for domestic politics it could be realised. In other words, an internal parliamentarisation, corresponding in some respects to the current of the age, would in all probability have encouraged the tendency to external expansion rather than controlled it. In the decades after 1890, however, the understandable craving for clear solutions in the field of foreign policy – albeit not inevitably – led to a formation of blocs which polarised the international system and finally committed diplomats more strongly to the cultivation of alliances than to the preservation of peace. As is indicated by the strengths and weaknesses, opportunities and limitations, stabilities and susceptibilities of German foreign policy in the age of Bismarck, in some respects there was no alternative to the 'system of stopgaps'.

Furthermore, no foreign policy builds for eternity, and each is always reliant on stopgaps. In Germany, stopgaps had indeed developed in an unusual and extreme form, implying that the external norm of the Reich lay in its immobility whereas, for all the other Great Powers, it was normal to expand. Domestic and foreign political forces, which were certainly modern and forward-looking by nature, even if ultimately they also had unforeseeably detrimental consequences, were

---

52. Peter Jakobs, *Das Werden des französisch-russischen Zweibundes 1890–1894*, Wiesbaden, 1968, p. 12.

thus either overcome or held in check during the 'Bismarckian Era' in order to secure the status quo of Imperial Germany, its existence and form. For to do what other powers did in this period, namely to expand, seemed far too risky to the founder of the Reich. Considered in retrospect, he was not so far out.

There remains the question of the extent to which this 'system of stopgaps' was characterised by the lack of future perspective or by the incapacity for development. The answers to that question, however, differing from case to case, show only what has already become clear in another context: the Reich's domestic and foreign *raisons d'état* which Bismarck had made compatible with one another in a quite deliberate but increasingly laborious fashion, fell virtually irreconcilably asunder. An increase in internal freedom which many desired would in all probability have unleashed precisely the unrest in foreign policy which it was imperative to avoid. But 'satiation', which secured Germany's existence, under substantially altered domestic conditions would have represented an internal contradiction for the Liberal public and a corresponding parliamentary majority since, after all, it was precisely the denial of this 'satiation' which characterised the new course in both domestic and foreign affairs.

This incompatibility between internal freedom and external peace was, at least to some extent, peculiar to the Bismarckian Reich. The 'tragedy' of its existence, characterised by Max Weber, with regard to Bismarck's 'career as a statesman', was that it would 'surely find its future in the fact that under him [Bismarck], the work of his hands, the nation to which he had given unity, slowly and irresistibly altered its economic structure and became another, a People which had to demand other arrangements than those which he was able to give it and to which his Caesarean nature could not adapt'.[53] Beyond this domestic, political side of history, it was neither the Great Power instincts of the Germans, fully awakened in the interim, nor the fundamentally changing world of states, which promoted the existence of a fully independent German nation state, as much as the historical developments which had once promoted its emergence.

Undoubtedly, what Bismarck did or omitted to do in the field of foreign policy was backward-looking in terms of the spirit of the age, and what he resisted or repressed was, viewed from this perspective, progressive. Germany's foreign policy had indeed reached the border of

53. Max Weber, 'Der Nationalstaat und die Volkswirtschaftspolitik' in his *Gesammelte politische Schriften* . . ., 3rd edn, Tübingen, 1971, pp. 19 f.

a new era into which it no longer appeared to fit properly and which at the very least mercilessly exposed its brittleness. Its pilot, Otto von Bismarck, altogether preferred 'the provisional in everything, because it is more elastic, to the definitive'.[54] This was profoundly alien to a period rapidly reforming and swiftly modernising in international and domestic politics, which sought immediate change and aimed at the ultimate in secular affairs.

Of course, beyond the German example of a particularly strongly developed incompatibility between internal and external *raison d'état*, the fundamental question is whether the classical European system of a balance of power instituted in 1815, the year of Bismarck's birth, was still capable of surviving for any length of time. At any rate, until the year 1890, the 'system of stopgaps', the alternative to which lay in an eventual general European war rather than in a stable solution, fulfilled its purpose in preserving peace. It had long seemed the most precious treasure to the generations moulded by the events of the French Revolution, by the wars which had emanated from it and by the Vienna peace settlement. Representatives and peoples of a new epoch, however, having grown more distant from such experiences, tended to see disadvantages in a policy of the status quo bought at the expense of domestic and national freedom. Since everything in history has its own time, they understandably pursued a different policy which, by no means inevitably, but as the result of decisions taken by those responsible, eventually produced fatal consequences.

54. Norman Rich and H.M. Fischer (eds), *The Holstein Papers*, vol. 2: *Diaries*, Cambridge, 1957, p. 137: 4.5.1884.

REINER POMMERIN

Germany's Reaction to the Globalisation of International Relations, 1890–1898: A Different Course

The nineteenth century, 'an epoque of world-wide expansion of European domination, European values and last but not least Europe's material culture', seemed not unreasonably to its contemporaries to be 'the European century'.[1] Nevertheless, the spheres of influence of the European states in the non-European world, acquired during the time of early colonisation as well as during the Age of Imperialism, were to influence the economic position and political power of every state in the Concert of Europe. On the other hand, the expansion of European states also influenced their position and weight in the world. If only to avoid the pressures of economic exploitation, colonies put forward claims of self-determination and independence which could not be suppressed in the long run. Although Europe, as represented mostly in its system of states, the pentarchy, appeared to Europeans as the navel of the world, by the end of the century this colonialist system had expanded to include new non-European members. International relations now covered the entire globe.

Before we consider when and in what way the still young German Reich reacted to the global expansion of the concert of power (if at all), we have to describe the conditions and participants of the change from the European to the global power system. The conditions will be considered first.

1. L. Gall, *Europa auf dem Weg in die Moderne 1850–1890*, Munich, Vienna, 1984, p. 98.

93

Even more important than closer political connections was the growing economic interdependence of the world. Increasingly, the economies of individual states circumscribed by political boundaries entered into contact – and competition – with one another and grew together into a system of world trade and world economy. This global growth, however, developed unevenly and not at all simultaneously. An important factor in this development was the 'second industrial revolution' then taking place in Europe. It started about 1870, at a time when non-European countries were just beginning to experience – if at all – their 'first industrial revolution': the revolution of coal and iron.

But in Europe began the century of steel, of electricity as a new source of light, warmth and power, of petroleum and chemistry.[2] World steel production in 1850 amounted to only 80,000 tons, but by 1890 it had increased to 28 million tons; inventions by Sir Henry Bessemer, Friedrich von Siemens and Sidney G. Thomas had created new technological conditions. By 1890 electricity was produced by water-powered plants; it lit up the darkness through the invention of the electric bulb in 1879 and also served as a source of power for various kinds of driving motors. By 1886 the newly developed process of electrolysis was employed in the commercial production of aluminium. Products of the distillation of mineral oil such as petroleum found their use in lamps and heating systems, and the internal combustion engine was invented. In addition to the other natural sciences, biochemistry and bacteriology emerged: vitamins and hormones were discovered in 1902. And as of 1899, one could fight a hangover with aspirin.

Baron von Rothschild is said to have stated: 'There are three ways to ruin: gambling, women and engineers. The first two are more agreeable, but the last is more certain.'[3] The conversion of scientific knowledge, new technologies and world-wide marketing of industrial products called for the readiness of investment capital. And this readiness existed. The Age of Imperialism put a new and particular emphasis on the credit market and the international circulation of money. Britain, until the end of the First World War the great financier of the world, had already had a gold standard since 1816. All other states had been on a silver standard or a double standard, and fluctuations in the value of silver made commercial calculations in the

2. See G. Barraclough, *An Introduction to Contemporary History*, London, 1964, p. 39.
3. Cited in G.A. Craig, *Europe 1815–1914*, New York, 1966, p. 290.

trade between states highly precarious.

Thus, by the turn of the century, after enough gold was found, all of the important states in the world had adopted the gold standard. Now, states involved in world trade could more readily balance the shifts and variations in price and service structure, as well as in the balance of services and balance of payments, since the international currency system was uniformly based on gold.[4]

At the same time a new system of banking and banknotes came into being in many states. Share banks, foreign banks and colonial banks simplified international payments, and non-cash payments were even more accelerated through the rapidly developing postal and telegraphic services.[5]

The development of the electrical telegraph was, indeed, of fundamental importance both economically and politically. At the outset, the electrical telegraph had come into existence along railway lines simply to serve the railways. But before long even the most remote villages were connected with one another by telegraph. Connections became necessary between states to overcome political borders and to help transmit information in the commercial, the political and, eventually, the military sectors.[6]

Britain, an island with world-wide commitments, assumed the leading position in opening the world through land and underwater cables. It began systematically to build up cable communication systems which bound together all parts of the Empire without touching foreign territories. The value of such a communications network and its control was displayed to the entire world when, for example, in 1895 the British government stopped all telegrams to and from Transvaal. The famous telegram from Kaiser Wilhelm II to President Krüger in 1896, congratulating him on his victory at Krügersdorp, found its way to Pretoria only after English evening papers had already published its contents in London. In 1898, during the Spanish-American War, the Spanish Admiralty sent two telegrams to Admiral Cervera, then cruising near Martinique. Both cables ordered him to return with the fleet to Spain. Neither one reached the Admiral, however, as they were

---

4. See A. Sartorius von Waltershausen, *Die Entstehung der Weltwirtschaft. Geschichte des zwischenstaatlichen Wirtschaftslebens vom letzten Viertel des achtzehnten Jahrhunderts bis 1914*, Jena, 1931, p. 495.
5. See F.-W. Hennig, *Die Industrialisierung in Deutschland 1800–1914*, 3rd edn, Paderborn, 1976, p. 253.
6. See R. Pommerin, 'Seekabel und Nachrichtenbüros. Determinanten des Deutschlandbilds im Zeitalter des Imperialismus 1871–1914', *Vierteljahresschrift für Sozial- und Wirtschaftsgeschichte*, 4, 1986, pp. 520–31.

intercepted by the Americans. He decided to proceed to Santiago de Cuba from where he was later unable to escape without great losses. Not without reason, the French government noted enviously in 1900 that 'England most probably owes its influence in the world more to its cable network than to its fleet. It controls information and makes use of it in its politics and its trade in a remarkable way'.[7]

World trade accelerated as a result of other changes, as well. The Suez Canal, opened in 1869, shortened the route from London to Calcutta from 12,000 to 8,000 sea-miles, i.e. by 30 per cent. Merchandise and passengers formerly having to circumnavigate Africa on their way to India, Singapore, Hong Kong or even Yokohama now arrived by steamship via Suez much sooner. Likewise, the 'Nord-Ostsee-Kanal' and the Channel of Corinth substantially reduced travelling time, thus encouraging more frequent travel. The tonnage and speed of ships, on the oceans as well as on rivers, also increased. On land railway lines continued to shrink distances, and thus the world moved closer together. Special importance was placed on the lines of communication between the Atlantic and the Pacific. In the film *East of Eden* the experimental transport of heads of lettuce to distant markets via railway ended in a disaster of thawing ice; nevertheless, frozen meat was already reaching New York from Kansas City as early as 1876, and it was shipped to Europe from Argentina beginning in 1877. Fruits and vegetables from the Mediterranean promptly reached northern European markets after the excavation of the Mont Cenis and St Gotthard tunnels in 1871 and 1882 respectively; Casanova informs us in his memoires that at the end of the eighteenth century, it had taken him three entire days to cross the St Bernhard. These changes opened the way for states outside of Europe, notably the United States and Japan, to contribute enormously to changes in the balance of power.

As previously mentioned, the expansion of European states through acquisition of territories abroad had awakened a desire for self-determination and independence among those held in subordination. This was even more the case when the dependent subjects were European emigrants. The basis of their demands can be found in the American Declaration of Independence of 4 July 1776.[8] A possible repercussion of American independence on Europe was already described by the journalist Posselt in 1796:

7. See P.M. Kennedy, *Aufstieg und Verfall der britischen Seemacht*, Herford, Bonn, 1978, p. 228.
8. The original version is to be found in the Exhibition Room, NA.

Until now small Europe has been able to treat other continents of enormous size as a sort of appendix, but the time will come when Nemesis, often late but never lacking, will execute her office. The time will come when Philadelphia [then capital of the United States] will discuss Europe's concerns as London does now those of Canada and Bengal.[9]

But the United States concentrated during the first century of its existence on an isolationist defensive policy. First of all, it rigorously defended the territorial and administrative integrity of North and South America: a continuation of colonisation by European powers was no longer to be tolerated in the western hemisphere. In addition, it continued its own relatively undisturbed colonisation of the West, and it acquired or obtained by war Florida, Texas, California and, finally, Alaska.

After the United States had overcome its internal ordeal at the end of the Civil War, the search for bases in the Pacific followed. A conflict between German, English and American interests in the islands of Samoa resulted in the Samoan Conference of 1889 in Berlin. Use of the English language for the first time at an international diplomatic conference serves as evidence that the United States had entered into a new era in its foreign policy; it had finally renounced George Washington's advice not to enter into agreements with European states. The result of this conference was a condominium of the three states over the Samoan Islands. A few years later this agreement appeared to the anti-imperialist Secretary of State, Walter Quintin Gresham, to be a deviation, hitherto avoided, toward co-operation with European powers. It marked – as he wrote – the break-down of 'our traditional and well-founded policy of not entering into entangling alliances with foreign states'.[10]

The then existing trade relations between the United States, European and non-European countries created a different set of international parameters. The new position of the United States as a Great Power was also reflected in its foreign policy; when, for instance, in 1895–7 Britain intervened in the question of the border between Venezuela and British Guiana, the United States supported Venezuela. Thus, Britain began to adjust its foreign policy regarding the United States, taking into consideration the real power relations in the western hemisphere and cultivating an Anglo-American *rapprochement*.

9. Cited in H. Gollwitzer, *Geschichte des weltpolitischen Denkens*, vol. 1: *Vom Zeitalter der Entdeckung bis zum Beginn des Imperialismus*, Göttingen, 1972, p. 259.
10. Cited in H.-U. Wehler, *Der Aufstieg des amerikanischen Imperialismus. Studien zur Entwicklung des Imperium Americanum 1865–1900*, Göttingen, 1974, p. 232.

The revolt in Cuba, an island which the United States had always regarded as belonging within its sphere of influence, led, after the explosion of the American warship *Maine* in the port of Havana in 1898, to a war between the United States and Spain in that same year. This war of a non-European against a European power ended favourably for the United States. The solidarity of the European powers (monarchs), which Kaiser Wilhelm II had tried to awaken, failed. They could only muster enough energy to send a rather ineffectual collective note to the American government. The contents of this note, moreover, had been negotiated beforehand by the British Ambassador Lord Pauncefote with the Department of State. Effective 'threat gestures' against the United States did not take place because of the commercial interests of European nations in transatlantic trade.

On the other hand, Europe's attention was more strongly directed at this time toward Asia. In the Sino-Japanese War of 1894–95 the United States offered its services – upon the request of China – for peace negotiations, thus signalling the end of American diplomatic reserve. In fact, America's interest in the Pacific region – Korea, Manchuria and China – as a large future American market, had increased steadily. To stop the partitioning of China into different spheres of influence by the various European states and to keep those markets open, Secretary of State John Hay dispatched a circular to all powers, asserting American interests in China. In this note the United States demanded acceptance of the principal of the open-door policy for trade, even in those spheres of influence already marked out. The agreement of the powers followed, readily enough since China's integrity, and thus the status quo, had been asserted in the note. There was henceforth no fear that one competing power could cut out any of the others.

When in the following year, in a kind of international police and punishment action, the Boxer Rebellion, was suppressed, the troops participating in the fight came from Europe as well as from the United States and Japan. During the Russo-Japanese war in 1904–5, Theodore Roosevelt created another opportunity to force the neutral powers to a positive decision regarding the open-door policy in China. And two years later, in January 1906, the United States participated in an important political conference of the European powers, the Conference of Algeciras: Kaiser Wilhelm II particularly, in utter ignorance of American policy, had considered Roosevelt an unselfish friend and had asked the United States to intervene in the Moroccan crisis between France and Germany.

This event, coming as it did after the consolidation of the American continental domain, its annexation of Hawaii in 1898, the installation of colonies on the Phillippines and Puerto Rico and the formation of a protectorate over Cuba, finally showed that the United States had become a world power. Its hegemonial position in the western hemisphere, its rapidly growing industrial and agricultural potential, as well as its influence on trade in Asia and Europe had contributed to an unsettling of Europe's global predominance. American military power, however, remained merely potential, and the assumption of political responsibility outside of the North American continent was in continuous opposition to isolationism. Nevertheless, after having played the role of 'balancer of power' due to its economic interests in Asia, the United States was now in a position to debate the concerns of Europe, if not from Philadelphia, then from Washington, just as the journalist Posselt had prophesied a hundred years earlier.

The second important partner in the transfer of the European state system into a world-wide state system was Japan. Japan, a country not colonised by Europeans, became a modern Great Power without breaking with its cultural heritage. Nevertheless, the history of Japan's incorporation into the concert of powers was tied to the world-wide expansion of the West. If cheap merchandise was to find a market all over the globe, then every country that obstructed western trade was an enemy to progress. According to a *New York Times* interpretation of 1852, there was a divine plan to transform the world into a realm of diligence, civilisation and happiness; Japan, which at that point still remained tightly shut to the world and its trade, was therefore 'a permanent stumbling block in the path of universal progress'.[11] A German author shared this view: 'the old obstinate powers who defy all foreign influence are like oysters. One has to open them forcibly, then they are dead and can be consumed by Europeans'.[12] The opening up of Japan was contrived in 1853 by Commodore Perry when he visited Japan with four torpedo-boats. This led to the first of the 'unequal treaties' which Japan had to contract with Britain, Russia, France, the Netherlands and Prussia. These treaties guaranteed foreigners ex-territorial rights and limited Japanese customs autonomy. Japan's effort to minimise the effect of this agreement failed, however, because of European pressure.

Japan finally obtained the annulment of the 'unequal treaties' in

11. Cited in W. Stingl, *Der Ferne Osten in der deutschen Politik vor dem Ersten Weltkrieg (1902–1914)*, Frankfurt a. M., 1978, vol. 1, p. 63.
12. Ibid., p. 64.

1899. That it succeeded in this was due in the first place to its internal modernisation process. This consisted politically in replacing the feudal government with an absolute bureaucratic government and socially in the transition from a corporate to a bourgeois society. With the aid of a tax system, Japan built its own monetary and banking system and remained, unlike China, largely independent of western capital to finance railway construction and industrialisation. Soon the Japanese became known as 'the most courteous and educated people of Asia'.[13] In 1891 a German author wrote somewhat prematurely that Japan was now in the position 'to be accepted by the Christian European nations as a fully civilised and recognised nation with equal rights, into the circle of civilised nations with all rights and duties'.[14]

Initially, Japan knocked very faintly at the door of the Great Powers, almost simultaneously with two young European states – Italy and the German Reich. In 1871 Japan obtained the Rio-Kio Islands from China and in 1876 received extra-territorial rights in an agreement with Korea. The dispute over sovereignty on the Korean Peninsula led to the Sino-Japanese war in 1894, which ended successfully for Japan in 1895. As much as Europe admired Japan's military success, there remained a distance based on racial as well as cultural differences. These found their expression in Europe and the United States in the slogan 'the yellow peril'.[15]

Nevertheless, Japan's victory was politically limited by the intervention of European powers, namely, Germany, France and Russia; Britain deserted this group at the last moment. On the peninsula, Japan had to renounce Liaotung and Port Arthur, which it had won at the peace of Shimonoseki from China. Interestingly, the German papers noted in this intervention of the European powers that what Europe had failed to do in time with the United States now had to be done with a timely move against Japan.[16] Kaiser Wilhelm II therefore tried to prevent Japanese intervention, as suggested by England, in the Boxer Rebellion in China. In the end, however, Japanese troops fought side by side with European and American soldiers. Japan could no longer imagine being absent from decisions on Asia's destiny.

From the point of view of contemporaries, it was Japan's victory in the war against Russia in 1904–5 which was regarded as its 'coming of

13. Ibid., p. 53.
14. Ibid.
15. See H. Gollwitzer, *Die gelbe Gefahr. Geschichte eines Schlagworts. Studien zum imperialistischen Denken*, Göttingen, 1962.
16. See R. Pommerin, *Der Kaiser und Amerika. Die USA in der Politik der Reichsleitung 1890–1917*, Cologne, Vienna, 1986, p. 68.

age' as a Great Power. During the Boxer Rebellion, German officers had talked about their Japanese fellow combatants as the 'little yellow apes'. British naval officers, after the announcement of the British-Japanese agreement in 1902 before Yokohama, toasted 'our brothers the monkeys'. The assault on Port Arthur in January and the sea battle at Tsushima in May 1905 changed the estimation of Japan enormously. An Asiatic, non-European state had provoked a confrontation with Russia, a European Great Power (Russia was then regarded as a leading military power). Reich Chancellor Bülow declared in the Reichstag: 'Japan has won its place amongst the great powers through its outstanding efficiency, its brilliant army and its courageous fleet.'[17]

Let us now examine the ways in which the German Reich reacted to the incisive changes in the system of world powers and, as a highly industrialised state, met the challenge of technological changes and new conditions.

Bismarck's reaction to a proposal of the Reichspost is indicative of the importance of technology in European thinking. Secretary von Stephan had suggested installing a submarine cable from Emden to Bilbao or Santander in Spain, to be independent from French cables in case of war. Bismarck dismissed this suggestion since he still believed that, in the case of a conflict with France, Germany could use the British cable network. The argument offered by Post-master von Stephan that, in the interest of its colonial policies, Germany needed its own cable connections similar to the British 'all-red connections' did not at all convince Bismarck. 'The development of colonial matters', he wrote, 'will show whether the necessity of our own cable connections is unavoidable!'[18] Bismarck's seemingly hostile attitude toward modernisation finds its explanation in his distrust of a colonial policy for Germany. This was his firm conviction when he said to the colonial enthusiast and traveller Eugen Wolf on 5 December 1888: 'Your map of Africa is indeed very pretty, but my map of Africa lies in Europe. Here is where Russia lies, and there lies France, and we are in the middle; that is my map of Africa.'[19] The German Chancellor, who felt himself under obligation to preserve peace in Europe as a prerequisite for the existence of the German Reich, was not able to perceive the

17. Cited in W. Stingl, *Der Ferne Osten*, vol. 2, p. 461.
18. See R. Pommerin, 'Seekabel und Nachrichtenbüros', p. 522.
19. Quoted from L. Gall, *Bismarck. Der weiße Revolutionär*, Frankfurt a. M., 1980, p. 623.

general change in the state system. His world remained Europe.

His successor, Chancellor Caprivi, also overlooked the political dimensions of the emergence of the United States and Japan. Caprivi remained spellbound by continental Europe and by hopes of realising his concept of 'Middle Europe' through commercial agreements. Thus the second Chancellor also remained attached to the central European concept of his predecessor. In his foreign policy, Japan played no role at all, and he regarded the United States as merely an economic power. He intended to oppose this economic power, however, with the aid of his trade agreement policy. He planned 'the creation of the United States of Europe with the goal of making the continent independent of America'.[20] But even this weak political trade offensive failed. The German Reich had to give up any anti-American trade policy and in principle also its middle-European conception as a result of the Saratoga Convention of 22 August 1891.

The most important development in American foreign policy up to 1897–8 was completely ignored by the German leadership. As demonstrated by America's offer to settle the Sino-Japanese War and its China policy in general, the United States was cautiously beginning to play a more active role within the power concert. Only the so-called *Weltpolitik* re-orientation of German foreign policy under the leadership of Bülow made it obvious to the Reichsleitung that they should secure at least the sympathy of the United States. With its victory in the war against Spain, the United States had entered, according to Bülow, into the 'circle of German political interest'. In fact, America not only tolerated the acquisition of the Carolines, the Marianas and the Palau Islands by Germany; it also made possible the partition of the Samoan Islands. The close co-operation of the United States with China followed.

Consequently, the German Reich avoided everything that might lead to conflict with the United States, including the deliberate acceptance of domestic conflicts in order not to offend American feelings in trade policy. This went as far as a self-imposed abstinence from interfering with American interests as laid down in the Monroe Doctrine. The German Reich tried to win the United States by cultural activities, by visits of the fleet and manoeuvers, as well as the training of American officers, and finally through a sort of goodwill tour of Prince Heinrich in 1902. To win the goodwill of the United States was clearly the aim of German foreign policy after 1901, when Bülow had

20. Cited in R. Pommerin, *Der Kaiser und Amerika*, p. 26.

dismissed British efforts to improve relations with Germany.

However, the instrumentalisation of German-American relations never really produced a reaction to the change in the power concert. Europe remained the centre for German foreign policy despite Germany's showing of the flag throughout the world. This reality changed only somewhat when in 1907 the plan for an American-German-Chinese *entente cordiale* was developed and encouraged by Kaiser Wilhelm II. Bülow tried to pull his rather unsuccessful foreign policy out of a blind alley with the aid of America after the French-British *entente cordiale* of 1904 and the Russian-British convention of 1907. He offered the American government a joint *entente*, with China as the third partner, only because he hoped to procure breathing space for the German Reich, which was feeling increasingly encircled. Allusion to a threat to American interests in Asia from Japan, in association with England, could be used as a lever in the Pacific. This initiative failed, however, because the United States reached an agreement with Japan in the Root-Takahira Agreement.

After the failure of Bülow's political concept of *Weltpolitik* in 1906–7, which in reality was nothing more than a continuation of European politics, German-American relations played only a minor role until the beginning of the war. Germany believed that it should acquire at least some small colonies and not remain an insignificant Middle Power amongst the European Great Powers. The importance of the United States as a new world power emerged in the German consciousness only after 1917, and then very painfully.

The second power which contributed to the globalisation of international relations was Japan. But this country continued to play a subordinate role in German foreign affairs. After the Triple Intervention of 1895, when Germany generated Japanese antipathy as a result of the exaggerated bearing of its Ambassador Gutschmid, Germany demonstratively and unreservedly supported Russia's offensive policies in East Asia. Continental European calculations guided German foreign policy in Asia, influenced especially by the fact that Russia's forces had left Europe in order to proceed offensively to the Far East. As a result the German Reich appeared for some time to be rid of the threat of a war on two fronts. At the same time, a new opportunity developed, quite in the sense of Bülow's *Weltpolitik*, to achieve territorial expansion without risks. German diplomats did not realise, however, that it was necessary for Russia to remain unthreatened in Europe in order to reach out in the Far East. Nor did they anticipate the almost automatic Russian decision to ally with

France and reach an accommodation with Britain, above all in the Persian region.

Likewise, German foreign policy makers realised far too late that the periphery was not a suitable terrain for easing European tensions. Germany's interest in the vast Chinese trade market – then widely overrated – and the securing of its own spheres of interest in Kiao-Chow, as well as Russian-Japanese differences, subordinated German policy towards Japan to its China policy.[21] In addition there were feelings of racial superiority toward Asians as a whole, as expressed in the slogan 'yellow peril', despite the fact that Germany had honoured the Japanese as 'East Asian Prussians'. As far as German foreign policy was concerned, Japan remained above all a very distant Asiatic power. Japan's victory over the highly touted military power of Russia finally made Japan a world power in German eyes. Nevertheless, this world power had already been a firm alliance partner of Britain since 1902.

To sum up, the German Reich participated actively in the perceptions and technical developments which made the world a smaller place. Since the foundation of the Reich, however, the view of those who steered the course of German foreign policy remained centred on Europe. Germany's so-called *Weltpolitik* remained at its root essentially centred on Europe. In spite of all endeavours to acquire mini-colonies anywhere in the world, German foreign policy makers hardly realised, and then too late, that the game of international relations was being played on a wider and more cosmopolitan court. Neither did Germany realise that the number of players had increased by two: Japan and the United States. The obvious weakness in German foreign policy was a lack of direction. But more importantly, the rules by which the nineteenth-century concert of powers played would have limited the German Reich to the role of ball boy in the new game of international relations.

---

21. See R.-H. Wippich, *Japan und die deutsche Fernostpolitik 1894–1898. Vom Ausbruch des Chinesisch-Japanischen Krieges bis zur Besetzung der Kiautschou-Bucht. Ein Beitrag zur Wilhelmi-nischen Weltpolitik*, Wiesbaden, 1987, p. 404.

IMANUEL GEISS

The German Version of Imperialism, 1898–1914: Weltpolitik

The German Reich and its *Weltpolitik* have been justly singled out as the decisive factors leading to the First World War, and for understandable reasons much moralising has gone into condemning them.[1] But the time has come to look at both more dispassionately, without dividing the world moralistically into 'goodies' or 'baddies', one way or the other. This is only possible by analysing the German Reich and *Weltpolitik* in a functional way, as part of complex historical processes that should be studied in scientific terms, like a chemical process which leads to an explosion. To identify the workings of complex and universal historical mechanisms as they apply to Germany does not cancel out the personal, moral responsibility of individuals, but it may help to avoid smugly condemning (or defending) developments that may have similarly taken place in other states which were subject to the same universal mechanisms or principles, only to a lesser degree and with less devastating effect.

This approach also requires us to transcend any kind of rivalry between the primacy of domestic or foreign policy. Neither the traditional dogma of 'Primat der Außenpolitik' nor the more recent counter-dogma of 'Primat der Innenpolitik', which Hans-Ulrich Weh-

1. This is a free version in English of the relevant material taken from my recent book *Der Lange Weg in die Katastrophe. Die vorgeschichte des Ersten Weltkriegs 1815–1914*, Munich, 1990. See also 'The First World War as a World War' in Solomon Wank et al. (eds), *The Mirror of History. Essays in Honor of Fritz Fellner*, Santa Barbara, Oxford, 1988, pp. 33–49, with some additional references to the literature.

ler has fortunately dismissed,[2] can help. Only the dialectical combination of both 'primacies' can yield fruitful results and contribute to a more objective view. But 'primacy' loses its absolute meaning if given equal status to another 'primacy'. Factors in foreign and domestic policies are rarely to be neatly separated. More often, 'external' and 'internal' factors are linked, forming only two sides of the same coin. Thus, Pan-Germanism was a domestic factor with external consequences for Germany, but a factor in foreign policy for all other Powers in Europe, great and small. To allege the primacy of either foreign or domestic policy reveals a conceptualisation based on categories of the national state, but Europe – or, before 1914, the European System – provides a more decisive frame of reference, which contains both national states or Powers and their domestic and foreign policies.

The trouble with studying German *Weltpolitik* is that, almost thirty years after Fritz Fischer's *Griff nach der Weltmacht*, no comprehensive monograph on it exists. Only special aspects have been treated, e.g. Peter Winzen on Bülow's *Weltpolitik*[3] or Barbara Vogel on Bülow's foreign policy towards Russia.[4] *Weltpolitik* is sometimes seen to figure as part of the immediate German background to world war,[5] sometimes as part of the foreign policy of the Second German Empire[6] or the 'Anglo-German Antagonism'.[7] Volker Berghahn's *Tirpitz-Plan*[8] deals with the hard core of *Weltpolitik*. Finally, Gregor Schöllgen's treatment of Germany's policy towards the Ottoman Empire[9] offers a kind of prologue for the future monograph, because it covers both the whole period of *Weltpolitik* and one of its most central aspects. The longest and broadest view is still offered by the oldest work in question, Langer's monumental study of imperialism, which, unfortunately, does not cover the pre-war years after 1902.[10] A sweeping analysis of the whole is still sadly missing.

2. Hans-Ulrich Wehler, 'Geschichtswissenschaft heute' in Jürgen Habermas (ed.), *Stichworte zur 'Geistigen Situation der Zeit'*, Frankfurt a. M., 1979, vol. 2, p. 735.

3. Peter Winzen, *Bülows Weltmachtkonzept. Untersuchungen zur Frühphase seiner Außenpolitik 1897–1901*, Boppard, 1977.

4. Barbara Vogel, *Deutsche Rußlandpolitik. Das Scheitern der deutschen Weltpolitik unter Bülow 1900–1906*, Düsseldorf, 1973.

5. Fritz Fischer, *War of Illusions. German Policies from 1911 to 1914*, New York, London, 1975.

6. Imanuel Geiss, *German Foreign Policy 1871–1914*, London, Boston, 1976.

7. Paul M. Kennedy, *The Rise of the Anglo-German Antagonism 1860–1914*, London, 1980.

8. Volker Berghahn, *Der Tirpitz-Plan. Genesis und Verfall einer innenpolitischen Krisenstrategie unter Wilhelm II*, Düsseldorf, 1971.

9. Gregor Schöllgen, *Imperialismus und Gleichgewicht. Deutschland, England und die orientalische Frage 1871–1914*, Munich, 1984.

10. William L. Langer, *European Alliances and Alignments, 1871–1890*, 2nd edn, New York, 1962; idem, *The Diplomacy of Imperialism 1890–1902*, 2nd edn, New York, 1968.

Since German *Weltpolitik* was no more or less than the German
version of imperialism, it is necessary to start from that more general
aspect. Imperialism, in its turn, was a particularly western variety of
the phenomenon of power and power politics, which has existed since
the emergence of articulate states in the Ancient Orient, 5000 years
ago.[11] Power politics are characterised by a constant and varying
interplay between power centres, based on concentrations of man-
power, economic and military potentials, and power vacua, in which
no central power existed for one reason (fragmentation into tribal
societies) or another (fragmentation of former power centres, e.g.
Greece, Italy, Germany). *All* power centres expanded after their
emergence, sooner or later, usually from the periphery of an established
power centre: from there they could safely expand beyond the periphery into 'barbarous' power vacua, subsequently taking over the old
power centre, as well. But they would decline and collapse again, once
their expansion had suffered a severe setback. In all these processes –
emergence as a power centre, expansion and collapse – there were and
are many factors at work, both internal and external, economic and
social, military and political, that brook no 'primacy' of one or the
other over the rest.

Historically, imperialism can be seen in the continuity of European
expansion overseas since the time of Columbus and Vasco da Gama. It
was originally prompted by the western desire to control the interconti-
nental long-distance trade between the Far East and the Latin Far
West. The cotton and spice trade with the East Indies, the transatlantic slave trade and slave trading in the West Indies and the Americas
all had long-term historical after-effects. The early colonial empires,
formed from the late fifteenth century onwards, laid the foundations for
and set the patterns of the modern European colonial empires, with
due allowances for modification and structural changes. For instance,
most European colonists in the Americas had wrung sovereignty from
their respective mother countries. The early colonial powers, Portugal,
Spain, Holland, had, as the structure of imperialism demanded, been
replaced by newcomers, England and France, in bitter rivalry at home
and abroad. On the whole, evidence of long-term continuities from the
older colonial empires after 1492–8 is more impressive than the many
short-term discontinuities that seem to be receding in importance with
the passage of time.

11. William H. McNeill, *The Pursuit of Power*, Chicago, 1982; a more sociological
approach in Michael W. Doyle, *Empires*, Ithaca, NY, London, 1986.

The trend towards collective European world domination overseas, complemented by Russian expansion overland in Eurasia, was characterised by the well-known plurality and rivalry of European powers. This gradually crystallised into the European Pentarchy from the late seventeenth to the late eighteenth century with the emergence of new Great Powers to join France – Austria in 1683, England in 1713, Russia in 1721 and Prussia in 1763–72.[12] The Concert of Powers that institutionalised itself at the Congress of Vienna in 1815 also had a kind of legislative power for the colonial empires annexed to European powers. Competition propelled expanding powers into a tremendous dynamism, which escalated into modern imperialism. But, as Sallust once remarked, the same principles that make a state are also its undoing: competitive growth of states expanding into power vacua on the globe escalated into deadly rivalries, exacerbated by the rise of industrialism once expansion had become global. Imperialist expansion filled most power vacua and found its limits around 1900 only in the physical form of planet Earth – Latin expansion proceeding west through the Americas reached the Far East in the Philippines on its way to China; Russian expansion proceeding east reached the Far West, Alaska and California. East and West did meet, confounding all traditional categories, and despite Rudyard Kipling's imperialistic poetry.

By the late nineteenth century imperialism had become a general phenomenon amongst all world powers sufficiently strong to claim their part in it. At first, these were European powers, great and small, including Tsarist Russia, which carried out its imperialist expansion by land, annexing territories adjacent to its imperial core, Great Russia. They were later joined by Japan and the United States. Among the regions or peoples that were objects or victims of largely European expansion, some had imperial power structures that were declining (China, Persia) or had actually dissolved (India). They formed huge power vacua that attracted, as usual in history, the expansion of active power centres. They themselves had missed the chance of participating in imperialist expansion for internal structural reasons.

With the formation of new national states in Europe in the course of the nineteenth century, new participants in the race for colonial expansion overseas appeared – Belgium, Italy, Germany. They all, sooner or

12. Derek McKay and H.M. Scott, *The Rise of the Great Powers 1648–1815*, London, 1983. For a systematic analysis, see Hans J. Morgenthau, *Politics among Nations*, New York, 1948. For a recent historical analysis, see P.M. Kennedy, *The Rise and Fall of the Great Powers. Economic Change, Military Conflict from 1500 to 2000*, London, 1988.

later, in one form or another, plunged into the business of colonial empire building, further complicating established patterns of rivalries, especially between England and France. Outside of Europe, Japan and the United States joined hands, as well. After going through severe internal conflicts on the way towards modernisation, and relatedly through cruel wars at about the same time, they became dialectically connected to one another, the United States having forced Japan to open herself to American trade, then western trade in general, in 1853–4, before their respective internal conflicts.

The most sudden, powerful and explosive of all arrivals on the scene of imperialist expansion was Germany, for reasons which were not the fault of the Germans themselves but which have to be taken into consideration just the same. The German Reich of 1871 was, as it turned out, only an interim answer to the much quoted but never defined 'German question'.[13] Again for reasons beyond German responsibility, the 'German question' was the biggest, most complex and most explosive of all European national questions in the nineteenth century. It also had the most shattering consequences for Germany, Europe and the world.

The reason is both simple and complicated. Simple, because the 'German question' can be seen as the German version of other national questions and can be formally characterised in the same way as the Polish, Irish, South Slav and Italian questions: should the Germans (like the Poles, Irish, South Slavs and Italians) have a national state of their own? And if yes, within what frontiers, what internal structures and with what consequences for their neighbours and Europe? The Germans were quantitatively for long the second biggest nation in Western Europe but overtook France around 1871, being overtaken in their turn by the Russians to the east; they had also qualitatively become a powerful factor in Europe. This had started with the cultural explosion of around 1800, centring on or symbolised by Vienna and Weimar, and was followed by their industrialisation. In the end, Germany emerged as the best educated and best organised state in the world. The creation of even the lesser German Reich under Prussian leadership had thrown into the midst of Europe one of the strongest of all continental powers, a kind of super-power (as Paul M. Kennedy has called it).

The answer to the 'German question' becomes extremely compli-

13. I. Geiss, 'The Continuity of the German Question', *John and Mary's Journal* (Carlisle, Pa.), 10, Winter 1985, pp. 12–26.

cated, however, if we fully take into account its many intricacies. Germany was by no means following the recently much-quoted *Sonderweg* throughout the nineteenth century and the first third of the twentieth century.[14] Rather, it often represented, as David Blackbourne has so brilliantly put it, only 'the most intensified version of the European norm'[15] or, one might add, the most extreme variation of European possibilities. Combined, they add up to a substantial difference from whatever might be considered the 'European norm', certainly from the western model. Some exceptions even further increased its difference from the rest of Europe. Only the 'German question' was linked with *all* Great Powers and smaller nations surrounding Germany. The size, skills and central position of the Germans automatically gave them, once they were united into one national state, a tremendous lever as the hegemonial power in Europe. Germany alone bordered on all the other Great Powers of the Pentarchy, by either land or sea.

Thus, the new German Reich of 1871 burst upon the scene of world history with shattering effects on the balance of power, first in Europe, then also in the world. As with every newly constituted power centre, Germany wanted to expand. Because of its central position in Europe, hemmed in by the three other continental Great Powers plus neighbouring smaller states, the new Germany could only have expanded overseas without coming into direct conflict with any other Great Power, and was therefore bound for collision with Britain, the greatest sea and colonial power. Thus, expansion overseas, called *Weltpolitik* by the Germans of the time, became the German version of imperialism.

The same reasons that had made the 'German question' the most explosive of all national questions in Europe also conspired to make German *Weltpolitik* the most explosive version of modern imperialism. By the very size of territory settled or claimed by Germans, by their central position in Europe surrounded by three Great continental Powers and more neighbours, great and small, than any other nation in the world and by their sheer quantitative and qualitative weight, Germans after 1871 occupied a unique position in the world. Their weight further increased following rapid demographic and economic growth after the founding of the Reich. That the new German Reich had not been created through war was the most aggravating problem.

---

14. Helga Grebing with Doris von der Brelie-Lewien and Hans-Joachim Franzen, *Der 'deutsche Sonderweg' in Europa 1806–1945. Eine Kritik*, Stuttgart, 1986.
15. David Blackbourne and Geoff Eley, *The Peculiarities of German History*, London, 1984, p. 292.

All other national questions before and after were settled through wars, either directly, as with the Greeks and Italians before 1871, or indirectly, as with the Poles and South Slavs after, through and at the end of the First World War. Much more serious was that emerging Germany had beaten two Great Powers with alarming ease and was threatening to outclass the remaining two: backward Russia by its rapid modernisation and even Britain after 1900 both by overtaking it in the most recent key sectors of industrialisation, the electrical and chemical industries, and by an attempt to become a first-rate sea power as well, through the building of a modern battlefleet.

Lightning victories over Austria and France in 1866 and 1870 only demonstrated the crushing superiority in power that automatically thrust upon the Germans a kind of latent hegemony over the Continent. The question was whether they would transform their covert hegemony into an overt one, and if so, how and when. The answer to that question was provided, after a quarter of a century of consolidating their gains in the period of Bismarck's 'Continental Policy' (*Kontinentalpolitik*), by Wilhelmine *Weltpolitik*, starting from about 1896–8.

Although *Weltpolitik* is linked with the Kaiser, it was far from being the personal spleen of an erratic monarch, imposed from above by a Kaiser who combined a brilliant, though superficial mind with fits of near-insanity (or, if you prefer, who combined insanity with fits of intellectual brilliance).[16] In contrast to a personalising and moralising view, that makes it so easy to single out the Kaiser as a scapegoat for Germany's political defaults, realities are much more complex. Firstly, Wilhelm II in fact represented the leading social classes in Germany almost perfectly.[17] Secondly, there is the question of whether there existed a viable political alternative. The SPD around 1900 was too numerically weak and too unprepared to govern alone, and their only domestic allies, the Liberals, were the very party of *Weltpolitik*, while those forces that mistrusted *Weltpolitik*, the East Elbian junkers and the Prussian Conservatives, were the bulwark of political reaction. Potential coalition partners for a realistic alternative to *Weltpolitik* worked at cross-purposes and, therefore, could not unite. The Liberals, potential coalition partners at home, pressed for imperialist *Weltpolitik* abroad, while the Prussian Conservatives, who seemed to agree with the SPD in their opposition to *Weltpolitik* abroad, were too reactionary on bread-and-butter issues at home.

16. John C.G. Röhl, *Kaiser, Hof und Staat*, Munich, 1988.
17. I. Geiss, 'Wilhelm II.' in his *Das Deutsche Reich und der Erste Weltkrieg*, Munich, 1985, pp. 211–23.

This kind of structural dilemma remains hidden, as long as one looks at history bound by shackles of either the 'Primat der Außenpolitik' or the 'Primat der Innenpolitik'. The split between internal and external policies in Germany around 1900 had devastating results for Germany and the world, but such splits are likely to be found in other historical constellations, if they are considered with a mind open to the ambivalences and dilemmas of historical (and political) forces.

Two more exceptions to world historical patterns worked in the same direction. Firstly, it took all other new centres of power a very long time, indeed, decades or even centuries, from the moment they established themselves until they reached the status of a hegemonial power in their region. Alone in history, the new German centre of power of 1871 propelled itself from a position as a relative power vacuum into one of at least latent hegemony literally overnight. In fact, it was inevitable that the union of all or most Germans in a single state would become the strongest power in its region.

Secondly, the German Reich alone in world history was thrust into the centre of an existing constellation of powers, the European System, that collectively dominated most of the world, either directly through colonial empires or indirectly through spheres of interest or client states. Germany's central position within the European power concert made for what was called in Germany *Einkreisung* (encirclement). It had two consequences, pulling in different directions. On the one hand, since Germany was hemmed in on all sides by three continental Great Powers and the one maritime Great Power, Britain, she was denied the kind of expansion after 1871 that, in all other cases, was deemed 'normal' once a new centre of power had emerged. After 1871 the European concert of powers was not prepared to accept the further defeat of a Great Power by the already towering Reich, because this would have transformed Germany's latent hegemony into an open one. Instead, a Great War of all the other Powers against a hopelessly isolated Germany would have been the inevitable consequence, despite Germany's tremendous power.

On the other hand, as long as Germany remained on the defensive under the auspices of Bismarck's Continental Policy, it had nothing to fear strategically from its 'encirclement' by three Great Powers, all weaker than prospering Germany, and after the Dual Alliance with Austria-Hungary in 1879 had modified the balance of power on the continent in favour of Germany, it had even less to fear. It was only when Germany launched its *Weltpolitik* by maritime expansion overseas, as a replacement for impossible continental expansion after 1871, that latent 'encirclement' became fatal for Germany's imperial ambitions, because the mechanisms of the European System carried over to the level of global imperialism. Germany again had to look for at least one valid ally or partner on the world scene.

Before further pursuing the German problem of finding a globally powerful ally, two other consequences of the German decision to turn imperialist by moving from *Kontinentalpolitik* to the *Weltpolitik* must be discussed. Firstly, there was no public debate in Wilhelmine Germany about the decision, carefully weighing the pros and cons of *Weltpolitik*. The reason for the remarkable absence of public debate on such a crucial matter around 1895 may lie in a fact only discovered by recent research: that debate had actually taken place half a century earlier among German Liberals, well before 1848.[18] Before the Revolution of 1848 Liberals, then shaping public opinion in Germany, were thrashing out their differences over the question of whether Germany, after re-forming an empire (which was taken for granted somehow or other), should expand overseas. Over the years, majority opinion seems to have wavered for and against overseas expansion. But advocates of overseas expansion after the founding of a future empire represented the Liberal mainstream at that time. This majority opinion was carried over into the actual founding of the new German Reich in 1871 and spilled over into the period of *Kontinentalpolitik*. When Germany, after its first period of colonial expansion under Bismarck in 1884–5, had become powerful enough to enter the imperialist race for expansion overseas, the pre-1848 majority consensus re-emerged and came to the surface of Wilhelmine Germany. The drive for German expansion overseas had become a matter of course among the German middle-classes, as brilliantly spelled out by Max Weber in his famous Inaugural Lecture at Freiburg University in 1895: 'We must understand that the unification of Germany was a youthful prank, which the nation committed in its declining days and which would have been better dispensed with because of its expense, if it should be the conclusion and not the starting point for a German *Weltmachtpolitik*.'[19]

The next problem concerns the way Germany looked at itself and its place in the world of imperialist expansion, literally the *Weltanschauung* of German *Weltpolitik*. Until 1914 there was uncertainty in the German

18. Hans Fenske, in a paper to the Bamberg Historical Conference, in October 1988, soon to be published in a collective volume. Until then, see provisionally Günter Wollstein, *Das 'Großdeutschland' der Paulskirche. Nationale Ziele in der bürgerlichen Revolution 1848–49*, Düsseldorf, 1977.
19. Max Weber, *Gesammelte politische Schriften*, ed. Johannes Winckelmann, 5th edn, Tübingen, 1988, p. 23.

mind as to whether Germany was already a World Power or whether it was still aspiring to that status. This wavering had serious psychological and political consequences and is still reflected in older German historiography right up to Gerhard Ritter.

Even more seriously, just before 1900 Germans saw great changes taking place in the world, in which they themselves took a prominent part. Industrialisation and expansion overseas converged in the rise of huge concentrations of imperialist and economic power in large political units. Russia was entering her first phase of intensive industrialisation since the emancipation of the serfs in 1861 had opened the way to modernisation. In Britain the call for imperial preferential tariffs was to be heard for the first time. If instituted, it would have made the British Empire into the greatest trading block of the world. Behind Britain and Russia, the United States to the west and Japan to the east were looming large, still beyond the horizon of the European System proper, but clearly aspiring future world powers. At the threshold of their own imperialist expansion and of further industrial growth Germans, trying to escape the narrowness of the European System, found themselves hemmed in as well on the global level by the economic and imperialist giants of the immediate future. This is what has been called the new *Weltreichslehre* (Fritz Fischer).

Thus far, German analysis of the world around 1900 was reasonable enough. There was even nothing wrong with the conclusion, drawn by Germany's leaders from the way they looked at the world, that Germany and continental Europe west of Russia would only be able to hold their own if Europe pulled together. And a united Europe would fall almost automatically under the leadership of the strongest power – Germany. This kind of reasoning was perfectly in accordance with the logic of power politics anywhere and at any time. But for Germany at that time universal historical mechanisms inherent in their global analysis clashed with the harsh realities of the European System. From then on, conclusions drawn to implement *Weltpolitik* became disastrous, for Germany and the world.

The prime reason for this was the anti-hegemonial and anti-imperial structure of the European System which would brook no hegemonial or imperial domination of Europe by one European power. German leadership over a united Europe in order to brave the coming giant economic and political power blocs would have to overcome that ingrained reluctance of Europeans to domination by one of their peers. Germany would have to persuade Europe to accept German leadership, not by the show or application of force, but patiently with subtle means, convincing Europe of the correctness of German global analysis and of German disinterest in any ambition beyond the normal consideration of surviving on honourable terms. Above all, Germany would have to make crystal clear that the overall interest of Europe would coincide with the enlightened self-interest of Germany. In short, Germany would have to perform an almost superhuman feat of self-restraint, subtlety and intellectual honesty in order to achieve in the years after 1900 something like the position of the Federal Republic today.

German *Weltpolitik*, as is well known, followed a course contrary to that which intelligent, enlightened and restrained self-interest would have demanded from Wilhelmine Germany. Instead, understandably enough, since it had been until then quite 'normal' in world history, it fell back on sheer power politics, based on military power. Wilhelmine Germany, and one world war later Hitlerite Germany, became the eternal young man in a hurry, plunging into short-cuts that turned out to be blind alleys, rushing about in world politics with the elegance of a bull in a china shop – hectic, nervous, because it knew that time would be against this sort of violent activity on a global level.

Once on the heady global trip with its expanding horizons, German leaders discovered with dismay that elemental mechanisms of the European System had also crept into the emerging World System, modified and extended by the United States and Japan. The European System of the Pentarchy had seen the prevalence of something like *horror isolationis* – every Great Power tried to avoid having to stand alone in any major conflict. Having at least one ally amongst the Five Powers was essential for survival, because no Power going it alone stood a chance against a coalition of all the other four Powers. Napoleonic France had to pay bitterly for that lesson. In the European System, Germany did have an ally, Austria-Hungary with the Dual Alliance of 1879, even extended to form the Triple Alliance by the accession of Italy in 1882. But ever since the Revolution of 1848–9 and the Compromise (*Ausgleich*) of 1867, Austria-Hungary was in reality a declining power, on the verge of becoming a power vacuum in her turn, comparable to that of the Ottoman Empire – Europe's second sick man on the Danube. And Italy, with her historical resentments against Austria dating back to the days of the Risorgimento and her political irredentist hostility against Austria-Hungary, was an ally of doubtful value, indeed, weak inside and out.[20] On the global level of *Weltpolitik*,

20. Risto Ropponen, *Italien als Verbündeter. Die Einstellung der politischen und militärischen*

both were more liabilities than assets for Germany and could not count as valid allies.

From the outset of *Weltpolitik*, therefore, Germany had to decide whether it wanted to rise to the status of a World Power as an ally of one of the two real European World Powers, Britain or Russia, the 'whale' or the 'bear' in the political clichés of the time, or whether it wanted to go it alone.

The same internal structural reasons, first set out so brilliantly by Eckart Kehr and George W.F. Hallgarten, that had blocked an alliance with either Power on the European level,[21] also worked against an alliance of Germany with either Britain or Russia on the world level. East Elbian Prussian Conservatives, ideologically depending on Tsarist Russia, clashed in their bread-and-butter-interests over Russian agrarian exports ever since Germany had industrialised. As agrarian producers they supplied the German domestic market and had gone from being grain exporters, standing for Free Trade, .o exponents of an agrarian Protective Tariff to keep cheaper Russian and American grain out of Germany. Their agrarian Protective Tariffs of 1879, escalated in 1887, amounted to a kind of economic declaration of war against Russia of the kind that often preceded real international wars. On the other hand, industrialists, largely in the west of Germany, had been looking ideologically towards the West, more to Britain than to France. With their industrial Protective Tariffs, again since 1879, they initiated the 'Anglo-German Antagonism', not so much through economic rivalry as, coinciding with the new *Weltpolitik*, through the building of a German battlefleet, which became a direct vested interest of German heavy industry.[22] Thus, recent economic interests, on both main frontiers of Germany, cancelled older ideological inclinations and led to paralysis of Germany's capability to conclude an alliance with either Britain or Russia. For internal structural reasons alone, Germany, by default, had to launch its *Weltpolitik* on its own.

According to Admiral von Müller in 1896, there was a widespread feeling in German society that Germany would have to fight Britain first to rise to the status of a World Power.[23] From a minority position,

Führung Deutschlands und Österreich-Ungarns zu Italien von der Niederlage von Adua 1896 bis zum Ausbruch des Weltkrieges 1914, Helsinki, 1986.

21. I. Geiss, *German Foreign Policy 1871–1914*, pp. 14 f.

22. Still valuable is the first critical study by Eckart Kehr, *Schlachtflottenbau und Parteipolitik 1894–1901. Versuch eines Querschnitts durch die innenpolitischen, sozialen und ideologischen Voraussetzungen des deutschen Imperialismus.* Berlin, 1930; reprint Vaduz, 1965.

23. His memorandum 'Zukunftspolitik' in *Der Kaiser. . . . Aufzeichnungen des Chefs des Marinekabinetts Admiral Georg Alexander v. Müller über die Ära Wilhelm II.*, Göttingen, 1965,

he pleaded for an alliance with Britain against Russia first, leaving it to future generations to fight it out between Britain and Germany as to who would rise to eventual world domination. After some hesitations, Germany decided to go it alone, following the slogan of a 'free hand' for Germany in world politics.

The consequences were inevitable. All the other imperialist powers, frightened by the breath-taking dynamism of the German upstart, pulled together mending their fences and patching up their rivalries. The rivalries between Britain and the other powers were of varying durations – with France they went back to the Middle Ages, with the United States only one century to the bitterness of the American War of Independence, while the Anglo-Russian antagonism had started only in 1815 or 1829 over the protection of the Ottoman Empire against Russian expansion. The Triple Entente was the natural outcome of German *Weltpolitik*, natural in terms of power politics. The Triple Entente, however, was perceived in Germany as *Einkreisung*, wicked 'encirclement' by invidious and treacherous rivals who wanted to strangle innocent Germany. By contrast, Britain, the key power in the Triple Entente, only had the aim of containing German *Weltpolitik*, as perceptively analysed in the famous Crowe Memorandum of 1 January 1907.

A rational analysis of the European System and of the new imperialist World System also leads logically to the overall aims of German *Weltpolitik* – expansion overseas, taking over a modernised Ottoman Empire and the building of the German battlefleet. Expansion overseas aimed at building up a viable colonial empire centring on 'Mittelafrika' by joining and regrouping the disparate German colonies in Africa. The Belgian Congo and parts of Angola and Mozambique figured as the main components of future 'Mittelafrika', which in the First World War emerged as the great colonial counterpart to 'Mitteleuropa' on the European Continent.[24]

German expansion into the Ottoman Empire linked expansion overseas to the European Continent, because the Ottoman Empire still had a substantial footing in south-east Europe until 1912. The literal backbone of German expansion into the Ottoman Empire was the building of the Baghdad railway, which cut across traditional lines of expansion of both Britain and Russia and, therefore, provoked the

---

pp. 36–41; almost complete in English translation in I. Geiss, *German Foreign Policy 1871–1914*, pp. 192–4.
24. F. Fischer, *Germany's Aims in the First World War*, London, 1967.

marked hostility of both Powers. British anxieties were additionally fuelled by the apprehensions of Lord Curzon, the British Viceroy of India, who felt very strongly that the final part of the Baghdad railway should not end in Kuwait and not be under German control.[25]

However irritating and conflict-producing those two aspects of *Weltpolitik* – 'Mittelafrika' and Germany's position in the Ottoman Empire – may have been, its real hard core was the building of the German battlefleet. Seen from a global perspective, it was the main instrument of ensuring Germany's free access to the Atlantic, which was barred by Britain and her powerful fleet.[26] Despite Tirpitz's political camouflage, the battlefleet was clearly built against Britain, because it could only operate against the coast of eastern England. The decision of the strongest land power with the most efficient army also to build the second strongest battlefleet was a direct challenge to the pre-eminent sea power, Britain. All other outstanding problems between Germany and Britain could have been solved in peace – economic competition, Germany's bid for more colonies, Germany's role in the Ottoman Empire and the Baghdad railway. But Germany's refusal to come to terms with Britain on curbing the costly arms race at sea by a naval agreement blocked any kind of *rapprochement* between two countries. Germany wanted the guarantee of British neutrality in a continental war beforehand, which would have ensured victory for Germany in advance and handed it hegemony over the continent.[27] Russia and France would have been at Germany's mercy, because on their own they stood no chance against the continental 'super-power'.

Britain's turning against Germany by forming the Triple Entente marked the failure of German *Weltpolitik*, war or no war. Germany's retreat at the end of the second Moroccan crisis in August 1911 in the face of Britain's threatened intervention provoked a drastic change of German foreign policy, a return to the continent. There, only one avenue was left for German surplus energies, the Ottoman Empire. The by now traditional outlet into and through the Ottoman Empire required safe lines of communication to Constantinople, preferably by a continuous railway line under German control. The consequences of this were clear. Austria-Hungary had to be made safe against the imminent onslaught of South Slav nationalism, and this, in its turn, drew Germany into the powder-keg of the Balkans. By 1912, German leaders were beginning to develop a kind of Serbophobia, because

25. G. Schöllgen, *Imperialismus und Gleichgewicht*, pp. 152–63.
26. A.J. Marder, *From the Dreadnought to Scapa Flow*, 5 vols, London, 1961.
27. P.M. Kennedy, *Anglo-German Antagonism*, pp. 450 f.

Serbia was, indeed, the spearhead of South Slav nationalism and Pan-Slavism against the Dual Monarchy, supported by Tsarist Russia.[28] Thus, the scene was set for the clash of South Slav nationalism with Austria-Hungary, more with the Hungarians than with the Germans of Austria but involving the German Reich as well. Sarajevo was the logical and most extreme outcome, with Germany using the outrage as a welcome excuse to make recalcitrant Serbia, blocking German communications and the railway route to Constantinople, into a German client state, through the agency of a declining Austria-Hungary.

There are certainly more scenarios for different world wars imaginable, but in the way the First World War did break out, German *Weltpolitik* played a central part, because of the tremendous energies of Germans united into one national state, even one as incomplete as the lesser German Reich.

It is one of the supreme ironies of modern history that today the Federal Republic (and for that matter, Japan) have achieved through the stint of hard economic work – and geographically only with much smaller West Germany rather than the Reich of 1914 – most of what Germany might have legitimately aspired to around 1900 through a non-violent alternative to *Weltpolitik* in two world wars (only in the Second World War for Japan). The Federal Republic has become an economic world power, but is fettered militarily and politically by international structures, the European Community and NATO, because of the disastrous effects of *Weltpolitik* in two world wars. Much depends on the way Germans today are prepared to look at their history, because any attempt at loosening or even breaking those benevolent fetters could result in a disaster comparable to that of *Weltpolitik* almost a century ago.

---

28. Analysed in greater detail by I. Geiss, 'Die deutsche Politik gegenüber Serbien in der Julikrise 1914' in his *Das Deutsche Reich und die Vorgeschichte des Ersten Weltkriegs*, Munich, Vienna, 1985, pp. 159–89.

GREGOR SCHÖLLGEN

Germany's Foreign Policy in the Age of Imperialism: A Vicious Circle?

In the decades before the outbreak of the First World War, the German Reich felt itself to be confronted by a serious dilemma. It was a European great power; as such, it desired – and was indeed compelled – to pursue great-power politics in order to maintain its position. But in the Age of Imperialism, great-power policy was synonymous with world-power policy or, as it was called in Germany, with *Weltpolitik*. By pursuing world-power politics, the German Reich actually contributed substantially to the destruction of the balance of power which was in many respects essential for the existence of a German great power in Europe. This 'vicious circle' is the subject of the following investigation.

Even contemporaries had no doubt that the German Reich had been a European great power since German unification in 1871. Its military and economic strength and potential provided the clear and essential external signs of great-power status. In combination with the sheer size and vital geostrategic position of the Reich, these factors ensured that Germany was regarded by its neighbours as a potential threat from the outset. It was thus no accident that the victorious powers of the First World War acted to change the situation in 1919, with their demands for reparations, the demilitarisation of Germany and the reduction in its territory. Significantly, the victorious powers were aiming to contain Germany rather than to eliminate it as a great power; to a certain extent, their proposals were designed to restrict the German world power to a (more controlled and controllable) great-power status. The decision taken in Paris to eliminate the German colonial empire provides important evidence of this intention. The existence of a German Reich capable of defending itself was apparently regarded by its European neighbours as a significant factor in the European balance of power after 1871. Though the Reich was certainly feared, it was thought to have an important role in maintaining the balance of forces on the continent even after the events of 1918–19.[1]

Attitudes towards Germany as a *world* power were different. Its policies were believed to have made a vital contribution to the breakdown of the balance of power in Europe. In truth, as one of the strongest European great powers, Germany had possessed all the necessary attributes for its rise to world-power status; even more important, it had also developed the will and desire to pursue *Weltpolitik*.[2] But what motives lay behind this decision, which had so many consequences for the development of international relations before 1914?

> Even today I am still of the conviction which filled both of us when we were appointed Secretaries of State at the same time, 27 years ago . . . that our people by virtue of its ability, its culture (in the best sense of the word) and its past had a right to the position which I called then a place in the sun, i.e. *the right to equality with other great nations.*[3]

These lines were written as late as 26 November 1924 by Bernhard von Bülow to Alfred von Tirpitz. They reveal the most important motive behind the conduct of the German Reich, which contemporaries had already labelled *Weltpolitik*. At the precise moment when the European system of states had begun to expand into a world system under the impact of the powerful imperialist drive of the 1880s,

1. The 'bolshevist menace' and the problem of checking it undoubtedly played an important role here. See esp. A.J. Mayer, *Politics and Diplomacy of Peacemaking. Containment and Counter-Revolution at Versailles 1918–1919*, London, 1967. The elimination of Germany as a great power became the dominant theme only in the course of the Second World War. See most recently G. Schulz, '"Dismemberment of Germany". Kriegsziele und Koalitionsstrategie 1939–1945', *HZ*, 244, 1987, pp. 29 ff.

2. See for example F. Fischer, *War of Illusions: German Policies from 1911 to 1914*, London, New York, 1975; P. Winzen, *Bülows Weltmachtkonzept. Untersuchungen zur Frühphase seiner Außenpolitik 1897–1901*, Boppard a.Rh., 1977; P.M. Kennedy, *The Rise of the Anglo-German Antagonism 1860–1914*, London, 1980. For a more detailed analysis of the criteria for the great- and world-power status of nations in the Age of Imperialism, see the extended German version of this article: G. Schöllgen, 'Die Großmacht als Weltmacht. Idee, Wirklichkeit und Perzeption deutscher Weltpolitik im Zeitalter des Imperialismus', *HZ*, 248, 1989, pp. 79 ff.

3. Bundesarchiv/Militärarchiv Freiburg i.Br., Nachlass Tirpitz, Bd. 173 (emphasis by author).

Germany felt virtually compelled to take part in the scramble to acquire overseas territories. According to this theory, great-power status *within* Europe could only be maintained by activity and self-assertion *outside* Europe. Only in this way was it possible to guard against the danger that the equal standing which had been achieved in Europe would be offset in the world terms now regarded as valid.[4] In Berlin, especially after 1890, there was little doubt that a great power *had to act* as a world power.

This contemporary view was expressed with clarity and precision in the famous dictum of Max Weber, which was formulated *before* the public announcement of German *Weltpolitik* by Bernhard von Bülow in 1897. In his Freiburg inaugural lecture in 1895, Weber had outlined a situation in which 'the unification of Germany was a youthful prank which the nation perpetrated in its old days and which, on account of its extravagance, had been better left undone if it was to be the conclusion and not the starting-point of a German world power policy'.[5]

In this case, Weber's implicit demand for a German world-power policy was in accord with the opinion of a majority of his contemporaries – a fact which is generally overlooked in the historical criticism of German imperialism which became fashionable some years ago. The subjective views of contemporaries play a vital part in shaping political relations, even though these may well appear mistaken and even disastrous to historians who specialise in being wise after the event. From the 1890s onwards most Germans – whether conservative, liberal or social democratic in allegiance – were convinced that a great power such as Germany must also pursue great-power politics and that, in the Age of Imperialism, meant *world*-power politics. The differences between political groups, some almost insuperable, emerged only over the means by which such policies should be achieved.[6]

The main reasons for the basic agreement among Germans about their country's involvement in *Weltpolitik* were also the driving forces behind imperialism in general.[7] From the 1880s, economic motives in

4. See A. Hillgruber, *Die gescheiterte Großmacht. Eine Skizze des Deutschen Reiches 1871–1945*, Düsseldorf, 1980, p. 21.

5. M. Weber, 'Der Nationalstaat und die Volkswirtschaftspolitik' in his *Gesammelte Politische Schriften*, ed. J. Winckelmann, 3rd edn, Tübingen, 1971, p.23. On this subject see G. Schöllgen, *Max Webers Anliegen. Rationalisierung als Forderung und Hypothek*, Darmstadt, 1985, pp. 101 ff.

6. Thus, even Social Democrats took the view that the desire for a 'great colonial empire, which our exporters entertain . . . [is] in itself very legitimate'. E. Frei, 'Zur Flottenpolitik', *Socialistische Monatshefte*, 4, 1900, pp. 37–8.

7. On the following see G. Schöllgen, *Das Zeitalter des Imperialismus*, Munich, 1990.

their widest sense led the European powers to renew their efforts to acquire overseas colonies or, where this was impossible or inopportune, to secure spheres of interest. These, it was hoped, would satisfy the growing domestic demand for raw materials and also serve as outlets for the products of expanding industries or as regions for financial investment, for example in the sphere of railway construction. There were also other, less important motives. They included the desire for missionary activity and conversion overseas, the suppression of the slave trade, and so-called 'cultural work' in the less developed parts of the world. Such high expectations about the consequences of the acquisition and control of overseas territories were rarely fulfilled, though the phenomenon cannot be treated in detail here.[8]

One further motive made a vital contribution to the last, simultaneous expansion of the powers. This was the issue of prestige, which had been of only minor significance during earlier periods of colonial expansion but became very important for the latecomers among the European great powers in particular. It could also be regarded as a matter of equal rights, connected in the case of Germany with the attempt to create an appropriate *Stellung und Geltung* (position and recognition) for the Reich in the European system of states. In the Age of Imperialism – and here the circle is closed – such a position could only be achieved by participation in the struggle for territory outside Europe. After 1890, the German Reich regarded itself as an equal partner in the middle of the continent and even (with some justification) as the decisive factor in European events. What choice was there for such a power? Was it not forced to adopt those policies which contemporaries regarded as economically necessary and which also seemed essential in order to uphold the prestige of a great power?

The enormous and increasing significance of this motive in German *Weltpolitik* can only be fully understood after a comprehensive analysis of the relevant documents. These also reveal that the issues of 'assertion' and 'humiliation' acquired even more importance for German foreign policy as the Reich came to perceive itself – whether through its own fault or not – as increasingly forced onto the defensive. One example is sufficient to illustrate the response: the events of 1904–5, the establishment of the Anglo-French *entente cordiale* and the first Morocco crisis, produced clear reactions of this kind from German politicians and diplomats.

8. This was already suspected, or indeed recognised, by some contemporaries. See, for example, J.A. Hobson, *Imperialism. A Study*, London, 1902.

Five days after the conclusion of the *entente*, Max Fürst von Lichnowsky, a senior official in the German Foreign Office and later the German ambassador in London, noted: 'We need a success in foreign policy, as the English-French rapprochement . . . is generally regarded as a defeat for us.'[9] Friedrich von Holstein, one of the most experienced analysts within the German Foreign Office, then predicted that if Germany allowed its 'toes to be trodden on silently' in Morocco, this would be tantamount to encouraging a 'repetition elsewhere'.[10] The crux of the matter was defined by the Bavarian envoy in Berlin, Graf Lerchenfeld, when he wrote to Munich on 13 October 1905:

> If I understand the interests of Germany correctly, the issue in the entire Morocco affair has been less the position of the Reich in this African state so much as the German world position. The attempt had been made to isolate us and to immobilise us in the concert of nations. Against this attempt the Morocco action was initiated with every justification and carried through successfully. *Germany has proved that it cannot be slighted with impunity.*[11]

The 'first and main point' in any settlement of the conflict with France would therefore be, according to Holstein's typical view of the importance of the affair, 'that France does not attempt to disgrace us before the world'. In that case there would have to be intervention, even if Germany's own future interests were damaged, in this case in Morocco.[12]

The Germans themselves obviously believed that their *Weltpolitik* was both the logical consequence of the foundation of the Reich as a great power and also, in the Age of Imperialism, a question of 'equality with other great nations' (Bülow) and thus a form of self-assertion in the new international order. But how was this analysis translated into concrete policy?

At this stage, it must be said that the reality of German *Weltpolitik* was fairly 'modest', particularly when measured against its expectations and the achievements of other great powers like Great Britain or France. That, in any event, was the view of many contemporaries, among whom Max Weber was only one prominent example.[13] This fact

9. Minute of Lichnowsky, 13 April 1904, in *GP*, vol. 20/I, No. 6516.
10. Minutes of Holstein, 3 June 1904, *GP*, vol. 20/I, No. 6521.
11. Bayerisches Hauptstaatsarchiv München, Abteilung II: Geheimes Staatsarchiv, Außenministerium, Bd. 2686.
12. Holstein to Radolin, 2 July 1905, *GP*, vol. 20/II, No. 6757. On this entire complex of issues see the early study by E. Wächter, *Der Prestigegedanke in der deutschen Politik von 1890 bis 1914*, Bern dissertation, Aarau, 1941.
13. Thus Weber claimed in 1916: 'If one compares the colonial acquisition of Ger-

needs to be emphasised today, particularly in view of the enduring myth about unique German successes in *Weltpolitik* which has been accepted by Germany's neighbours and was stated most recently by Raymond Poidevin.[14] German advances in 'world political' activity were unimpressive after 1890, even in comparison with those achieved by Bismarck's colonial policy in the years 1884–5. At that time, the Reich had gained possession of the territories in the South Seas and in Africa which were to remain the centre of its empire until 1914–18. Apart from the acquisition of smaller territories and bases, such as those of Kiao-Chow, part of Samoa and the Carolines, the Mariannes and the Pelew islands, German successes *after* 1890 lay mainly in some progress in the sphere of informal imperialism, particularly in the Near East.[15] This region became increasingly important in German foreign and world policy as other parts of the world were shown to be unavailable for penetration by German interests. German politicians and diplomats also found themselves faced by a sobering fact: the German Reich was denied spectacular political triumphs of the kind which could be enjoyed by the second newcomer to the circle of European great powers, Italy, with its occupation of Libya in 1911–12. In fact, comparable actions by the Reich tended to end in a débâcle, as indicated by the two Morocco crises of 1905 and 1911.[16]

In that case, why did the world-power activities and ambitions of the German Reich arouse such suspicion among the established great and world powers of Britain, France and Russia that they agreed to combine in *entente* by 1907? It was no accident that the Triple Entente was achieved over 'peripheral' questions and was quickly directed against the German world and great power, even within Europe itself.[17] The established powers feared that Germany would be able to exploit

---

many with that of other states in the same period, it is really absurdly modest' from 'Deutschland unter den europäischen Weltmächten' in M. Weber, *Gesammelte Politische Schriften*, pp. 159–60.

14. R. Poidevin, *Die unruhige Großmacht. Deutschland und die Welt im 20.Jahrhundert*, Freiburg, Würzburg, 1985.

15. For specific details see G. Schöllgen, *Imperialismus und Gleichgewicht. Deutschland, England und die orientalische Frage 1871–1914*, Munich, 1984.

16. On the first Morocco crisis see an analysis of 1930 which remains valuable: E.A. Anderson, *The First Morocco Crisis 1904–1906*, Chicago, 1930. On the second Morocco crisis, which continues to stimulate investigation because of its consequences in the international sphere, see most recently J.C. Allain, *Agadir 1911, Une crise impérialiste en Europe pour la conquête du Maroc*, Paris, 1976; E. Oncken, *Panthersprung nach Agadir. Die deutsche Politik während der Zweiten Marokkokrise 1911*, Düsseldorf, 1981; G. Barraclough, *From Agadir to Armageddon. Anatomy of a Crisis*, London, 1982.

17. Also vital here was the fact that the German side saw the development in this way. For example, on 27 September 1907 the German chargé d'affaires in St Petersburg, von Miquel, wrote to the Reich Chancellor (*GP*, vol. 25/I, No. 8537): 'However skilfully the

even modest triumphs in *Weltpolitik* on the periphery of European events and use them to strengthen its great-power position on the continent; in this way, it might complete the establishment of hegemony *in Europe itself.*

The individual actions of German *Weltpolitik*, in themselves, still need not have aroused sustained alarm among the other powers, including Britain. Yet the British in particular came to regard these activities as highly dangerous, because they appeared to be the product of a consistent line of German foreign policy which ran counter to British interests. The German Reich seemed to be entering into direct competition with Great Britain in many areas at once: the entire legacy of the island power might even be under threat. The British found frequent confirmation for their suspicions: in the Kaiser's Kruger telegram;[18] in the attitude of German public opinion during the Boer War[19] or the two Morocco crises; and in German Middle Eastern policy in general, since its most important project, the Baghdad railway, appeared to be aimed directly at the heart of the British Empire.[20] Last but not least, the expansion of the German navy was regarded as extremely dangerous.[21] From its original conception under Tirpitz, this could scarcely be regarded as a part of German *Weltpolitik* in the narrow sense but seemed to pose a direct threat to the security of Britain itself.[22] Furthermore, the actions of Germany's partners in the Triple Alliance after 1908, particularly in south-east Europe and north

wording of the agreement may be phrased, the impression is inevitable that the powers have founded a syndicate with which we will have to reckon. This requirement for close alliance is a compliment . . . to the German army, the German navy, our merchants and the viability of the German people in general.'

18. *GP*, vol. 11, No. 2610.

19. On this issue see R.W. Bixler, *Anglo-German Imperialism in South Africa, 1890–1900*, Baltimore, 1932.

20. On this subject see G. Schöllgen, '"Germanophobia". Deutschland, England und die orientalische Frage im Spiegel der britischen Presse 1900–1903', *Francia*, 8, 1980, pp. 407 ff.

21. The expansion of the German navy naturally drew the attention of historians of the inter-war period. Today it is one of the best-researched chapters of pre-war history. In particular see S. Thalheimer, *Das deutsche Flottengesetz von 1898*, Bonn dissertation, Düsseldorf, 1926; E. Kehr, *Schlachtflottenbau und Parteipolitik 1894–1901. Versuch eines Querschnitts durch die innenpolitischen, sozialen und ideologischen Voraussetzungen des deutschen Imperialismus*, Berlin, 1930; W. Hubatsch, *Die Ära Tirpitz. Studien zur deutschen Marinepolitik 1890 bis 1918*, Göttingen, Berlin, Frankfurt a.M., 1955; J. Steinberg, *Yesterday's Deterrent. Tirpitz and the Birth of the German Battle Fleet*, London, 1965; V. Berghahn, *Der Tirpitz-Plan. Genesis und Verfall einer innenpolitischen Krisenstrategie unter Wilhelm II.*, Düsseldorf, 1971; H. Schottelius and W. Deist (eds), *Marine und Marinepolitik im kaiserlichen Deutschland 1871–1914*, Düsseldorf, 1972; B. Kaulisch, *Alfred von Tirpitz und die imperialistische deutsche Flottenrüstung*, Berlin (GDR), 1982; I.N. Lambi, *The Navy and the German Power Politics 1862–1914*, Boston, London, Sydney, 1984.

22. It must nevertheless be said that the significance of the naval question has generally been somewhat exaggerated by researchers, at any event during the period

Africa, provided additional evidence to support a negative assessment of German foreign policy. In fact, German foreign policy was not directly involved in preparing the annexation of Bosnia and Herzegovina by Austria-Hungary in 1908,[23] or the occupation of Tripoli and the Cyrenaika by Italy in 1911.[24] But it is clear that German foreign policy was often held jointly responsible for such actions *ex post facto* and was sometimes accused of being wholly to blame for them.[25]

German policy itself did much to encourage analyses of this kind. From the German point of view the Morocco policy of 1911, which culminated in an international crisis, was at least in part a 'Flucht nach vorn' (escape forward). It was designed to prevent a shift in the balance of power to the detriment of the Reich and its alliances by provoking the desired split in the Triple Entente.[26] The desire for self-assertion may have been the real motive behind German foreign policy; with hindsight, it may even appear understandable. Yet there was little prospect that it would meet with sympathy or even with understanding in the foreign ministries of Britain and France. On the contrary, with a consistency that was increasingly removed from reality, the German Reich was now held responsible for the next international crisis, which emerged in the shape of the Italian ultimatum to Turkey.

As early as 26 September 1911, Sir Arthur Nicolson, the influential Under-Secretary of State and co-ordinator of anti-German tendencies in the Foreign Office, was asked if he thought it possible that Germany

---

1911/12–1914. At the turn of the century the problem had genuinely been at the forefront of British political and military plans and eventually led to the 'dreadnought' leap. However, after the second Morocco crisis, even strongly anti-German officials in the Foreign Office were prepared to let the question of naval armament and limitations rest in favour of a prospective political settlement over 'peripheral' issues. Eyre Crowe, for example, noted in a minute on Goschen's letter of 10 February 1913 (which was also signed by Grey and even Nicolson): 'I am firmly convinced that one of the main reasons why Anglo-German relations are now more cordial (– I do not overlook the obvious other reasons –) is that we have entirely ceased to discuss the question of a limitation of armaments. I feel equally certain that any resumption of that discussion will have the inevitable effect of making relations worse again. I am therefore earnestly hoping that the matter will not be revived by us' (*BD*, vol. 10/II, No. 457).

23. On the Bosnian annexation crisis see the works by B.E. Schmitt, *The Annexation of Bosnia 1908–1909*, 1937; New York, 1970; M. Nintchich, *La crise bosnique (1908–1909) et les puissances européennes*, 2 vols, Paris, 1937; H.A. Gemeinhardt, *Deutsche und österreichische Pressepolitik während der Bosnischen Krise 1908–1909*, Husum, 1980.

24. See F. Malgeri, *La Guerra Libica (1911–1912)*, Rome, 1970; C. Zaghi, *L'Africa nella coscienza europea e l'imperialismo italiano*, Naples, 1973; R.A. Webster, *Industrial Imperialism in Italy 1908–1915*, Berkeley, Los Angeles, London, 1975.

25. At the beginning of the Bosnian annexation crisis, many Turkish politicians were actually of the 'view that Germany was the driving force in the matter'. So, at any rate, Marschall reported to Berlin on 4 October 1908 (*GP*, vol. 26/I, No. 8980).

26. See E. Oncken, *Panthersprung nach Agadir*, p. 419.

had 'been marking time for' the Italian-Turkish tensions 'in order to secure an atmosphere more suited to thunderbolts'. Remarkably, the enquiry came from Winston Churchill, the man who was to become the bitterest opponent of German *Blitzkrieg* some thirty years later and was then to contribute to the final elimination of Germany's great- and world-power status.[27] But he was not alone in his opinion. Against the background of the recent and difficult Morocco crisis and the war begun by Italy in north Africa, Sir Charles Hardinge, Viceroy of India, was convinced 'that it would not be long before a similar situation arises owing to the demands of Germany for territory in some part of the globe. I have always thought – and still think – that in 1913 the great Armageddon will occur.'[28] Hardinge even thought he could predict where Germany would intervene: 'It is not unlikely that Spain might be the next victim, or even Portugal.'[29]

Analyses and predictions of this kind may well surprise and even amuse later observers. Nevertheless, they reveal an attitude which had momentous consequences for the further development of international relations before the First World War: after the turn of the century in particular, all the events mentioned here – including those for which Germany was *not* responsible – were regarded in Paris, St Petersburg and especially in London simply as various aspects or direct consequences of a single, internally consistent line of German world-power politics.

This perception of events is not likely to be shared by historians today. The German documents do not reveal anything like a lineal German foreign policy during the Wilhelmine era. Instead, they give an impression of inadequate conception and planning underlying foreign policy, which was mainly the result of the methods applied after 1890. These were characterised increasingly by their incalculability, a fact which distinguished them from the policies pursued by Bismarck. Even British statesmen, who were decidedly sensitive on the subject, regarded Bismarck's policies as calculable; this continued to be the case during those periods – such as 1884–5 – when they were far from being pro-British.[30] But even incalculability can be consistent or can at

27. Churchill to Nicolson, 26 September 1911, *BD*, vol. 9/I, No. 240. At this time Churchill was First Lord of the Admiralty.
28. Hardinge to Nicolson, 15 October 1911, Public Record Office London, Foreign Office (PRO/FO), Nicolson papers, 800/357.
29. Hardinge to Nicolson, 30 November 1911, PRO/FO, Nicolson papers, 800/352.
30. On the importance of calculability in Anglo-German relations, see the work of K. Hildebrand, in particular, and esp. 'Zwischen Allianz und Antagonismus. Das Problem bilateraler Normalität in den britisch-deutschen Beziehungen des 19. Jahrhunderts

least – particularly in the field of international relations – have consistent effects.

It was these methods of German foreign policy, combined with their 'world political' thrust, which aroused fears in London about the deliberate 'aggrandisement of the German Empire at the expense of Great Britain'. Hardinge's predecessor in India, Lord Curzon, had made the prediction in 1901:

> In my opinion, the most marked feature in the international development of the next quarter of a century will be, not the advance of Russia – that is in any case inevitable – or the animosity of France – that is hereditary – but the aggrandisement of the German Empire at the expense of Great Britain; and I think that any British Foreign Minister who desires to serve his country well, should never lose sight of that consideration.[31]

For many British observers, German *Weltpolitik* after the 1890s was simply a contemporary variation on an aggressive basic theme of Prussian-German politics which, *with hindsight*, was thought to be perceptible even in the eighteenth century. The famous memorandum of Sir Eyre Crowe in January 1907 provides a typical example of this point of view. This influential civil servant in the British Foreign Office drew a direct line from the 'sudden seizure of Silesia in times of profound peace' by Frederick the Great, through the 'annexation of Schleswig-Holstein' or the 'reconquest of Alsace-Lorraine' by Bismarck, to the *Weltpolitik* of his successors. His description of the rest of German foreign policy as 'vague, confused and unpractical' is certainly significant, given the methods of Wilhelmine foreign policy as reflected in British reports.[32]

It is also significant that, a full three decades later, one of Crowe's most prominent successors in the Foreign Office was to reach a very similar conclusion. In a memorandum of 14 March 1940 entitled 'The Nature of the Beast', Robert Vansittart drew the same direct line from the policies of Prussia under Frederick the Great through to the most recent events of his own time, i.e. to the German attack on Poland.[33] But Vansittart did not rest his case there. Two major wars had broken out since Crowe's memorandum; in the view of the British, these had

---

(1870–1914)', in H. Dollinger et al. (eds), *Weltpolitik, Europagendanke, Regionalismus. Festschrift für Heinz Gollwitzer zum 65. Geburtstag am 30. Januar 1982*, Münster, 1982, pp. 305 ff.
  31. Curzon to Hamilton, 25 September 1901, India Office London, Hamilton papers, vol. 9.
  32. *BD*, vol. 3, Appendix A.
  33. PRO/FO 371/24389. The 'beast' is not Hitler or National Socialism, but the 'German character' which had to be fought.

the same causes and the same originator. In March 1940, the Foreign Office official was convinced that the 'German danger' could only be dealt with by the eradication of its Prussian roots. Thus, a development was contemplated, and in some respects actually begun, which was to find its logical conclusion in the final dismemberment of Germany as a great and world power.

But we must return to the years before the First World War, where the theory which was realised in 1945–7 had its origins. Beyond any doubt, national perceptions and interpretations of the supposed intentions of the other side played a significant role in the formulation and implementation of individual foreign-policy strategies. Furthermore, it seems clear that the politicians and diplomats of all the European great powers were convinced that, first and foremost, they were only *re*acting to the (subjectively perceived) political actions of the other side. This widespread attitude is one of the most interesting features of the period, and one which has yet to be adequately researched. As the course of the July crisis revealed, the politicians were thus doing much to deprive themselves of that freedom of manoeuvre which was and remains essential in crises of this kind. Looked at in more detail, all the military and political plans of the powers were calculated not to take the first step, but to supply a rapid and decisive response to an action taken by the other side.

However important the perceptions at the root of such decisions may have been, they do not provide a comprehensive explanation of the developments studied here. Further investigation must be made of the factors which underpinned the subjective perceptions of the powers and which made such a vital contribution to the changes in the system of international relations that were to culminate in the outbreak of the First World War.

Of course, many of these changes were also caused by the mistaken assessments and blunders of the leading politicians involved (in this case) in the implementation of German world-power policies and by the sometimes aggressive course of German foreign policy in the Age of Imperialism. Such factors have been at the centre of the important debate triggered by the work of Fritz Fischer, which has continued for thirty years.[34] Nevertheless, though German foreign policy did appear to its neighbours to be growing perceptibly more aggressive, it was not

34. Starting with F. Fischer, 'Deutsche Kriegsziele, Revolutionierung und Separatfrieden im Osten 1914–1918', *HZ*, 188, 1959, pp. 249 ff. More recently, the position of research has been surveyed by G. Schöllgen, 'Griff nach der Weltmacht? 25 Jahre Fischer-Kontroverse', *Historisches Jahrbuch*, 106, 1986, pp. 386 ff.

the actual and specific course of that policy which did most to under-mine and ultimately to destroy the European balance of power. In-stead, there were two impulses, located in the development of the international order during the Age of Imperialism itself, which played the major role in overstraining and disrupting the balance of forces in Europe.

Firstly, the imperialist drive of the powers had acquired a new quality which distinguished it from earlier phases of colonising activity. The strength and the prestige of states now appeared to be intimately connected with the success they could demonstrate in their imperialist ventures and thus in their rivalry on the periphery of Europe. From the 1890s onwards, the tensions produced overseas found their expression in a continuing deterioration in relations between the powers within Europe itself. The periphery had caught up with the centre; imperial-ism was overlaid by its consequences. To a certain extent the First World War was, among other things, an inevitable consequence of this development.[35]

The second impulse which decisively undermined the European balance of power can be seen in the fundamental incompatability of two factors. On the German side, there was the will to pursue world-power politics, which seemed to flow inevitably from the great-power status of the Reich and was even regarded as wholly natural for a great power in the Age of Imperialism. Yet, Germany was confronted by the resolute determination of the established great powers to maintain their traditional positions in world-power politics without significant restriction. Such an approach permitted no effective concessions to be made to the rising world power, which remained unsatisfied in this field. After all, who will voluntarily encourage a powerful potential competitor? Behind this attitude lay the fear that the German Reich might be able to exploit its successes in world politics in order to strengthen its position as a *continental* great power. And since Germany was already, on account of its sheer size and military and economic strength, the most important European great power, any additional strength accumulated by the process of colonial expansion would

---

35. It was therefore no accident that the *détente* endeavours of 1911 onwards began with attempts to improve the international climate in general by means of (contractual) agreements in such 'peripheral spheres'. The hope was that there could then be a second step, on a new basis of trust, leading to an agreement on the 'central' questions and thus to a general relaxation of tension. For details see G. Schöllgen, 'Richard von Kühlmann und das deutsch-englische Verhältnis 1912–1914. Zur Bedeutung der Peripherie in der europäischen Vorkriegspolitik', *HZ*, 230, 1980, pp. 293 ff; G. Schöllgen, *Imperialismus und Gleichgewicht*, pp. 329 ff.

inevitably conflict with the balance of power in Europe. This, at any rate, was how the situation appeared to Germany's neighbours. In summary, the 'world political' *idea* which was so compelling to Germans was incompatible with the no less compelling *reality* of the European system of states.

Consequently, even today it is very difficult to dismiss the idea that German policy in the Age of Imperialism was characterised by a vicious circle. On one hand, 'the belated nation'[36] was convinced that its creation as a national state and a great power also made it essential and legitimate for the Reich to achieve world-power status. German statesmen therefore sought to translate this belief into practical politics. On the other hand, in taking these steps the Reich was also – against its will – removing the foundations from beneath this policy itself. Even more significantly, it was also making a decisive contribution to the *Selbstentmachtung*[37] (political and military suicide) of the European system in which the German nation, if ever, had any prospect of being a *great* power. In 1731, Crown Prince Frederick of Prussia had commented that in 'grand policy', the power that 'does not advance' is bound to 'decline'.[38] This may well be true. Nevertheless, the observer of Prussian-German policy before 1914 is left with a quite different impression: in this case, it appears that *because* German policy advanced, it was also *bound* to decline.

---

36. The usage stems from H. Plessner, *Die verspätete Nation. Über die Verführbarkeit bürgerlichen Geistes*, Frankfurt a.M., 1971.
37. The title of the book by E. Hölzle, *Die Selbstentmachtung Europas. Das Experiment des Friedens vor und im Ersten Weltkrieg*, Göttingen et al., 1975.
38. Letter to his chamberlain von Natzmer, February 1931, in *Die Werke Friedrichs des Großen*, ed. G.B. Volz, vol. 7, Berlin, 1913, p. 197.

GUSTAV SCHMIDT

Contradictory Postures and Conflicting Objectives: The July Crisis

So much has been written about the July crisis that another attempt is justified only if a convincing new argument can be put forward.[1] The structure of my argument, the 'abstract', is therefore presented first. There were two patterns of diplomatic activity during the pre-war crisis; their precarious balance constituted a stable crisis in international relations until the outbreak of war. The members of the military alliances and diplomatic alignments, pursuing economic and strategic aims of their own, were not yet acting as 'bloc partners', and Britain in a sense was still an uncommitted principal power. The first pattern prevailed during the first (28 June–mid July) and second phase (17–23 July) of the crisis: Grey and Bethmann Hollweg stuck to 'doves versus hawks' parameters and shared to a certain extent the desire to localise the conflict, although with different intentions. An uneasiness about Russia's (and France's) assertiveness still influenced the policy-makers in London, as well as in Berlin. The second pattern relates to Britain's regard for the Triple Entente as the only chance to resist German *Drohpolitik* and to Germany's attempts to exploit the Reich's advantages over the 'enemy'.

The second pattern corresponded to the *idées fixes* on which the 'military' of the major powers based their offensive strategic concepts.

---

1. This text stands as it was delivered on 3 March 1989. For the background of this article see my *Der europäische Imperialismus*, Munich, 1985; 'Great Britain and Germany in the Age of Imperialism', *War & Society*, IV/1, 1986, pp. 31–51.

The politicians and diplomats did not become aware of the implications of the military strategies and only learned of some of the crucial
elements at the last moment. However, they had provided the military
with the means and – even more importantly – the autonomy to
prepare for the contest, which almost all of them at one moment or
another regarded as inevitable.

This chapter will illuminate diplomatic patterns and strategic plans
and demonstrate the contradictions between the positions of the major
powers and their conflicting objectives.

I

The crisis scenario in the period between the Sarajevo
assassination (28 June) and the Austrian ultimatum to Serbia (23 July)
is a familiar one, i.e. the July crisis started as previous conflicts had
done. Berlin exerted pressure on its ally to make a determined stand
against Serbia, lest Austria-Hungary lose control over the Serbs within
the Dual Monarchy; at the same time, the military exploited the
situation to mount a new drive for rearmament to improve Germany's
strategic capabilities of meeting the rapidly growing power of Russia.
The powers that be in the Habsburg monarchy vacillated between
recklessness and suspicion of Germany's war-mongering. There were
doubts as to whether France would act as a restraining influence on
Russia; whether the Tsar's regime, aroused by public opinion and
pressed by the top military echelons, would rather take up arms and
extend the war by proxy into a continental war, or whether St Petersburg would become assertive only if Russian diplomacy succeeded in
mobilising the solidarity of France and Britain.[2] London, distracted by
serious domestic strife, was watching, hoping on the one hand to get a
chance to mediate between and contain the parties directly involved in
the conflict, while on the other determined not to tolerate the suppression of France under any circumstances.

---

2. At the Imperial Council on 13 January 1914 General Sukhomlinov (Minister of
War) categorically declared that the 'army was perfectly prepared for a duel with
Germany, not to speak of one with Austria'; see L. Albertini, *The Origins of the War of 1914*,
London, 1965, vol. I, p. 548; L.C.F. Turner, 'The Russian Mobilization in 1914', *JCH*,
III/1, 1968, p. 69; D.W. Spring, 'Russia and the Coming of War' in R.J.W. Evans, H.
Pogge von Strandmann (eds), *The Coming of the First World War*, Oxford, 1988, pp. 70, 64
ff. In January 1914, the Imperial Council adopted Kokovtsov's point of view – that a
war at present would be a great calamity – and decided to solve the Liman von Sanders
crisis by diplomatic settlement.

To explain why the July crisis exploded into a major war, whereas previous conflicts had not, two problems have to be faced:

- what is special about the conjunction of the July crisis, apart from the simple fact that an explosion was becoming more and more likely after a series of acts of brinkmanship?
- are the general explanations of the causes of the First World War satisfactory, if the structural elements of the crisis – (1) escalation in the use of force in international politics, (2) domestic conflict,[3] (3) imperialism, (4) militarism and navalism – did not result in the outbreak of war during any of the other Balkan crises since the breakdown of the Austro-Russian political armistice in 1908?

The recurrent features of the pre-war crises, which were bound to strain the relationships, are the following:

Firstly, the situation in St Petersburg came to the point of a power struggle between the advocates of an inevitable war of the 'Slavs against the German central powers' and the moderates, who warned that a war would wreak havoc on the finances of the Tsarist Empire and intensify the crisis of the political regime.[4] The parties to this conflict, which culminated in meetings of the Imperial Council in December 1913 and January 1914, linked the outcome of their contest to the support which France and Britain provided for the postures of either the 'doves' or the 'forward policy' strategists. 'In contrast to previous comparable crises a request was made for the Tsar to order

3. Even proponents of the original Fischer thesis now argue that: 1) 'the economy was booming. A brief recession in 1913 had by the spring of 1914 come to an end . . . industrialists like Stinnes and Rathenau were convinced that Germany would achieve its economic predominance in Europe without a war'; 2) 'there were no indications that Wilhelmine Germany could not continue to muddle through politically for years to come'; H. Pogge von Strandmann, 'Germany and the Coming of War' in R.J.W. Evans, H. Pogge von Strandmann (eds), *The Coming of the First World War*, Oxford, 1988, pp. 121 ff. My own interpretation of the domestic scenario on the eve of war has been summarised (in English) by V.R. Berghahn, *Germany and the Approach of War in 1914*, London, 1973, pp. 161 f. There is also agreement by now that the economic disputes between Russia and Germany – in view of the renewal of the Commercial Treaty in 1915–16 – had an impact on the crisis 'psychosis' but that economic factors were not the driving forces towards war in the July crisis.
4. D. Geyer, *Der russische Imperialismus*, Götingen, 1977, esp. pp. 232 ff.; D.C.B. Lieven, *Russia and the Origins of the First World War*, London, 1983; D.W. Spring, 'Russia and the Coming of War', p. 57; B. Bonwetsch, 'Rußland und der Separatfrieden im Ersten Weltkrieg', *Geschichte und Gesellschaft*, 1, 1977, pp. 125–49; G. Schramm, 'Das Zarenreich: ein Beispielfall für Imperialismus. Folgerungen aus einem Buch von Dietrich Geyer', *Geschichte und Gesellschaft*, 7, 1981, pp. 297–310, all argue that Sazonov succeeded in bringing the Tsar around to act boldly (30 July 1914) by insisting that Russia would never forgive the Tsar if he capitulated to the Central Powers; this argument had been put to Sazonov a few hours earlier by the Chairman of the Duma.

Secondly, for the first time, in October 1913[6] expressions of support
for Russia from France (Poincaré) paralleled Germany's backing of
Austria.[7] This had partly to do with the new belief of the French

Secondly, for the first time in October 1913[6] expressions of support
for Russia from France (Poincaré) paralleled Germany's backing of
Austria.[7] This had partly to do with the new belief of the French
general staff that they could defeat Germany in war, and partly to do
with the enormous financial interests that France had by then acquired
in Russian industry and 'state' credit. France shared the Tsar's point of
view that 'to abandon the Straits to a powerful state would be synonymous with subordinating the whole economic development of
southern Russia to that state'. This markedly contributed to French
policy, in that Russian loan repayments in grain and her industrial
imports were flowing through the Straits, and any dislocations would
bring disaster.[8] French policy became materially interested in strengthening Russia's posture in the Balkans.[9] The Tsarist government, for its
part, was confident that France was ready to go to extreme measures in
supporting Russia.[10]

Thirdly, Britain and Germany participated in the pre-war crises
partly as stalwarts of international 'interventionism' (Concert of
Europe), partly as partisans of their allies; in the latter sense Grey had
considered – in April–May 1913 – the unity of the Entente more
important than working with Germany within the Concert.

Parallels to the July crisis are most conspicuous in early December
1912.[11] The dramatic, conflict-ridden component in the Anglo-German

5. D.W. Spring, 'Russia and the Coming of War', p. 57; he emphasises that the
decisions of 24–25 July still aimed at a peaceful conclusion. They aimed, however, at
deterring Germany from supporting Austria-Hungary by taking a firm stand early on
and were thus of the same kind as Berlin's backing up Vienna in early July. The
diplomatic strategy was to make 'Little Serbia' appear the victim of German aggression.
6. L. Albertini, *The Origins of the War of 1914*, I, pp. 402–18; R.J. Crampton, *The
Hollow Detente: Anglo-German Relations in the Balkans 1911–1914*, London, 1971; P.W.
Reuter, *Die Balkanpolitik des französischen Imperialismus 1911–1914*, Frankfurt, New York,
1979.
7. R. Langhorne, *The Collapse of the Concert of Europe: International Politics, 1890–1914*,
London, 1981, pp. 106 ff.
8. R. Girault, *Diplomatie européenne et imperialismes. Histoire des relations internationales
contemporaines* , vol. I: *1871–1914*, Paris, New York, 1979; on French-Russian tensions
resulting from the dependency of Russia on French capital see Girault, *Emprunts et
investissements français en Russie*, Paris, 1973.
9. G. Krumeich, *Armaments and Politics in France on the Eve of the First World War*,
Leamington Spa, 1984; J.F. Keiger, *France and the Origins of the First World War*, London,
1983.
10. D.W. Spring, 'Russia and the Coming of War' p. 72; the sense was 'that Paris did
not want to be associated with another humiliating climb-down by Russia'.
11. K.M. Wilson, 'The British Démarche of 3 and 4 December 1912: H.A. Gwynne's
Note on Britain, Russia and the first Balkan War' in his *Empire and Continent: Studies in*

pattern took shape when Wilhelm II considered Haldane's and Grey's rigorous warning that 'England would not tolerate a suppression of the French under any circumstances' as a moral declaration of war. The conversations between these two members of the British Cabinet and Ambassador Lichnowsky took place only ten days after the exchange of letters between Grey and Cambon. Although the 'majority of the non-interventionist Cabinet' regarded the notes affirming the plans for naval disposal as a safeguard against Britain's involvement in a continental war, Grey had thought that Bethmann Hollweg's affirmation of Austro-German solidarity on 2 December 1912 had made Germany an interested party in the settlement of the Balkans and thus rendered impossible the sort of mediation which Britain, Germany and France, as disinterested powers, might otherwise have been able to undertake with their respective friends and allies. Grey hoped that Russia would not find itself in the situation that had arisen in the Bosnian crisis of 1909: 'If . . . a European war were to arise through Austria's attacking Serbia, and Russia, compelled by public opinion, were to march into Galicia . . . thus forcing Germany to come to the aid of Austria, France would inevitably be drawn in and no one could foretell what further consequences might follow.'[12]

But to Grey the real danger – in December 1912 at least – was not a conflict of the Powers; what he was really afraid of was that 'Germany will go to St Petersburg and propose holding Austria in, if Russia will leave the entente . . . We are sincerely afraid lest out of the hurly-burly of the crisis Russia should emerge on the side of the Alliance . . . if we can get the two Powers to settle matters themselves, we are prepared to keep the ring for them . . .'[13] This fear constitutes the driving force behind 'pattern two'. The two dramatic elements of the December 1912 crisis – a) Germany's demand that Vienna should make a determined stand against Serbia, and b) Berlin's attempt at exploiting the prospect of splitting the Entente[14] – were defused in 1912. The so-called German 'Kriegsrat' on 8 December 1912 resulted in no call for immediate action, although Moltke had coined his famous 'je eher, desto

---

British Foreign Policy from the 1880s to the First World War, London, 1987, pp. 141 ff. The following is based on Wilson and on J. Röhl, 'An der Schwelle zum Weltkrieg: Eine Dokumentation über den "Kriegsrat" vom 8. Dezember 1912', *MGM*, 1, 1977.
12. Ambassador Lichnowsky reported Grey's warning – 4 December 1912 – to Bethmann Hollweg.
13. K.M. Wilson, 'The British Démarche of 3 and 4 December 1912', pp. 144–5.
14. Kurt Riezler, *Tagebücher, Aufsätze, Dokumente*, ed. K.D. Erdmann, Göttingen, 1972, 8 July 1914. The controversy about the Riezler diaries with respect to Erdmann's edition does not affect these particular entries.

besser' (the sooner, the better) on this occasion. Rather, it was agreed to improve Germany's strategic and political position.[15] Since the message got through, Grey was keen to return to 'joint crises' management. Therefore 'pattern one' of the crisis scenario could evolve. The German Chancellor attempted to steer the Reich away from the critical point which Moltke felt had been reached and to enlarge his government's room for manoeuvre both at home and abroad.[16] The pressure on Grey to meet Germany on terms corresponded to Bethmann Hollweg's line of action.

II

After these preliminaries, sketching the considerations for action in a crisis situation, I turn to the first theme: the instability of the 'international system'. The major powers had been unable to prevent the Balkan states from resorting to war or to introduce stable settlements. Among the parties to these local conflicts, Austria-Hungary was the only major power, but Vienna had to fight to maintain that status; the Habsburg Empire represented an out-dated concept of political organisation, a multi-national Empire in the shape of a dual monarchy, and it was thus at a disadvantage in its struggle against its neighbouring countries and their claim to national self-determination. 'In the light of Serbian actions and attitudes on both sides of the frontier, [Berchtold] henceforth perceived little difference between peace and war anyway.'[17] 'The war between Austria and Serbia which broke out on 28 July was a war which both sides wanted;'[18] the First World War

15. On the new German army bill – which increased the 'Friedenspräsenzstärke' by about 140,000 men – see V.R. Berghahn, *Germany and the Approach of War in 1914*, pp. 156 ff., 108 ff.; P.-Ch. Witt, *Die Finanzpolitik des Deutschen Reiches von 1903–1913*, Lübeck, Hamburg, 1970; B.F. Schulte, *Europäischer Krieg und Erster Weltkrieg: Beiträge zur Militärpolitik des Kaiserreichs, 1871–1914*, Frankfurt, 1983; G. Ritter, *The Sword and the Sceptre*, trans. H. Norden, London, 1972.
16. K.H. Jarausch, *The Enigmatic Chancellor: Bethmann Hollweg and the Hubris of Imperial Germany*, New Haven, Conn. 1972; H.J. Henning, *Deutschlands Verhältnis zu England in Bethmann Hollwegs Außenpolitik 1909–1914*, Cologne, 1962; V.R. Berghahn, *Germany and the Approach of War in 1914*, pp. 169 ff.
17. R.J.W. Evans, 'The Habsburg Monarchy and the Coming of War' in R.J.W. Evans, H. Pogge von Strandmann (eds), *the Coming of the First World War*, Oxford, 1988, p. 36; S.R. Williamson, 'Vienna and July 1914: The Origins of the Great War Once More' in P. Pastor, S.R. Williamson (eds), *Essays on World War One*, New York, 1983.
18. Z.A.B. Zeman, 'The Balkans and the Coming of War' in R.J.W. Evans, H. Pogge von Strandmann (eds), *the Coming of the First World War*, Oxford, 1988, p. 29; J. Remak, '1914: The Third Balkan War – Origins Reconsidered', *JMH*, 43, 1971, pp. 353–66; H. Hantsch, *Leopold Graf Berchtold*, 2 vols, Graz, 1963; F.R. Bridge, *The Habsburg Monarchy among the Great Powers, 1815–1918*, Oxford, 1990.

was in the first instance the Third Balkan War.

The second conflict between Austria-Hungary and Russia may be described – since 1908 – as 'organised peacelessness' (organisierte Friedlosigkeit), in that Germany's support for the Dual Monarchy had been more direct and decisive than French intervention on behalf of Russia. 'Whereas Russia had been humiliated before in the Balkans and been able to restore her authority',[19] it was the only European great power assured of its future world-power status, whatever short-term setbacks due to domestic constraints or external defeats it might have to suffer. The Tsar's regime was prone to resort to war even if circumstances were not all that favourable.[20]

The third field of conflict, the Anglo-German rivalry, involved the competitive pursuit to shape the relationships between the Triple Alliance and the Triple Entente; 'Germany's crime was to be Britain's isolator'[21] and vice versa. In Anglo-German relations there was a sort of uneasy co-existence emerging between, on the one hand, the naval arms race and compromise on side-issues (pattern one)[22] and, on the other, a secret competition for collaboration and good understanding with Russia (pattern two). Berlin and London both regarded Russia – once it had recovered its position of strength, i.e. since 1913 – as the one major power which could redraw the political map of Europe and which would start to do so at its own convenience.

Likewise, the French top military echelon and French diplomacy under the guidance of Poincaré became more and more inclined to demonstrate France's regained strength. Asked by Poincaré on his return from Russia to assess the probable consequences of military intervention by Austria in the Balkans, the General Staff gave – on 2 September 1912 – as its considered opinion 'that such intervention would put Germany and Austria at the mercy of the entente'; the French military doubted whether Germany would permit Austria to indulge in a Balkan adventure, but if it did, a general war would result in which the Triple Entente would have the best chances of success and

---

19. M. Howard, 'Europe on the Eve of the First World War' in R.J.W. Evans and H. Pogge von Strandmann (eds), *The Coming of the First World War*, Oxford, 1988, p. 7.
20. B. Bonwetsch, 'Rußland und der Separatfrieden'.
21. K.M. Wilson, 'The British Démarche of 3 and 4 December 1912', p. 155.
22. From Britain's point of view neither Tirpitz's 'grand design' – because of the concentration of the High Fleet and the naval arrangements with France – nor German *Weltpolitik* (such as 'German India in Middle Africa') posited the German threat; rather it was the likelihood that Berlin might succeed with repeated *coups de force* (going to the brink of war) to blackmail St Petersburg and disentangle Russia from her alliance respecting the Entente with the western powers.

might gain a victory which would shake up the European balance of power.[23]

For his part, Moltke had to confess that 'We are not superior to the French', when asked at the Carlsbad meeting in May 1914 by Conrad, his opposite number in the Austrian General Staff, what Germany would do if she lost on the Western Front. This query was a rebuttal to Moltke's claim (10 February 1913) that 'in the outcome of the conflict between France and Germany lies . . . the essential of the whole European war, and even the fate of Austria will be decided not on the Bug, but on the Seine'.[24] Fearing the consequences of this reversal in the relative strengths of the military blocs, namely that in the future St Petersburg and Paris would submit Vienna and Berlin to the kind of blackmail that Berlin had exerted in the Moroccan and Balkan crises in the past,[25] both the German Chancellor and the Chief of the General Staff had every reason to back up Austria-Hungary in order not to lose their one and only ally. 'Unless the Reich stiffens Austria-Hungary's back, she will seek a rapprochement with the Western powers whose arms are wide open, and we shall lose our military ally.'[26] Against this background, the British Liberal Government may have been justified in thinking of France and Russia as the equals of Germany and Austria-Hungary and in concluding that British foreign policy should aim at keeping Britain at peace if a 'continental war' broke out.[27]

To sum up these remarks: the first 'dramatic' component of the crisis

23. S. Williamson, *The Politics of Grand Strategy: Britain and France Prepare for War, 1909–1914*, Cambridge, Mass., 1969; *idem*, 'Joffre Reshapes French Strategy, 1911–1913' in P.M. Kennedy (ed.), *The War Plans of the Great Powers, 1880–1914*, London, 1971, pp. 133 ff.; L.C.F. Turner, 'The Russian Mobilization in 1914' in ibid., pp. 252–68, esp. p. 256.

24. N. Stone, 'Moltke and Conrad: Relations between the Austro-Hungarian and German General Staffs, 1909–1914' in ibid., pp. 233 ff.; F. Fischer, *War of Illusions: German Policies from 1911 to 1914*, London, New York, 1975.

25. R. Langhorne, *The Collapse of the Concert of Europe*, p. 99; J. Dülffer, *Regeln gegen den Krieg? Die Haager Friedenskonferenzen von 1899 und 1907 in der internationalen Politik*, Frankfurt a. M., Berlin, Vienna, 1981; H. Raulff, *Zwischen Machtpolitik und Imperialismus. Die deutsche Frankreichpolitik 1904–1906*, Düsseldorf, 1976. On German *Drohpolitik* see V.R. Berghahn, *Rüstung und Machtpolitik. Zur Anatomie des 'Kalten Krieges' vor 1914*, Düsseldorf, 1973; G. Schmidt, *Der europäische Imperialismus*.

26. K. Riezler, *Tagebücher*, 7 July 1914. On Vienna's approaches to the French government and various rumours about Austria-Hungary's intent to change sides, see F. Fischer, *War of Illusions*; D. Löding, 'Deutschlands und Österreich-Ungarns Balkanpolitik von 1912–1914 unter besonderer Berücksichtigung ihrer Wirtschaftsinteressen', Hamburg, 1969 (Ph.D. thesis); F.R. Bridge, *The Habsburg Monarchy*.

27. M. Brock, 'Britain enters the War' in R.J.W. Evans, H. Pogge von Strandmann (eds), *The Coming of the First World War*, Oxford, 1988, pp. 147, 151 f., 159, argues this case to explain Asquith's stances during the July crisis. Grey, the 'military' and the Conservatives held different views; see below.

scenario consisted of the contradictory postures of the two alliance systems. If one ally backed down, either the Entente or the Alliance would collapse; France and/or Russia might come to terms with Germany, or contrarily Austria could incline towards France and Britain, leaving Germany isolated rather than Britain.[28]

The counterbalancing factor was that both Britain and Germany were still in a position of strength to decide whether to opt for co-operation with a view to avoiding the calamity of a major war. Alternatively, Britain might be forced to conclude that it had to fulfil its role as a stumbling block to Germany's domination of Europe. 'An entente between Russia, France and ourselves would be absolutely secure. If it is necessary to check Germany, it could then be done.'[29] The fear of alienating Russia by refusing to support it over its 'Balkan mission' was widely shared in the British diplomatic establishment; that might make Russia turn its back on the undertaking to hold Germany in check in Europe, while it renewed its advance towards India via Persia and Tibet.[30] This explains why British foreign policy on the eve of the outbreak of war regarded Russia's self-assertiveness ('mangelnde Friedensfähigkeit') with many qualms but, nevertheless, decided to counter the German drive to domination, since Germany's policy made the alternative a separation of Russia from the Entente.[31]

The second 'conciliatory' component of the crisis scenario involved moving away from the idea of the Triple Entente as an anti-German bloc. The progress that had been achieved in 1912–14 in discussions about bilateral problems, as well as in diplomatic crisis management in the Balkan conflicts, nourished some hope that the defusing of the rivalry could develop into a marked interest in jointly working out solutions for regional conflicts. 'We are on good terms with Germany now and desire to avoid a revival of friction with her, and wish to discourage France from provoking Germany.'[32] If the co-operative

---

28. Z.S. Steiner, *Britain and the Origins of the First World War*, London, 1977, p. 43; Lord Grey, *Twenty-Five Years*, London, 1925, vol. II, pp. 15 f.

29. Grey, February 1906, *BD*, vol. III, No. 299.

30. Grey, July 1910; see K.M. Wilson, 'British Power in the European Balance, 1906–1914' in D. Dilks (ed.), *Retreat from Power*, vol. I, London, 1981, p. 39: 'France and Russia would regard [any political arrangement with Germany] with suspicion and all the blessings of the entente with France and Russia would go, and we might again be on the verge of war with one or the other of these powers.'

31. Ambassador Buchanan (St Petersburg) to A. Nicolson, 16 April 1914, *BD*, vol. X/2, No. 538, pp. 784 f.: 'Russia is rapidly becoming so powerful that we must retain her friendship at almost any cost'; for similar views – held by Nicolson, Hardinge – see K.M. Wilson, *Empire and Continent*, pp. 150–1.

32. M.G. Eksteins, 'The Triple Entente on the Eve of the Sarajevo Crisis' in F.H. Hinsley (ed.), *British Foreign Policy under Sir Edward Grey*, Cambridge, 1977, pp. 346–7.

pattern were to persist, the parameters which had determined British and German 'world/global policy' in general and their 'Orient policy' in particular had to be examined with a view to:

- their compatibility with regard to a diplomacy of 'settlement';
- the question of whether domestic constraints imposed serious limitations on the room for political manoeuvre;
- the question of whether other 'metropolitan powers' (Paris, St Petersburg) offered the local parties to the conflict an alternative, thus denying Germany and Britain the opportunity for acting as 'joint pacifier' in the turbulent Balkan arena.[33]

III

The process of reviewing the advantages and disadvantages of 'alliance politics' was in progress when the July crisis began to unfold in late June 1914. The assessments in London and in Berlin of the European power constellation on the eve of the July crisis converged to a certain degree. Grey realised that Britain's friends capitalised on Britain's fear of the German threat and used the German card to their own advantage;[34] this induced him to seek improved relations with Germany:

> The truth is that whereas formerly the German government had aggressive intentions . . . they are now genuinely alarmed at the military preparation in Russia, the prospective increase in her military forces and particularly at the intended construction at the instance of the French Government and with French money of strategic railways to converge on the German frontier.[35]

By way of contrast, Grey thought at this moment (late June 1914) that 'the German government are in a peaceful mood and . . . anxious to be

---

33. The main issue in the aftermath of Serbia's territorial and diplomatic gains in the Balkan wars – i.e. during the first and second phase of the July crisis – was how to find a solution which offered Austria-Hungary the prospect of determining the course of restructuring the Habsburg Monarchy independently, without at the same time implying that this strengthening of Austria-Hungary's posture had to be at the expense of her 'unfriendly neighbours', provoking them to balk at any bargain that might favour the Dual Monarchy. Sazonov's diplomacy aimed to prevent any split between Serbia and Russia and therefore counterbalanced the 'localisation' policy of Bethmann Hollweg.

34. Z.S. Steiner, 'Foreign Office Views, Germany and the Great War' in R.J. Bullen et al. (eds), *Ideas into Politics*, London, Sydney, 1984, p. 39.

35. Bertie to Grey, 27 June 1914; Grey, 16 July 1914, quoted in Z.S. Steiner, *Britain and the Origins*, pp. 122 ff.

on good terms with England.'[36] Riezler noted on 7 July 1914 in a similar manner:

> Recent general staff studies had reinforced Bethmann Hollweg's fear of Russia's quickly growing military might. After the completion of their strategic railroads in Poland our position will be untenable . . . Austria was growing weaker and more immobile by the day. Vienna was increasingly undermined from north and south-east, at any rate incapable of going to war for German interests as our ally. The Entente knows that we are, therefore, completely paralysed.

and added on the following day: 'if war comes from the East so that we have to fight for Austria-Hungary and not Austria-Hungary for us, we have a chance of winning . . . if war does not break out, if the Tsar is unwilling or France, alarmed, counsels peace, we have the prospect of splitting the Entente.'[37] Bethmann Hollweg – via Ambassador Lichnowsky – had explained his troubles to Grey on 6 July and enquired what Grey would do to save the situation. Obviously, the German Chancellor expected some sympathy for his dilemma, for both had shown understanding during the Liman von Sanders crisis and at many stages of the Balkan crisis.[38]

Bethmann Hollweg's decision on 5 July to back up Austria-Hungary, the so-called 'blank cheque',[39] was accompanied by a sort of mandate to the Chancellor and Foreign Secretary Jagow to try out their plan, i.e. to achieve a *fait accompli* and then be friendly towards the Entente, with a view to localising the conflagration. The military – Falkenhayn and Waldersee, substituting for Moltke, who was already on leave – were prepared to acquiesce. Two essential conditions were involved:

(1) Vienna must act quickly, i.e. overwhelm the Serbs and then make peace, just as Prussia did in 1866: 'if the Serbian business

---

36. K. Robbins, *Grey*, London, 1971, p. 287.
37. K.H. Jarausch, 'Statesmen versus Structures: Germany's Role in the Outbreak of World War One re-examined', *Laurentian University Review*, 5, 1973, p. 139.
38. Grey attempted to explain his predicament to the German government; see M.G. Eksteins, 'The Triple Entente', p. 345: 'I do not believe that the whole thing is worth all the fuss Sazonov makes about it; but so long as he does make a fuss it will be important and embarrassing to us for we cannot turn our backs on Russia.'
39. I agree with R.J.W. Evans's statement, 'The Habsburg Monarchy', pp. 34–7, 'that the high policy makers of the [Habsburg] Monarchy actively provoked that war'; Vienna was not waiting for instructions from Berlin, as F. Fischer and I. Geiss had stated at the beginning of the Fischer controversy. This is not to deny that the 'final decision' in Vienna was pressed through the ministerial Council when Germany's 'blank cheque' had been presented.

comes off well without Russia's mobilisation and hence without war, Germany might perhaps come to an agreement with her on the question of stabilising the Dual Monarchy.'[40] This aim was compatible with Grey's position; Grey regarded a renewed Austro-Russian understanding as the best hope for stability in the Balkans. The hope of keeping Russia passive collapsed, however, when the Central Powers opted for an ultimatum to Serbia, which was intended to clear the way for military action, and when Russia and France reassured each other during Poincaré's state visit (20–23 July 1914).

(2) The Triple Entente must not become suspicious of the German Central Powers; the latter had to avoid for the time being all steps liable to arouse political attention.[41] 'Since England is absolutely peaceable and France as well as Russia likewise do not feel inclined towards war (17.7.1914, Riezler), Bethmann Hollweg could expect his "blitz plan" to succeed.'[42] Hearing nothing from Berlin and Vienna, Grey did become disturbed but was not yet convinced that it was necessary to check Germany and side with Russia and France.[43]

The crucial aspect of this calculated 'risk' diplomacy was that Bethmann Hollweg had to face a target date, i.e. he had to reckon with the intervention of the military top echelon in German and Austrian policies if his strategy did not achieve results, and he had to expect French and Russian counter-offensives, at the latest after Poincaré's state visit to St Petersburg, including pressure on Britain to join forces in rebutting German *Drohpolitik*.[44] Although the German military did not take Britain's continental commitment seriously,[45] Bethmann Hollweg's strategy for avoiding a major conflict – which Moltke on 2 July designated as the only alternative, if the diplomatic offensive came to

40. K. Riezler, *Tagebücher*, 18 July 1914.
41. V.R. Berghahn, *Germany and the Approach of War in 1914*, pp. 188 ff.
42. K.M. Jarausch, 'Statesmen versus Structures', pp. 145 ff.; V.R. Berghahn, *Germany and the Approach of War in 1914*, pp. 198 ff.
43. Russian Ambassador Benckendorff (London), to Sazonov, 16 July 1914; Bertie, 16 July 1914; see Z.S. Steiner, *Britain and the Origins*, pp. 215 ff.
44. G. Schmidt, *Der europäische Imperialismus*; V.R. Berghahn, *Rüstung und Machtpolitik*.
45. F. Fischer, *Krieg der Illusionen*, pp. 566 ff. (Moltke–Jagow interview , May 1914); G. Ritter, *Der Schlieffen-Plan. Kritik eines Mythos*, Munich, 1956. On British defence planning before the war; see D. French, *British Economic and Strategic Planning 1905–1915*, London, 1982; J. Gooch, *Plans for War*, London, 1974; N. d'Ombrain, *War Machinery and High Policy*, Oxford, 1973; K.M. Wilson, *The Policy of the Entente*, London, 1985; P.M. Kennedy in Kennedy (ed.), *The War Plans of the Great Powers* on British naval strategy and planning, and S. Williamson, *The Politics of Grand Strategy*.

nought – had to concentrate on Britain. This was the lesson of past conflicts: Berlin had been warned by the British government that Britain would stand 'on the other side if continental war proved inevitable'.[46]

The Chancellor managed to keep the military – when they returned from their leave on 25–26 July – from proceeding with their preventive war plan; both Moltke and Falkenhayn maintained an attitude of restraint and caution, accepting the Chancellor's ambivalent position of remaining calm in order to allow Russia to put herself in the wrong, 'but then not [to] shrink from war if it were inevitable'.[47] In spite of the first news about Russian war preparations since 25–26 July, Moltke[48] did not yet hamper Bethmann Hollweg's belated attempts to put the brake on Austria during the period 26–29 July.[49] On 30 July, Moltke asked Conrad to respect the strategy of waiting for Russia to attack rather than declaring war on Russia themselves,[50] i.e. the strategy which Moltke himself accepted as a result of the 'Kronrat' on 29 July. It was up to Bethmann Hollweg to prove the correctness of his reassurance (23 July 1914) to the Kaiser that 'it is improbable that England will immediately enter the fray.'[51]

In Britain, Grey was encountering resistance to his advice, which from now on (26 July) shifted to 'pattern two'. The Liberal government refused to honour their moral obligations towards France; rather they indulged in the search for alternative views. There are various indications that Asquith – unaware of France's war plans and of the German General Staff's strategic calculations – might have tolerated the passage of German troops south of the Meuse-Sambre river line as the shortest way to get at France.[52] On the assumption that France and Russia were a match for Germany, the Asquith government searched for ways to keep Britain at peace (26 July – 1 August).

46. V.R. Berghahn and W. Deist, 'Kaiserliche Marine und Kriegsausbruch 1914', *MGM*, 1970, p. 48 (Note by Zimmermann, 9 July 1914).

47. K. Riezler, *Tagebücher*, 27 July 1914.

48. Moltke and Bethmann Hollweg restrained Falkenhayn, who demanded the declaration of a 'state of imminent danger of war'; J. Joll, *The Origins of the First World War*, London, New York, 1984, p. 20.

49. Moltke did, however, on 26 July work out the ultimatum for Belgium; Moltke to Bethmann Hollweg, 29 July 1914, 'Zur Beurteilung der politischen Lage' (Assessment of the political situation), D.D. 349; L. Albertini, *The Origins of the War of 1914*, II, pp. 488 ff. Here and in the notes that follow, D.D. stands for *Die deutschen Dokumente zum Kriegsausbruch 1914*, ed. by the German Foreign Office, 4 vols, Berlin, 1921.

50. Berghahn, *Germany and the Approach of War in 1914*, pp. 202 ff.

51. K.H. Jarausch, 'Statesmen versus Structures', p. 142.

52. M. Brock, 'Britain enters the War', pp. 147 ff.; C. Hazlehurst, *Politicians at War*, London, 1971.

On the German side, Bethmann Hollweg does not seem to have been told until 31 July 1914[53] of the decision by the German General Staff – April 1913 – to focus on the capture of Liège as the *sine qua non* for the success of the revised Schlieffen strategy. However, the Chancellor knew of and approved the central aim of the German military to crush the French opponent as soon as a war began; yet this feature of German policy was bound to provoke the Asquith government to stand by France, whatever happened about and in Belgium. The preliminary question was, however, whether Germany and Britain could see a way to localise the 'eastern conflict'. As to this matter, there were still influential voices in the British Cabinet (H. Samuel) pleading for support of the 'peace party' in Berlin against the 'warmongers'; Grey no longer believed that this distinction was relevant.[54]

IV

If Bethmann Hollweg's diplomatic strategy to localise the conflict by means of co-operation with Britain failed, Germany's contradictory postures would become a predicament. The question of who ruled in Berlin – Bethmann or Moltke? – was then bound to arise. This was due to the conflicting objectives inherent in that the diplomatic strategy of instigating Vienna to a decisive and speedy *Strafaktion* correlated with Plan B, i.e. Conrad's preferred option for a preventive war against Serbia, an option, however, which was anathema to Moltke.[55] For Plan B, if executed, deprived Austria-Hungary of the forces it should deploy in Galicia in order to help check Russia's advance through East Prussia towards Berlin and would therefore endanger the implementation of the revised Schlieffen Plan.

When the news of Russia's partial mobilisation on 29 July was confirmed,[56] Moltke stepped in. On the morning of 30 July, he urged

53. G. Ritter, *The Sword and the Sceptre*, vol. II, pp. 266 f.

54. See below.

55. Conrad put Plan B into operation when Vienna ordered partial mobilisation on 25 July; he did not reverse that decision until 5 August. The bombardment of Belgrade by Austrian mortars on 29 July 1914 was a futile operation in so far as Conrad had to tell Berchtold that the invasion of Serbia could not begin until 12 August 1914; the political-diplomatic pressure in favour of 'quick results' ('halt at Belgrade') contrasted with the postures of military strategy. See brief analyses of Conrad's war plans in N. Stone, 'Moltke and Conrad', pp. 223 ff.; L.F.C. Turner, 'The Russian Mobilization of 1914', pp. 86 ff.

56. On the withdrawal of the decree for general mobilisation by the Tsar in favour of a partial mobilisation (on 29 July) and the reversal of this decision as a result of Sazonov's intervention (in accordance with the Minister of War, the Chief of Staff and the General

the Austrian military attaché to press for immediate mobilisation against Russia and thereby – unauthorised – contermanded the Chancellor's demand for a 'halt at Belgrade' as a platform for a diplomatic settlement.[57] London, and even Sazonov (by then), had come around to giving this formula a try. Moltke brought pressure to bear on Vienna on 30 July after he had failed to obtain Bethmann Hollweg's consent to proclaim a *Kriegsgefahrenzustand*. On 31 July the Kaiser appealed to Franz Josef to mobilise Austria's main force against Russia and not to fragment her resources through any simultaneous offensive on Serbia![58] But the German Kaiser also made an offer to the British – on the evening of 31 July – that he would restrain Austria if London persuaded St Petersburg to delay the general mobilisation: the King, woken by his Ministers, appealed to the Tsar directly at 1.30 a.m. on 1 August, but the move came too late.

Moltke had become desperate, because Conrad had inaugurated partial mobilisation on 25 July, i.e. put Plan B into force. In other words, Conrad decided to proceed with the punitive action against Serbia and, thus, had to remain on the defensive against Russia in Galicia.[59] Moltke was, therefore, confronted with a worst-case scenario. In the spring of 1913 – in the aftermath of Austro-German staff talks – he had shelved the *Aufmarsch* in the East and thus had no alternative but to stick to the rigid time-schedule of the revised Schlieffen Plan and to remind Vienna of the importance of standing by its agreements: Austria was expected to bear the thrust of the Russian war machine.[60] Conrad had promised to do so, but on one condition (21 January

Quartermaster) in *Die Internationalen Beziehungen im Zeitalter des Imperialismus* (Russian Documents), series I, vol. 5, Doc. Nos. 224 and 284; D.W. Spring, 'Russia and the Coming of War', pp. 73 ff.

57. Wilhelm II to Jagow, 28 July 1914 (*DD* 293); Bethmann Hollweg to Tschirschky, 28 July 1914 (*DD* 323); K.H. Jarausch, 'Statesmen versus Structures', pp. 148 ff. The main German documents are printed in I. Geiss, *Julikrise und Kriegsausbruch 1914. Eine Dokumentation*, 2 vols, Hanover, 1963–4.

58. Moltke to Bethmann Hollweg, 29 July 1914 (*DD* 349); Franz Freiherr Conrad von Hötzendorff, *Aus meiner Dienstzeit 1906–1918*, Vienna, Leipzig, Berlin, 1922, vol. 4, p. 152; on the interaction between Vienna and Berlin, see N. Stone, 'Moltke and Conrad'; L.F.C. Turner, 'The Russian Mobilization in 1914'; L. Albertini, *The Origins of the War of 1914*, vol. 3, pp. 8 ff.; G.Ritter, *Staatskunst*, pp. 320.

59. L.F.C. Turner, 'The Russian Mobilization in 1914', pp. 87–8; Conrad decided on 31 July 1914 to remain on the defensive against Russia in Galicia. See also N. Stone, 'Moltke and Conrad', pp. 223 ff.

60. In order to induce the Dual Monarchy to take the burden of the 'eastern conflict' and launch an offensive against the Russian southern army, Moltke had to give in to the demand to attack over the Narev in the early stage of the war. In fact, the German frontier with Russia was covered by only 13 divisions of the 8th Army, whereas the proportion of the German armed forces intended for the western front was increased from two-thirds to eventually eight-ninths; in addition to Ritter, Stone and Turner (note 58) see J. Terraine, *Mons*, London, 1960.

1909), which Moltke did not honour: Germany was to keep the 8th
German Army in West Prussia strong enough to launch an offensive at
the outset of the campaigns against the Russian railway communications running east of Warsaw, thus facilitating an Austrian offensive
from Galicia.[61]

Consequently, both Moltke and Conrad reneged on their promises:
the forces needed to reassure each respective ally that the 'risk' was
manageable were not deployed as they ought to be. No wonder, then,
that Moltke, as soon as he learnt of Russia's general mobilisation,
insisted on the immediate proclamation of a state of imminent danger
of war and urged the Chancellor to dispatch an ultimatum to
St Petersburg demanding that Russia should cease all military measures
against Germany and Austria within twelve hours; in the absence of a
satisfactory reply, Germany declared war on Russia on 1 August 1914
(6 p.m.).

V

Having fitted the second pattern into the crisis scenario, let
us return to the fate of the first pattern. Bethmann Hollweg based his
decision for a diplomatic offensive on the assumption that Britain
might co-operate in limiting the spread of a Balkan conflict, as had
happened in 1912 and 1913.[62] In December 1912 he had argued:
'England habe sich in der Balkankrise absolut loyal verhalten und
namentlich auf Rußland mäßigend eingewirkt. Es wolle eben keinen
Kontinentalkrieg, weil es selbst in einen solchen verwickelt werden
würde, aber nicht selber fechten mag . . . Insofern hätten Rußlands

61. N. Stone, 'Moltke and Conrad', pp. 233 f. The argument that there was no chance
for the Central Powers to match Russia's masses, but that Russia was slow to mobilise,
was repeated by Bethmann Hollweg during a meeting of the Prussian Ministerial
Council (Staatsministerium). Referring to this circumstance, D.W. Spring, 'Russia and
the Coming of War', and H. Pogge von Strandmann, 'Germany and the Coming of War',
both argue that the Russian government was not enthusiastic about using its military
power; thus, Russia could not be considered as driving to war. To use this as evidence to
'clear' Russia of her responsibility for the outbreak of war is to ignore the importance of
the prevailing conviction expressed during crucial meetings of the Imperial Council and
between Sazonov and the top military echelon that Russia had to take an energetic
stance in order: (1) to deter Germany from supporting the Habsburg Monarchy, and (2)
to impress France and Britain that Russia would not (again) back down and 'sacrifice'
Serbia. The reassurance of France's support (Joffre's pressure on Yanushkevitch) and the
'self-confidence' of the heads of the Russian armed forces combined to make the Russian
leadership willing to face the consequences of their new bellicosity.
62. Bethmann Hollweg to Lichnowsky, 27 July 1914 (*DD* 248).

Verpflichtungen gegenüber Frankreich doch etwas Gutes.'[63]
For his part, Grey thought of the dividends which co-operation with Germany had paid in the autumn and winter of 1912.[64] He took the line that Germany should preach moderation in Vienna, while Britain would try to temper Russia's demands. Grey had assumed that France, too, would shy from considering the lengths to which France and Britain were prepared to go in support of Russia.[65] Although he recognised the pressures on France in July 1914 to back up Russia, Grey resisted Franco-Russian attempts (supported by Ambassador Buchanan from St Petersburg) at mobilising Britain's intervention; instead, he expected the French government to act in unison with London, with a view to forcing St Petersburg and Vienna to formulate a way out.[66]

These considerations shaped Grey's strategy during the July crisis. He would work with the German government as far as might be possible without moving away from France and Russia. On 9 July 1914, responding to Bethmann Hollweg's appeal of 6 July to save the situation, which underlined the dangers of victory for the 'militarists', Grey told Lichnowsky: 'I would continue the same policy as I had pursued through the Balkan crisis . . . The greater the risk of war the more closely would I adhere to that policy.'[67] In case the conflicting interests of Britain and Germany threatened the continuation of collaboration, the international co-operation between the 'civilian peace parties'[68] constituted a second layer of crisis management by co-operation (zwischenstaatliches Zusammenspiel innerstaatlicher Kräfte). The 'doves versus hawks' parameter was the last resort and the

---

63. Bethmann Hollweg to Karl von Eisendecher, 20 December 1912, quoted in J. Röhl, 'An der Schwelle zum Weltkrieg: Eine Dokumentation über den "Kriegsrat" vom 8. Dezember 1912', *MGM*, 1977/1, doc. 36, p. 125, and Röhl's comment, p. 93.
64. R.J. Crampton, 'The Balkans, 1909–1914' in F.H. Hinsley (ed.), *British Foreign Policy*, pp. 262 ff.
65. Grey to Bertie, 3 February 1912, in ibid., p. 258.
66. Grey aimed at discussions between Russia and Austria-Hungary on the Serbian issue; this offer ran counter to views of Poincaré and Sazonov, who agreed during the French President's state visit in St Petersburg on a joint *démarche* of the Entente Powers in Vienna; see documents No 67, 79 and 86 in *BD*, vol. XI.
67. Grey to H. Rumbold, 9 July 1914, in *BD*, vol. XI, No. 41, pp. 33 f.
68. The 'doves versus hawks' figure of speech was instrumental in internal debates and domestic contests, esp. in relation to disputes as to whether new armaments programmes were necessary or whether some agreement could be attained on arms limitation. This parameter is not restricted to British-German relations. The 'long tradition' of successful German attempts to separate Russia from joint action with France (and Britain) must not be left out of the analysis, even if – during the July crisis – the 'link' – i.e. German diplomatic efforts to persuade Russia of the advantages of a settlement with Germany – is less present than, say, in the autumn of 1911 (Potsdam Agreement).

crucial element in Bethmann Hollweg's calculated-risk diplomacy, for
he knew that his image depended on the 'localisation' of the conflict
and on preventing the military from initiating their alternative
strategy. However, within certain limits Bethmann Hollweg could
expect Grey to take his warnings seriously; they confirmed Grey's own
reading of the divisions in the Kaiser's entourage; Ballin (23 July 1914)
repeated a similar message to Grey and Haldane.[69] Since Grey was
disturbed by the way France and Russia were asserting themselves, he
genuinely felt that the German Chancellor – if reassured about Russian intentions – would restrain Austria, as he had done in the past.[70]
Hoping that the 'peace party' in Berlin would hold out and impose
constraints on Austria, Grey tried to give the Germans time to act. He
was relying on their good will and, therefore, did not want to bring
pressure to bear on Germany until the very last stage of the July
crisis.[71] At first (23–25 July), Grey wanted Berlin to hold back Austria-
Hungary as a first step in four-power mediation; this proposition was
Grey's reaction to the warning of the French Ambassador, Paul Cambon, that once Austria marched against Serbia general war became
inevitable.[72] At that stage, Sazonov was telling everybody that an
attack on Serbia was equivalent to a declaration of general war.

With Sazonov making ever more pressing demands for support
(26 July) – implying that early British declaration of solidarity with
the Entente would frighten off the Central Powers and assure the Triple
Entente a resounding diplomatic victory – Grey realised for the first
time the seriousness of the contradictory postures of Germany and
Russia. The Serbian question had turned into a test of strength
between the Triple Entente and the Triple Alliance.[73]

69. Z.S. Steiner, *Britain and the Origins*, pp. 220 ff.; Z.S. Steiner and M.G. Eksteins,
'The Sarajevo Crisis' in F.H. Hinsley (ed.), *British Foreign Policy*, pp. 397 ff.
70. Z.S. Steiner, *Britain and the Origins*, p. 221; M.G. Eksteins, 'The Triple Entente . . .'
in F.H. Hinsley (ed.), *The British Foreign Policy*, pp. 346 ff. K.M. Wilson, *Empire and
Continent*, stresses the point that Grey had become wary of Russia's attempts at black-
mailing the British in Persia, Tibet and other areas. Russia was speculating that Britain
was too preoccupied with the balance of power in Europe to stand up to Russia's imperial
ambitions.
71. Z.S. Steiner and M.G. Eksteins, 'The Sarajevo Crisis', pp. 409 f.
72. The Austrian Ministerial Council had, however, resolved – 7 July 1914 – that
demands should be presented with such far-reaching objectives as to make their rejection
certain and clear the road for a radical solution by means of military action; V.R.
Berghahn, *Germany and the Approach of War in 1914*, pp. 193 ff.; Minutes of the meeting of
the Joint Ministerial Council, 7 July 1914, in *ÖU*, vol. VIII, No. 10118.
73. For Lichnowsky's report on his interview with Grey, 27 July 1914, see K.M.
Wilson, *Empire and Continent*, p. 162; and the documents and comments in I. Geiss, 'Juli
1914. Die europäische Krise und der Ausbruch des Ersten Weltkrieges', Munich, 1965,
pp. 221 ff.; K.H. Jarausch, 'Statesmen versus Structures', pp. 144 f.

Grey's approach, however, of a variety of offers at mediation, could not find favour with Berlin. The Reichsleitung likened the conference of ambassadors to a proposal to put Austria-Hungary in front of a tribunal; the 'Algeciras' trauma of German foreign policy re-emerged. By rejecting the British offer, Bethmann Hollweg had to look for an alternative in order to meet the British half-way. This alternative, however, induced Grey to give up any idea of operating further in accordance with 'pattern one' (see below).

Depending on Germany remaining calm, while concocting a chain of events to provoke Russia into putting itself in the wrong – a stance which Bethmann Hollweg impressed on the Kaiser on 27 July 1914[74] – Bethmann Hollweg expected Grey to use his influence in St Petersburg to try to prevent Russia committing a hostile act.[75] Berlin, however, regarded the Russian mobilisation as a hostile act, 'which would force Germany to take counter-measures against our will'. When the Chancellor instructed Lichnowsky to warn Britain 'that for us Russian mobilisation means war',[76] Grey became convinced that the German Chancellor had started borrowing phrases and tactics from the 'war party'. Indeed, a Russian partial mobilisation along the northern border of the Dual Monarchy would compel Austria to order general mobilisation, which in turn would invoke the Alliance and require general mobilisation by Germany. For this reason, German diplomacy promised full support to Vienna whenever Berlin wanted its ally to show strength. But for Grey the discovery was painful: the German government was preparing for the worst.

At the start of the last week of July (27 July), efforts were set in motion in Berlin: (1) 'to unite the nation', and (2) 'to keep Britain out of war'.[77] At the other end Grey sought to carry the Cabinet his way (27 July 1914), while extending his diplomatic activities. Grey's declar-

74. Bethmann Hollweg informed the Kaiser on 27 July of the situation and explained his strategy (*DD* 245); Bethmann Hollweg to Wilhelm II, 28 July 1914 (*DD* 323). On the 'Crown Council' (Admiral von Müller diary), see W. Görlitz (ed.), *The Kaiser and His Court*, London, 1961, p. 7.
The situation on 27 July was that Russia was heading for a collision course with Austria and Germany; Berlin was aware of the fact, as was St Petersburg of Berlin's intention to support Austria-Hungary's offensive against Serbia.
75. Bethmann Hollweg to Lichnowsky, 26 July 1914, and reply to Wilhelm II, 26 July 1914. Grey noted on 26 July 1914: 'Prince Lichnowsky called this afternoon with an urgent telegram from his government to say that they had received information that Russia was calling in classes of reserves, which meant mobilization', *BD*, vol. XI, no. 103, further no. 146. On the events in Russia see L.F.C. Turner, 'The Russian Mobilization of 1914', p. 79.
76. Bethmann Hollweg to Lichnowsky, 27 July 1914; I. Geiss, 'Juli 1914', pp. 229 ff.; L.F.C. Turner, 'The Russian Mobilization of 1914', p. 71.
77. V.R. Berghahn, *Germany and the Approach of War in 1914*, pp. 202 ff.; E. Zechlin,

ation that he could no longer keep Britain aloof from the Serbo-Austrian conflict rendered, in Bethmann Hollweg's phrase, 'localisation impossible . . . since no one was left to mediate between the alliances'.[78] Grey had used the same phrase on 3 and 4 December 1912 to justify his firm warning in his address to the German government. Nevertheless, the lingering danger that France and Britain might commit their support to Russia, in order not to alienate her,[79] spurred Bethmann Hollweg to work for collaboration with Grey in order to prevent the spread of the conflagration after the Austrian declaration of war on Serbia (28 July).

VI

The Chancellor's aim of localisation might have still been attained if Austria had seized Belgrade quickly and then negotiated with St Petersburg before the latter proceeded with mobilisation.[80] Grey, too, was bound to stop the rot – the more so since his endeavours to reassure France that their moral bonds were going to be honoured and their military planning implemented were opposed in Cabinet (27 July 1914). The Foreign Secretary made a last attempt to test whether he could count on Bethmann Hollweg to lead the 'peace party' in Berlin, in order to avoid the alternative which his Foreign Office staff and the French and Russian as well as his own ambassadors started to impress on him: 'to choose between giving Russia active support or renouncing her friendship'.[81]

Since Austria – under German influence – had offered to guarantee Serbia's integrity[82] and since Sazonov had come to accept that Serbia should be made to face some degree of punitive action,[83] there was

---

Krieg und Kriegsrisiko: Zur deutschen Politik im Ersten Weltkrieg, Düsseldorf, 1979; F. Fischer, *Germany's Aims in the First World War*, London, 1967.

78. Bethmann Hollweg to Lichnowsky, 27 July 1914 (*DD* 248).

79. As a first instalment of solidarity with their Entente partner, Grey agreed to publicising Churchill's decision to keep the Royal Navy together after the Spithead Review (26 July 1914); Z.S. Steiner, *Britain and the Origins*, p. 223; the decision might 'soothe the Russians and the French and serve a useful warning to Germany and Austria'. Cf. M. Brock, 'Britain enters the War'.

80. Bethmann Hollweg to Tschirschky, 28 July 1914 (*DD* 323); Wilhelm II to Jagow, 28 July 1914 (*DD* 293).

81. Ambassador Buchanan (St Petersberg) to Grey, 26 July 1914, *BD*, XI, No. 125, p. 94.

82. See I. Geiss, 'Juli 1914', ch. 7, esp. pp. 294 ff.

83. Pourtalès to Jagow, 27 July 1914 (*DD* 282); Pourtalès to Jagow, 30 July 1914 (*DD* 401).

some sign of a new situation.[84] German pressure on Vienna paralleled by British and French pressure on St Petersburg might combine to keep the 'mediation' option open.

Bethmann Hollweg, however, undermined his belated compliance with Grey's expectations – that Berlin should exert pressure on Vienna in favour of Grey's proposals for mediation – when he aimed at a British declaration of neutrality.

On 29 July, returning from the Potsdam Crown Council – where the Kaiser had shrugged off Grey's warnings and Prince Heinrich had reported King George V's comment that England would remain neutral in the event of war – Bethmann Hollweg made his clumsy[85] bid for British neutrality: if Britain stayed out, Germany would, in the event of a victorious war, aim at no territorial acquisitions at the expense of France (proper); he also pledged that the integrity of Belgium would be respected in the peace settlement. Afraid that the British government might pass the message to the French, Bethmann Hollweg shifted the emphasis: he sent urgent notes to Vienna, advocating mediation, in order to fend off the possibility of a war beginning in circumstances which might cast suspicion on the German government.[86] The military acquiesced for the moment but forced the Chancellor – on the night of 29 July 1914 – to send warnings to Paris and St Petersburg to desist from further military preparations.[87]

Against the background of the bombardment of Belgrade (29 July), Bethmann Hollweg tried to reverse the wheels of German policy: the 'halt at Belgrade' should help to keep the option of preventing the spread of the conflagration. Although Grey picked up these threads and backed the 'halt at Belgrade' proposal in St Petersburg (30–31 July 1914) – trusting that the renewed Austro-Russian talks in Vienna might be prolonged by and expanded into four-power mediation – he became convinced that the peaceful elements in Berlin were rapidly losing ground. In Cabinet on 29 July 1914, however, members (H. Samuel) indicated their belief that the 'doves' in Berlin might still be able to use their influence in favour of peace and, thereby, provided

84. Berlin and Vienna aimed at dispelling the effects of their previous refusal to agree to international (four-power) negotiations; Lichnowsky to Jagow, 29 July 1914; Bethmann Hollweg to Tschirschky, 30 July 1914 (*DD* 368, 395 ff.)

85. 'Clumsy' because the offer was similar to the kind which Tisza introduced into the package to be presented to Serbia; this type of offer was at best 'acceptable' to 'small powers' being faced by a group of major powers, but not with regard to France and Belgium as central elements of Britain's 'vital interests'.

86. Bethmann Hollweg to Tschirschky, 30 July 1914; cf. R. Langhorne, *The Collapse of the Concert of Europe*, pp. 118 f.

87. Bethmann Hollweg to the French and Russian governments (via Ambassadors Schoen and Pourtalès), 31 July 1914 (*DD* 490, 491)

a rationale for the Cabinet's decision that it would be better 'to maintain an equivocal position because, if both sides do not know what we shall do, both will be less willing to run risks'.[88] But Grey felt obliged to give the German Ambassador a private warning that Germany should not rely on British neutrality (this message rejected Bethmann Hollweg's neutrality offer). The Cabinet did not consider the German bid for Britain's neutrality; they wanted Germany and France to be asked to comply with the neutrality of Belgium (31 July) before further decisions were considered as to what constituted a *casus belli* and as to how far the naval agreements and military staff talks had committed Britain to defend France as Britain's first line of defence.[89] The Belgian and naval issues (defence of France's northern shores) were decided on 2 August in favour of upholding the commitments, whereas the issue of despatching the Expeditionary Force to France to take up its role of extending the left wing of the French left army was still being debated on 5–6 August, when Britain and Germany were – at the expiry of the British ultimatum at midnight (11 p.m. London time) – already at war.

VII

The 'Military' at first disputed and then actually challenged the foreign-policy monopoly of governments and 'foreign offices'.[90] When the diplomatic crisis turned into a test of strength, the military launched into a diplomacy of their own. The communications between Moltke and Conrad on the one hand and between Joffre and Yanushkevitch on the other (since 26 July) went far beyond the exchange of information about *Aufmarschpläne*, etc.; they collaborated

88. Z.S. Steiner and M.G. Eksteins, 'The Sarajevo Crisis', p. 401 ff.

89. Z.S. Steiner, *Britain and the Origins*, pp. 229 f.; K.M. Wilson, *Empire and Continent*, pp. 149 ff. and *idem*, 'To the Western Front: British War Plans and the "Military Entente" with France before the First World War', *British Journal International Studies*, 3, 1977, pp. 151–68; M. Brock, 'Britain enters the War', on the deliberations of the Liberal government.

90. This is not to say that the 'politicians' abdicated or that they invited the 'men on horseback' to take over the reigns of power. Both in Austria-Hungary and in Russia the civilian-dominated Councils of Ministers made the decisions (D.W. Spring, 'Russia and the Coming of War', pp. 72 ff.; R.J.W. Evans, 'The Habsburg Monarchy', pp. 37 ff.); in Berlin, Chancellor Bethmann Hollweg had the support of Wilhelm II to steer off a continental war. However, the military intervened to present the conditions on which the 'diplomats' could use – at an advanced stage of the crisis – military power; this implied that the options were narrowed to those which the military war planners had fixed; conscious of the narrow range of their own options, the military collaborated with their opposite numbers with a view to implementing offensive strategies.

with a view towards making their governments comply with the action-related programmes developed by the military for a contest between the two blocs. The risk of escalating the political conflagration into war had to be taken and – this was the main thrust of the message of the General Staffs – they were well prepared to face the risk *now*. But to guarantee success, the military demanded that they should run the affair according to the time-schedules agreed upon at their staff talks. There was only one chance of attaining military success, and this depended on the timely execution of the mobilisation schedules. The alliance mechanism implied a near-identity of mobilisation and resort to war.

Military strategies were fixed according to the need to match the main opponent in war and to deter the allies as far as possible from plans to exploit specific political opportunities. This involved an aversion on the part of both Germany and France towards partial mobilisation by Austria and Russia respectively with a view to intervening directly in the 'war by proxy'. Joffre and Messimy (French Minister of War) were alarmed at the indications that Russia was contemplating partial mobilisation and exerted pressure on St Petersburg to induce the Russian general staff to demand general mobilisation.[91] The 'technical' explanation that partial mobilisation would hamper general mobilisation later on was used to reverse the option;[92] this tipped the scale towards full-scale preparation for war. The French military requested the Tsarist government (27 July) to prepare for taking the offensive according to the agreements in the Military Convention, since the allies were heading straight for war. As to the Russian General Staff itself, there is little doubt that the senior members regarded the introduction of the period preparatory to war on 26 July – with measures taken over the whole of European Russia – as the first step towards general mobilisation. According to Turner they viewed the outbreak of a general European war with equanimity.[93] The postures of the military against partial mobilisation undermined the chances of diplomatic settlement.

91. Joffre to Ignatieff (Russian Military Attaché), 28 July 1914 (*Internationale Beziehungen*, ser. I, vol. V, No. 180); cf. I. Geiss, 'Juli 1914', pp. 216 ff.; L.C.F. Turner, 'The Russian Mobilization in 1914', pp. 82 ff.

92. In a partial mobilisation the Warsaw District would not have been affected in order to avoid offending Germany. The French General Staff had some information about (or correctly assessed) Austria-Hungary's 'Plan B', but did not want to encourage Russia to exploit such a situation, i.e. concentrate on partial mobilisation against Austria alone in order to support diplomatic efforts by threatening a show-down. On Conrad's schemes for offensive action against Serbia see note 55 above.

93. L.C.F Turner, 'The Russian Mobilization in 1914', pp. 76–7; cf. note 61 above.

Politicians and diplomats had at some point invited the 'military' to do their job for them. Governments regarded their being forced to attend conferences as an indication of defeat; they felt they had to rely on armed preparedness as a means to protect their freedom of action. Thus, governments had only to support the 'military' to obtain the material which they demanded to implement their offensive strategies. The military, however, were absolved from explaining their assumptions, i.e. the 'necessity' to plan for offensive operations in order to bolster the 'morale' of their allies. The military postures of the alliances were too competitive to entertain any pretence by politicians that they might serve diplomatic-political ends. The equation

$$\text{solidarity} = \text{offensive strategy} = \text{war action}$$

tied 'diplomacy' to the 'policies' of the defence establishment rather than tying military operations and defence to the conditions of foreign policy.

Summary

Ever since the re-emergence of a full-fledged arms race – Russia's programme of 1909; Germany's and France's expansion programmes of 1913 – the precarious co-existence between the military alliances and the diplomatic alignments was endangered. The pressure to support allies to the full and to prevent diplomatic settlements between the antagonists of the power system, Germany and Russia – and to a lesser extent Austria-Hungary's shift towards France – led in October 1913 for the first time to a confrontation between the two camps. The willingness of Russia and Germany to bolster Serbia and Austria-Hungary respectively, and of France to support Russia's assertiveness, were indications that the military build-up might really be put to the test. Until then (a) political-diplomatic steps, (b) financial (imperial) strategies and (c) the designs of the 'military' had operated towards different objectives and in different directions. The major countries had exploited 'crises' to pass through another armaments programme; but even the more demanding figures among the 'military' (Moltke, Ludendorff, Joffre) had emphasised that the 'enemy' was not inclined to adopt an aggressive posture in the near future. Therefore, the calculations of the 'military' in Germany, France and Russia cannot be said to amount to long-term preparation for war at a pre-set date.

The arms race had resulted in a system in which the players pursued a dynamic of their own; thus far, the 'rationale' had been to improve their position, i.e. add strength to strength, and not yet to engage the enemy in war. However, the more the General Staffs in Berlin and Vienna, as well as in Paris and St Petersburg, realised that the relative military strength was shifting in favour of France and Russia and the more the 'politicians' noticed the closing of the ranks between the allies and were told of the increasing threat posed to their country by the recent rearmament of the 'enemy', the more were both blocs inclined to risk a show-down. The 'new', escalating element was the fact that the German and French governments, wanting to reinforce the alliance spirit in the Dual Monarchy and Russia respectively, came to accept that the 'Balkan' interests of their partner were an integral part of the alliance; hitherto, Berlin and Paris had repeatedly warned Vienna and St Petersburg that they could not be expected to intervene just because of 'pure' Austrian or Russian 'local' interests. The 'politicians' and diplomats in Paris and Berlin were concerned with the double task of protecting their major ally against blackmail (by their 'senior' opponent) and at the same time assisting this ally to force through a number of its demands against their 'junior' opponent. The German and French 'military', on the other hand, were upset about such endeavours to localise the conflict; they reminded their 'political' partners that the whole purpose of the military alliance demanded concentration on the main enemy. Once the military might of each ally was shifted from the arena of competitive rearmament to the task of performing the duties of an ally with a view to attaining 'security gains' over the opposite bloc, the 'military' were bound to intervene and to employ their own crisis diplomacy in order to make sure that they could proceed along the lines of their pre-conceived *Aufmarsch* plans. Since neither the French nor the German General Staffs had alternative strategies at their disposal, the military options were tied to the rigid network of offensive strategies.

Although Britain was under constant pressure from France and Russia to become a party to the conflict, thus adding in decisive manner 'political' superiority to the already existent military balance between the two blocs, the Liberal government resisted the temptation to encircle the 'German' (Central) Powers. But the British were no longer the free agents they wished to remain. Militarily, their armed forces were assigned a certain task, even if the French designers of 'Plan W' did acknowledge the proviso that defence planning did not bind the British Cabinet to that duty. The central figures in the Asquith government, pressured by the opposition and by their own military and diplomatic advisers, had committed themselves, too. They were convinced of the necessity – under the spell of the Moroccan crises – of preventing Germany from starting to fight the Dual Alliance while Britain remained neutral; if Britain stood aside, this would endanger the future of the British Empire, whether Germany or the Franco-Russian Alliance prevailed. For one thing, Britain's leadership had every reason to work towards 'localisation' of Balkan conflicts (or any other 'war by proxy'). There was, however, another matter: Grey overestimated neither the deterrent effect of British naval force nor that of the British Expeditionary Force on German strategy. This was sound – but by implication it meant that, in the worst case, Grey was likely to opt for 'encirclement', if only to make sure that Britain would not be isolated, now or later on.

The July crisis, therefore, was both similar to and different from previous crises. The first pattern of diplomatic activity operated towards 'localisation', the second led to a war between the 'German' alliance and the Triple Entente. This essay has attempted to illuminate the political actions supporting 'pattern one', to outline the contradictory postures prevailing in the 'defence planning' of the General Staffs and to point to those conflicting objectives within British and German 'localisation diplomacy' which prepared the stage for the eventual predominance of 'pattern two'.

ANDREAS HILLGRUBER

The Historical Significance of the First World War: A Seminal Catastrophe

A variety of academic approaches can be adopted to deter-
mine the historical significance of a single caesura in world history, of
an event such as the First World War which transformed the politics of
the world. The following essay is written in the conviction that political
history is still predominantly a sequence of decisions, despite the
importance of trends and developments in the economic and social
spheres; any historical situation contains alternatives and various
options within it, and history remains open to the future. From this
standpoint, an appraisal will be made of the experiences of what had
been the greatest military catastrophe in the world to date and of the
possible alternative courses of action which had been available.

Initially, this will be done from the vantage point of 1918. An
attempt will then be made to assess the significance of new political
forces and of the trends towards social change which had begun to
emerge before 1914 and had made an impact either during the war or
at its end. There will be some description of major decisions taken
under the influence of these factors and of alternatives and options
which were rejected. Then, the path taken by Europe and the world
towards the even greater catastrophe of the Second World War, and
beyond it towards the threat of a third, will be outlined. Finally, a
cautious assessment of the significance of the First World War in the

The German original of this article was published in M. Funke et al. (eds), *Demokratie
und Diktatur. Geist und Gestalt politischer Herrschaft in Deutschland und Europa. Festschrift für
Karl Dietrich Bracher*, Düsseldorf, Bonn, 1987, pp. 109–23.

history of the twentieth century will be attempted.

It is useful to begin this task with a look back at the closing years of the eighteenth century. The war of 1914–18 was the culmination of a development in the European system of states spanning more than 100 years, since the French Revolution and the rule of Napoleon I, over much of the European continent. Statesmen at the Congress of Vienna in 1814–15 were profoundly conscious of the significance of these events; their impact had not been diminished by the defeat of Napoleon's 'grand empire' and what appeared, on superficial examination, to be a broad restoration of the principles if not the details of the *ancien régime*. The intellectual, political and social triumph of the French Revolution in Europe during the previous quarter century had shattered the confident sense of identity of the Europe of estates; the order in which the pre-revolutionary elites had lived was gone for ever. Though the defeat of Napoleon had allowed these elites to maintain or regain their dominant positions in most countries, the French Revolution and the Napoleonic era continued to pose a grave threat to the order which was established or reconstructed at the Congress of Vienna.

Similarly, the liberal and national movements, which had recently been used against Napoleon during the wars of liberation, had also come to be seen as a danger. In these circumstances, the concept of the solidarity of the great powers moved to the centre of international politics. The cornerstone of the new 'Concert of Powers' was a joint, European responsibility to act against the threat of social and national revolution in the interests of each and every power. Initially, the resulting solidarity of conduct placed strict limits on selfish state-power politics of the kind inherited from the later era of absolutism. But memories faded as time passed, diminishing the impact of those twenty-five years of war, which had claimed so many lives and endangered the social foundations of the great powers. For the next generation of European statesmen, the French Revolution and the supremacy of Napoleon were mere history rather than living memory. The longer the peace lasted, the stronger was the inclination of the great powers to return to an untrammelled form of state-power politics.

Nevertheless, it was some years before the obstacles erected in 1814–15, including the psychological barriers created by the proclaimed solidarity of the 'Concert of Powers', were dismantled. The limits set at the Congress of Vienna were first exceeded only in the generation of Napoleon III, Palmerston, Cavour and Bismarck. At that stage, the statesmen of many nations grew ready to use the liberal and national movements which they had previously opposed; they prepared to exploit these movements for the sake of selfish state-power politics, with the aim of revising the order established in 1815 in favour of their respective states and to the detriment of others. Yet even then, some inhibitions remained. The statesmen did not challenge the entire European order of powers and, thus, did not threaten its existence as a whole. Though no longer with complete success, they were still anxious to remain independent of the social and national movements they planned to use. There is no doubt that statesmen of this generation were attempting to jettison the ties of principle binding them to a conservative social order throughout Europe, since such concepts were now regarded as little more than ideological encumbrances (*Realpolitik* as against *Prinzipienpolitik*). They continued, however, to recognise a genuine solidarity of the European great powers, though this was more narrowly conceived than in the preceding generation. More precisely, statesmen recognised the necessity of respecting the interests of the other great powers. This outlook enabled them to step back from the brink of a new major war on a number of occasions, particularly in 1853–6 and 1878 in the perennially troublesome Near East and Balkans.

However, the following generation of statesmen was much more dependent than its predecessors on the dynamism of new social classes and on actual or ostensible political constraints and compulsions. It was these statesmen who finally lost the vital awareness of a solidarity of the great powers of Europe in the interest of every state. Unrestrained nationalism and imperialism consequently triumphed. At first, the aim was to establish imperial positions overseas. After the Russo-Japanese War of 1904–5, however, the focal point of tensions reverted back to Europe itself. Until then, the basic structure of 1815 had survived despite major revisions, caused particularly by the unification of Germany in 1871 and the developments in the centre of Europe. This order finally collapsed in the 'great seminal catastrophe' of Europe, in the world war of 1914–18.[1]

Among this last generation of statesmen who plunged Europe into the First World War, no great names spring to mind. This in itself is an indication of the lack of outstanding figures among them. There was no ability to look beyond everyday events and minor issues; statesmen showed no capacity to moderate their own objectives in order to make vital decisions which might have enabled Europe to avoid impending

1. George F. Kennan, *Bismarcks europäisches System in der Auflösung: Die französisch-russische Annäherung 1875 bis 1890*, Frankfurt, Berlin, Vienna, 1918, p. 12.

catastrophe. Sir Edward Grey's comment that 'The lamps are going out all over Europe' is revealing in this respect; it describes the characteristic tendency of his generation towards passivity, towards allowing themselves to be carried along with the tide. Equally significant is Bethmann Hollweg's admission, at the height of the July crisis, that 'direction has been lost, and the stone has been set in motion'. Typically, none of the statesmen of 1914 fully recognised the consequences of the coming war for the great-power position of their respective countries and for the European order as a whole.[2]

In general, the statesmen of 1914 were unable to weigh the interests of their own states against those of their opponents and partners in a rational manner and with the *raison d'état* of their own power as the yardstick. In Europe after 1890 these considerations were increasingly replaced by the constraints and compulsions of the alliance system and ultimately by the two opposing groups of the Triple Entente and Triple Alliance. As James Joll has recently demonstrated, *raison d'état* was now equated with alliances;[3] consequently, independent conduct outside the bloc system became impossible for any power as soon as a conflict began to affect a great-power partner or antagonist.

In the years before 1914, these restrictions on freedom of manoeuvre in foreign policy were accompanied by the growing dependence of governments on chauvinist, imperialist and even racialist elements in internal affairs. This was true even of those great powers which had not yet witnessed the introduction of a genuine parliamentary system. There was, thus, a general 'democratisation' – if it can be so called – of foreign policy, which in the nineteenth century had still been regarded largely as an 'arcanum' of governments.

The freedom of manoeuvre available to statesmen during crises was also enormously restricted by a third important trend. This was the decline in the traditional political conception of security and the subsequent reduction of the European balance of power to a purely military balance, to a question of the relative strength of navies and armies and the various weapons held by the opposing power constellations. As a result, actual or supposed shifts in favour of one's own position or – more correctly – the bloc to which one belonged, tended to be regarded as opportunities. The risk of war could thus be increased. Moreover, the opposite situation was equally dangerous; when

2. The most recent overall analysis is Klaus Hildebrand, 'Julikrise 1914: Das europäische Sicherheitsdilemma. Betrachtungen über den Ausbruch des Ersten Weltkrieges', *Geschichte in Wissenschaft und Unterricht*, 36, 1985, pp. 469–502.
3. James Joll, *The Origins of the First World War*, London, New York, 1984.

the rival bloc seemed to be catching up in terms of military strength, and even threatening to overtake one's own bloc, it was easy to assume that the current superiority of one's own bloc would have to be exploited before it was irrevocably lost within a few years. Against such a background a 'preventive' war, waged at a time when it could still be won, seemed a sensible choice.

This reduction of the idea of the 'balance of power' to a purely military balance had profound consequences. On one side, it encouraged the 'encirclement' syndrome of the central powers; on the other, it did much to fuel the fears of Great Britain, which were soothed only by forging the closest possible links with France and Russia (reaching far beyond its treaty obligations). Indeed, Britain became convinced that the alliance with Russia, which since 1907 had come to be regarded as a vital counterweight to Germany, must be retained at all costs. In the final crisis of 1914, the strength of these convictions prevented the free mediation of the British government, independent of its alliance partners and in accordance with the traditional British role as protector of the European balance of power.

Some pacifist sentiment did exist in the period before 1914. Nevertheless, opinion within governments and amongst the general public was dominated by the belief that war was a legitimate means of politics for sovereign states. Indeed, in line with a widespread social Darwinism, wars were widely regarded as a vehicle for progress, as a kind of selection process to establish the strongest forces in international politics. Translated into the military sphere, this ensured the pre-eminence of offensive thinking and an allied conviction that a ruthless offensive would bring the war to a swift end. The idea that future wars would be short was also supported by a general belief that modern civilisation, particularly the complex and interdependent world economic system, could not tolerate the burdens of long wars.

The outbreak of war in 1914 was welcomed with enthusiasm by the masses. This response, especially among the young, can be interpreted as a joyous rebellion against the tedium of bourgeois life and of even a proletarian lifestyle which had become increasingly pseudo-bourgeois. The reaction also contained an element of conscious irrationality, a rejection of the enlightened-liberal ideas which had apparently been so influential in the nineteenth century and the decade before 1914. Thus, the war seemed to promise a brief interruption of the prevailing boredom and monotomy. The crucible of war, it was felt, provided the greatest imaginable test of masculinity. 'In the spirit of 1914' – according to the thesis of Michael Howard – Europe marched 'into the field with shouts of joy'.[4] None of the great international movements, chief among them the Second Socialist International, was sufficiently strong to counter the integration of the working classes into their respective nations. This process, which was well under way before the war, was initially strengthened by its outbreak.

Hence, the early stages of the war produced an increased level of social integration. Existing domestic political and social tensions were diverted against the external enemy. As the war dragged unexpectedly on, however, the tendency towards integration was replaced by an opposite trend towards polarisation. Though there was no split along traditional political fault-lines for some time, the broad 'centre' of the political spectrum was challenged by the extreme 'left', with its rejection of national solidarity, and the extreme 'right' with its desire for a militarised society and a different, modern and 'total' state. But the development towards polarisation in the civilian sphere was not matched in the mass armies. Here, integration in the 'community of the trenches' was actually strengthened as the conflict grew more bitter. The contrast with civilian society grew more stark as the war became established.

In the sphere of international politics, the trend towards polarisation between the belligerent power blocs was exacerbated by the development of psychological warfare and virulent propaganda. It was also intensified by the addition of an ideological hostility to the original, traditional power-political antagonism between the powers and power blocs. During the course of the war a number of different efforts were made to restore the peace, but all of them foundered on this tendency towards the polarisation, radicalisation and totalisation of conflict. A sober and rational understanding of the situation was thus suppressed. Such an attitude was described by the German Secretary of State for Foreign Affairs, Richard von Kühlmann, to the central committee of the Reichstag. He made his remarks on 28 September 1917, a few weeks before the October Revolution in Russia. Though Kühlmann's thinking was restricted by the ideas of the preceding era, he showed some awareness of the problem:

> Europe! – today the word sounds like a fairy tale from times long ago . . .
> The little peninsula set against the Asiatic continent has had the mastery of
> the world in its hands before now, as regards trade politics and power
> politics . . . It is not too much to say that the situation existing over the last
> forty years has not been so intolerable for any of the states in this old Europe

4. Michael Howard, 'Ende der europäischen Ära', *Die Zeit*, No. 9, 22 February 1985.

that it was forced to eradicate it even at the risk of its own destruction. Even today, in the midst of this immense war, it is still perhaps a common interest of all the major states [to ensure that] Europe does not perish.[5]

But Kühlmann's tentative overtures to Britain were unavailing, as were his attempts in 1918 to avert the destruction of Russia as a great power and an important factor in the European order as a whole.

Between 1914 and 1917 an ideological hostility developed, based on the conflict between democracies and autocracies and intensified by the propaganda slogans of both sides. After the entry of the United States of America into the war and the Bolshevik revolution in Russia, this antagonism was overlaid with the global ideological programmes associated with these two new centres of world politics. According to American ideals, the world was to be prepared for a democratisation of all the states and then for their amalgamation into a 'league of nations'; on the Bolshevik side, the aim was to transform the imperialist war between the power blocs into a 'world revolution', into a triumph of the international proletariat over the bourgeoisie in every country. These new watchwords influenced opinion in the belligerent nations, where 'Wilson' and 'Lenin' parties appeared as a result. The new ideological and socio-political fronts cut virtually across the existing power politics of the hostile blocs without, however, being able to overcome them. Here, in the climax of the First World War, the 'age of ideologies' (K.D. Bracher) had its origins. Albeit with various changes of emphasis and fluctuations in intensity, this era was to last throughout the twentieth century.

Superficially, the ambitious war-aims programmes developed by all the belligerents during the first weeks of the war were not in harmony with this development, since they were based purely on considerations of power politics. Popular over-simplifications encouraged the extension of these programmes into objectives which ultimately won the support of the bulk of the various nations and their representatives. This development had profound consequences for the course of the war. In particular, it practically eliminated the possibility of a 'drawn' peace of the status quo ante 1914; even a 'meagre' peace of success, which individual government representatives would actually have regarded as 'victory', became unlikely. The notion of prestige, largely restricted to state governments during the nineteenth century, now

---

5. Quoted by Wolfgang Steglich, *Die Friedensversuche der kriegführenden Mächte im Sommer und Herbst 1917, Quellenkritische Untersuchungen, Akten und Vernehmungsprotokolle*, Stuttgart, 1984, p. v.

gained a wide quasi-democratic, national-chauvinistic following which was hugely encouraged by war propaganda and journalism. In this climate, the war aims of the powers were affected by a number of motives: by concrete economic interests; by the search for strategic security; by the desire to obtain strong initial positions for the next war (in case the current one was not, after all, the 'war to end wars'); and – last but not least – by cultural-ideological and even racial convictions about the superiority of one nation over another. Consequently, the belligerents developed the will to improve their own power position and to reduce that of the enemy states to such an extent that they became little more than medium-ranking powers dependent on the victors. At the very least, they were to be made incapable of pursuing 'grand policy' in future. Overt or latent attempts to create *Großraum* were thus based on more than political and military strategic thinking, the latter caused by the enormous increase in the range of modern weapons; they were also linked with the desire to create economically self-sufficient and militarily secure alliance systems, consisting of a larger body of states grouped around a leadership power. This idea had emerged as central Europe was cut off from the world economy after the outbreak of war and was associated with plans to continue the economic war effort after the ending of military hostilities.

War aims of this kind involved a willingness to ignore national state boundaries and to include smaller and medium-sized states either with their agreement or against their will. Their neutrality, as the cases of both Belgium and Greece had revealed, was no longer respected if strategic advantages could be obtained from violating it. This was particularly true in the case of the 'battle of destruction'[6] which formed part of the offensive approach and reflected the illusory expectation of a short war; here the aim was to ensure the military, and perhaps even political, capitulation of the enemy. In military theory, 'destruction' meant the complete elimination of a major part of the enemy forces (their capture).

During the First World War, however, the word began to acquire another meaning: 'destruction' already implied some element of physical elimination. The mass murder of Armenians in the Ottoman Empire in 1915, linked with mass deportations, was the first major indicator of possible future intensifications of 'people's wars'. In a different context, the treatment of the Serbs by the Bulgarians was

6. Jehuda L. Wallach, *Das Dogma der Vernichtungsschlacht. Die Lehren von Clausewitz und Schlieffen und ihre Wertungen in zwei Weltkriegen*, Frankfurt, 1967.

another. In a conversation with the journalist Guttmann of the *Frankfurter Zeitung* on 20 November 1917, Richard von Kühlmann described how 'the Serbs are being finished off; they are brought to delousing stations for cleansing and are killed by gas. That,' von Kühlmann stated, 'is the future in people's wars.'[7] In practice, these were isolated instances. Yet support for a 'national cleansing of fields and pastures', for major programmes of compulsory evacuation and resettlement, was widespread. Such programmes were designed to help create unified national blocs instead of the mixed population structures so typical of east-central and south-east Europe, in particular. At this stage they remained largely in the realms of oratory, despite the concrete nature of demands such as those made by the Pan-Germans in the east.

The social consequences of the war, caused particularly by its length and increasing bitterness, varied from country to country. Only in those major states least affected by the movement towards national integration in the war, Russia and Austria-Hungary, did they lead to complete disintegration and to new beginnings in transformed circumstances. With regard to war ideas of the future, two other tendencies can be detected. The first of these was the notion that a massive effort by the whole nation could enable it to stand firm through a war, which had become immeasurably more bitter than had seemed possible in 1914, and eventually to triumph. Significantly, it was thought that this war effort must include the militarisation of society, allied with the dismantling of traditional social barriers. The approach contributed to the belief that a 'total' war, linked with the removal of the classical distinction between combatants and non-combatants, between the military and civilian sectors, was appropriate to modern warfare. This belief had spread far beyond the circle of military thinkers long before it was summarised by Ludendorff in his book on 'Total War' in 1935. In the war of 1914–18 itself, the discrepancy between ideas and reality remained considerable despite every effort to incorporate the home 'front' fully into the nation under arms. Domestic constraints and difficulties, connected with the political structure of the German Reich and even that of its west European opponents, could not be removed so easily, especially in wartime.

The second tendency to emerge from the war was in contrast to these attempts at the militarisation of society. It involved the hope that the military balance of power could be overturned in one fell swoop, by means of a qualitative leap in military technology. A rapid victory was

7. Bernhard Guttmann, *Schattenriß einer Generation 1888–1919*, Stuttgart, 1950, p. 146.

to be achieved once the ossified fronts had been set in motion, probably as a result of dramatic advances in a previously disregarded field. Unrestricted submarine warfare, the development of air forces and tanks are examples of this intent; the use of gas, though it was less effective, is another. At the end of the war it was an open question which of the two tendencies would gain the upper hand in future. The first was a purely defensive fortress mentality, based on the total community of the nation for defence. It can be regarded as the consequence of 'Verdun', which was to become its symbol. The second possible course of action was based on the idea of a battle of destruction – the symbol of which was 'Tannenberg' – and depended on the further development of revolutionary weapons. In future, these weapons would be able to produce rapid, conclusive victories in so-called 'lightning wars', before any mobilisation of the whole resources of one's own or an enemy nation.

Another ambiguity came to light at the end of the war and in the transition to the post-war period. Despite numerous declarations of intent, the conflict was not waged until total victory and the capitulation of the enemy. Though the imminent defeat of the Central Powers and their leading state of Germany was clear, the conflict had actually been ended when the Central Powers broke off the fight. The international situation had been transformed by the emergence of Bolshevik Russia, with its ideology of world revolution; the Soviet state was now regarded as highly dangerous to the social foundations of every bourgeois-capitalist state, particularly since communist agitation was apparent in all the belligerent nations. This new factor in international politics made it seem advisable for the Entente powers to accept the situation when the German Reich broke off the war. Generally hard but none the less moderate conditions were imposed, at least in comparison with the stated war aims of the powers, including those made by Tsarist Russia against Imperial Germany during the war.

For the rest, the emergence of Soviet Russia was easily the most momentous result of the First World War. Despite the intervention of the allies and the unfulfilled intentions of part of the German leadership, the Soviet state could not be eradicated. By its apparent ideological and socio-political challenge to all other states, Soviet Russia changed the system of states, the relationship of the other states with each other, in a fundamental way. Here, there is a clear analogy between 1815 and 1919–20. As the structure established at the Congress of Vienna can be fully understood only with reference to the danger which was believed to emanate from France as the 'stronghold' of revolution, so the new system of states of 1919–20 can be properly interpreted only by taking account of the social-revolutionary threat of Soviet Russia.

Russia was thus excluded from the European peace arrangements. To counter the ideological and social threat, the Soviet state was forced behind a 'cordon sanitaire' stretching from Finland through the Baltic states to Romania. At the heart of the 'cordon sanitaire' stood a re-established Poland, allowed to exist as an independent state for the first time in 125 years and extended at the expense of both Germany and Russia. The defeated German Reich was to be greatly weakened but not destroyed, at least partly because of the problem of Soviet Russia. However, Germany did not participate in the Paris peace negotiations either. These twin developments showed that a fundamentally different basis was to be established for the reorganisation of Europe in 1919–20 than had operated in the order established at Vienna in 1815 and maintained with limited revisions until the Congress of Berlin in 1878.

In particular, 1919–20 was not a general European peace. Instead it was a compromise between the United States of America, which had intervened in a European war for the first time, and Britain and France. It was a compromise based on the long-term isolation of Soviet Russia on the periphery of Europe and designed to achieve an equally durable weakening – though not destruction – of Germany. As a result, a highly unstable constellation was created. The 'imperialist' powers – to use Soviet terminology – subsequently tended to fall into two distinct groups: the victorious established powers, or 'haves', with a natural interest in the status quo; and the 'have not' powers which had been defeated or left unsatisfied by their share in the spoils of victory (Germany, Italy and Japan, the latter forced by the United States to abandon the positions it had gained in China between 1914 and 1918). The imperialist programmes of the 'have nots' were not fully developed until the world economic crisis, the most significant belated consequence of the First World War. This crisis destroyed the liberal world economic order, produced the breakdown of state finances and encouraged inflationary tendencies; despite British endeavours, the liberal pre-war economic system could not be maintained on a world-wide basis. In this situation, the imperialist programmes of the 'have nots' were very different from those dating from the era of classical imperialism before 1914. Expansion was no longer motivated by a surplus of capital, people and goods, as before. Instead, reaction to political depression, economic crisis and impoverishment (with the addition of some ideological elements) were its distinguishing features, as Theodor Schieder noted in a survey of the old and new imperialisms.[8]

For different and largely ideological reasons, the Soviet Union was as interested as the 'have not' powers in forcing alterations to the international order of 1919–20. The inability of the established great powers to manoeuvre freely and constructively in foreign policy during the world economic crisis shows just how unstable this order had become. A 'triangular' relationship between the 'established' powers, the 'have nots' and the Soviet Union, initially containing within it every conceivable combination of forces, was the feature of the complex international situation.

Even before the economic crisis began, the structure created in 1919–20 had changed. Most of the democratic parliamentary structures established under the impact of the ideas of President Wilson had collapsed, particularly in the new states of east and south-east Europe. During the 1920s and early 1930s, these gave way to authoritarian regimes. Domestic instability in the major and successor states had been intensified by the disappearance of constitutional monarchies there as a result of the war. World politics after 1919–20 was most affected, however, by the fact that the First World War had failed to produce an unequivocal result; the defeated states had not been forced to come to terms with the new situation and make a new beginning. Wilson's principle of self-determination was actually somewhat ambiguous and could be applied to a number of different objectives. In consequence, it became little more than a tool used to accelerate the 'revision' of the Paris peace settlement. In the early stages these attempts at revision were made by peaceful means. However, as soon as international conditions allowed and domestic and socio-psychological circumstances were favourable, they were also made with the use of military threats.

Pacifist sentiments had been encouraged by the enormous losses of men and materials during the First World War. Some of them persisted after 1918, but they soon proved an inadequate counterweight to opposing trends. Chief among these were the protestations of journalists and other writers of the national will to hold firm, the loyalty of millions of soldiers to the 'comradeship of the trenches', despite the huge casualty lists, and the emphasis on the exemplary nature of the soldiers' community as an alternative to the apparent chaos of post-war

8. Theodor Schieder, *Einsichten in die Geschichte. Essays*, Berlin, 1980, pp. 137–55.

democratic and parliamentary conditions. National myths were rapidly created. The 'German trauma' concerned the supposedly unconquered German army, forced to accept defeat because of the collapse of the home front.[9] By contrast, the myth of the victor emerged in France. This held that France had borne the main burden of defence for four years and had suffered the most casualties, only to be 'betrayed' politically by its allies, the United States and Britain. After 1918, moreover, German demographic superiority had continued and even increased. France seemed to have no choice but to shut itself off militarily, politically and psychologically behind an apparently invulnerable set of fortifications on the Maginot Line; then, it seemed, there could be no repeat of the German advance on Paris in 1914, whatever the Germans might do in the rest of Europe and despite the fact that Germany had not been adequately disarmed in 1919–20.

During the First World War there was a change in the moral judgement of war, particularly in western Europe. This change was linked with trends which had become apparent at the Hague peace conferences of 1899 and 1907. The moral dimension had a profound effect on the German attitude towards the peace treaty, on the irritations which resulted from it and , eventually, on the basic assessment of the war which prevailed even after 1945. From the point of view of international law, there was no doubting the right of sovereign states to declare and wage war as in previous centuries. However, awareness of the enormous casualties of 1914–18 greatly encouraged the demand for a moral condemnation of the power which had started the war – the 'aggressor', to use a new key word. In response to this clamour, a moral judgement was incorporated into the famous Article 231 of the Versailles Treaty and linked with reparations obligations. (In fact, the condemnation was not quite as unequivocal as the Germans believed when they reacted so furiously to the text of the draft peace treaty.) In the 'have not' nations, which began a second round of expansion through war, the discriminatory terminology of 'aggressors' and 'aggression' was drowned out by social Darwinist arguments (introduction of a 'co-prosperity sphere', creation of a 'mare nostro' empire, establishment of *Lebensraum*). Nevertheless, the terminology reflected a theme which was to play a key role in twentieth-century politics and propaganda and – after 1945 – in international law, as well.

It is simultaneously easy and difficult to assess the significance of the

9. Michael Salewski, 'Der Erste Weltkrieg – ein deutsches Trauma', *Revue Internationale d'Histoire Militaire*, 63, 1985, pp. 169–85.

First World War in the history of the twentieth century. Easy, because we know the subsequent course of developments, the mistaken decisions which led to the Second World War and, later, threatened a third which may well destroy humanity. Difficult, because in the 1920s it was much less easy to assess the different trends of the period and to recognise which would eventually be strong enough to prevail over other influences.

To summarise the previous arguments, a lasting impression must be that the war of 1914–18 failed to produce an unequivocal result which promised to endure. Instead, its conclusion permitted the nations of Europe to pursue a policy of 'as if'. With hindsight, it is obvious to us that Europe as a whole had lost the war. Its supreme position, unchallenged until 1914, had been threatened by the undeniable emergence of the United States and Japan as great powers in a new global order and by the undermining of the imperial position of the European powers. The colonial possessions of the European states were now to be challenged in three ways: by nationalist movements, initially strongest in India, the Arab world and China; by the world communist movement, which sought to link itself with the emancipation of colonial peoples; and, finally, by the American idea of the right of all peoples to self-determination, including those living under colonial rule. It was clear that a second great war between the European powers would cause the collapse of colonial empire. 'The world history of Europe', as Hans Freyer has called the colonial-imperial age, was visibly coming to an end.

The trend was delayed,   wever, by the separation of Soviet Russia from the heart of Europe oefore 1930 and by the withdrawal of the United States from political involvement in the continent in the 1920s, followed by its financial and economic withdrawal during the world economic crisis. These developments permitted the Europeans to continue with their 'as if' politics – that is, to behave as if the European powers still had only each other to reckon with, as in 1914. There was a positive side to this state of affairs. The League of Nations, which the United States and the Soviet Union did not join, offered some prospects for a restoration of Europe's role in the world. Success in this attempt remained within the bounds of possibility in the 1920s, when some positive steps were taken. But at the end of the decade, the world economic crisis made its catastrophic impact on world politics, and the 'have not' powers began their fateful changes in policy. Another major war became increasingly likely, since the foreign-policy paralysis of the established powers prevented an early response to the first endeavours of the 'have nots' to break the restrictions imposed on them in 1919–20. During the 1930s, the British then attempted to win over the 'have not' powers to a peaceful solution, by making concessions in the interest of an empire and commonwealth in danger of disintegration. These efforts, too, were unsuccessful. In Germany, the dynamic forces which had broken through in the First World War – and had been only temporarily suppressed in 1918 – became dominant once again, and in their most radical form.

Despite the severity of its defeat in 1918, Germany remained the strongest power in central Europe in economic – and potentially in military – terms. With hindsight, it seems obvious that the German state had the opportunity to regain the hegemonic position it had lost in the First World War. In some ways the events of 1919–20 actually made such a development more, not less, likely; the disintegration of the Habsburg monarchy and the creation of the anti-Soviet 'cordon sanitaire' in east-central and south-east Europe made it almost inevitable that an economically revived Germany would regain its leadership role as soon as the restrictions of the post-war era were lifted (which happened from the end of the 1920s). The gradualist path was finally rejected by Hitler, with his programme of a solo military effort to achieve world supremacy. The dictator's programme had some links with conditions in the east as they had existed in 1918, when Germany was *de facto* master over a defeated Russia; in it, racial and ideological elements were thus superimposed on the old power-political and economic considerations. Adoption of this programme meant the rejection of an alternative course which had remained open until the summer of 1939, involving European co-operation between Britian, France, Germany and Italy. This new 'concert of powers', adapted to the conditions of the twentieth century, would have been established on the basis of a defensive front against the perceived social-revolutionary threat of Soviet Russia.

Hitler chose the radical alternative. In pursuit of his goals, he was able to exploit the experiences of the First World War in technological and strategic matters. For a time the dictator succeeded where Imperial Germany had failed, in subjugating the whole European continent between Great Britain and the Soviet Union. In 1939 there was no repetition of the mass enthusiasm which had greeted the outbreak of war in 1914; the true nature of war was still too clear in the memory of the European nations. Nevertheless, a grim resolve was forged by the notion of *Volksgemeinschaft* (people's community), derived from the comradeship of the front line and intensified by the totalitarian elements of

Nazi rule. This determination developed after the 'lightning campaigns' were over and Germany was forced into a strategic defensive. It persisted even when the number of casualties – initially smaller than in 1914–18 – rose to many times the level of those incurred in the First World War, not least because of the mass exterminations in German-ruled Europe.

Only the intervention of the United States and the Soviet Union, the two states outside the inner-European circle which had become the leading world powers, finally forced the collapse of Hitler's continental empire. Unlike 1918, they also forced an irrevocable decision against the continuation of Germany's *Eigenweg*, its unique path through history between the capitalist West and the communist Soviet Union.

In 1945, the armies of the United States and the Soviet Union penetrated to the centre of Germany and Europe. Supported by their enormous resources and promoting rival socio-economic ideals, these two states embarked upon a period of dominance in the world. The role of Europe as an independent force, shaken in the First World War and maintained with difficulty in the inter-war years, was thereby ended.

Despite the enormous losses incurred, the First World War was predominantly a European conflict with only a temporary and limited military effect on the world outside. By contrast, in the Second World War the originally separate regional wars in Europe and East Asia grew into a genuine *world* war. And when the atom bombs were dropped on Hiroshima and Nagasaki, the ultimate intensification of the conflict had occurred not in Europe, but in the Far East. Yet even in 1939–45 the continents did not bear an equal share of suffering. To that extent, the term 'second world war' refers more to the tendency than to the reality. In a third world war between the only true victors of the second, even this restriction would no longer apply because of the range and power of modern nuclear missiles. For humanity there is only the hope of a lasting peace between the two powers, of the kind which was not achieved after the First World War and which must be based on a sober and rational understanding of the situation by the governments involved. Only in this way can the catastrophe begun in 1914, heightened for Europe and the world in the Second World War, finally be averted. Only then would the 'age of world wars' begun in 1914 be brought to an end.

Select Bibliography

Albertini, L., *The Origins of the War of 1914*, 3 vols, 1952–57, repr. Westport, CT, 1980

Balfour, M.L., *The Kaiser and his Times*, New York, 1972

Behnen, M., *Rüstung – Bündnis – Sicherheit. Dreibund und informeller Imperialismus 1900–1908*, Tübingen, 1985

Berghahn, V., *Der Tirpitz-Plan. Genesis und Verfall einer innenpolitischen Krisenstrategie unter Wilhelm II.*, Düsseldorf, 1971

——, *Germany and the Approach of War in 1914*, London, Basingstoke, 1973

——, *Rüstung und Machtpolitik. Zur Anatomie des 'Kalten Krieges' vor 1914*, Düsseldorf, 1973

Canis, K., *Bismarck und Waldersee. Die außenpolitischen Krisenerscheinungen und das Verhalten des Generalstabes 1882 bis 1890*, Berlin (GDR), 1980

Carlson, A.R., *German Foreign Policy, 1890–1914, and Colonial Policy to 1914: A Handbook and Annotated Bibliography*, Metuchen, NJ, 1970

Craig, G.A., 'The Historian and the Study of International Relations', *American Historical Review*, 88, 1983, pp. 1 ff.

Dehio, L., *Gleichgewicht oder Hegemonie. Betrachtungen über ein Grundproblem der neueren Staatengeschichte*, Krefeld, n.d. [1948]

Dülffer, J., *Regeln gegen den Krieg? Die Haager Friedenskonferenzen von 1899 und 1907 in der internationalen Politik*, Frankfurt a. M., Berlin, Vienna, 1981

Erdmann, K.D., Zechlin, E., *Politik und Geschichte. Europa 1914 – Krieg oder Frieden*, Kiel, 1985

Eyck, E., *Das persönliche Regiment Wilhelms II. Politische Geschichte des deutschen Kaiserreiches von 1890–1914*, Erlenbach, Zürich, 1948

Farrar, Jr, L.L., *Arrogance and Anxiety. The Ambivalence of German Power, 1848–1914*, Iowa City, 1981

Fiebig-von Hase, R., *Lateinamerika als Konfliktherd der deutsch-amerikanischen Beziehungen 1890–1903. Vom Beginn der Panamerikapolitik bis zur Venezuelakrise von 1902/03*, 2 vols, Göttingen, 1986

Fischer, F., *Germany's Aims in the First World War*, London, New York, 1967

——, *World Power or Decline: The Controversy over Germany's Aims in the First World War*, New York, London, 1974

——, *War of Illusions: German Policies from 1911 to 1914*, London, New York, 1975
——, *From Kaiserreich to Third Reich. Elements of Continuity in German History, 1871–1945*, London, Boston, Sydney, 1986
Förster, S., *Der doppelte Militarismus. Die deutsche Heeresrüstungspolitik zwischen Status-Quo-Sicherung und Aggression 1890–1913*, Stuttgart, 1985
Friedjung, H., *Das Zeitalter des Imperialismus 1884–1914*, 3 vols, Berlin, 1919–22
Geiss, I. (ed.), *Julikrise und Kriegsausbruch 1914. Eine Dokumentation*, 2 vols, Hanover, 1963–64
——, *German Foreign Policy 1871–1914*, London, Boston, 1976
——, *Das Deutsche Reich und die Vorgeschichte des Ersten Weltkriegs*, Munich, 1983
Gollwitzer, H., *Europe in the Age of Imperialism 1880–1914*, London, 1969
Gutsche, W., *Der gewollte Krieg: der deutsche Imperialismus und der I. Weltkrieg*, Cologne, 1984
——, *Monopole, Staat und Expansion vor 1914. Zum Funktionsmechanismus zwischen Industriemetropolen, Großbanken und Staatsorganen in der Außenpolitik des Deutschen Reiches 1897 bis Sommer 1914*, Berlin (GDR), 1986
——, 'Außenpolitische Ziele, Rüstungspolitik und Kriegsdisposition der deutschen Reichsleitung vor 1914', *Zeitschrift für Geschichtswissenschaft*, 36, 1988, pp. 963–77
Hale, O.J., *The Great Illusion 1900–1914*, New York, et al., 1971
Hallgarten, G.W.F., *Imperialismus vor 1914. Die soziologischen Grundlagen der Außenpolitik europäischer Großmächte vor dem Ersten Weltkrieg*, 2 vols, 2nd edn, Munich, 1963
——, 'War Bismarck ein Imperialist? Die Außenpolitik des Reichsgründers im Lichte der Gegenwart', *GWU*, 22, 1971, pp. 257 ff.
Hauser, O., *Deutschland und der englisch-russische Gegensatz 1900–1904*, Göttingen, 1958
Hildebrand, K., 'Imperialismus, Wettrüsten und Kriegsausbruch 1914. Zum Problem von Legitimität und Revolution im internationalen System', *Neue Politische Literatur*, 20, 1975, pp. 160–94, 339–64
——, 'Staatskunst oder Systemzwang? Die "Deutsche Frage" als Problem der Weltpolitik', *HZ*, 228, 1979, pp. 624–44
——, 'Zwischen Allianz und Antagonismus. Das Problem bilateraler Normalität in den britisch-deutschen Beziehungen des 19. Jahrhunderts (1870–1914)' in H. Dollinger, H. Gründer, A. Hanschmidt (eds), *Weltpolitik, Europagedanke, Regionalismus. Festschrift für Heinz Gollwitzer zum 65. Geburtstag am 30. Januar 1982*, Münster, 1982, pp. 305–31
——, 'Julikrise 1914: Das europäische Sicherheitsdilemma. Betrachtungen über den Ausbruch des Ersten Weltkrieges', *GWU*, 36, 1985, pp. 469–502
——, *Deutsche Außenpolitik 1871–1918*, Munich, 1989
Hillgruber, A., *Bismarcks Außenpolitik*, Freiburg, 1972
——, *Deutsche Großmacht- und Weltpolitik im 19. und 20. Jahrhundert*, Düsseldorf, 1977
——, *Deutschlands Rolle in der Vorgeschichte der beiden Weltkriege*, 2nd edn, Göttingen, 1979
——, *Die gescheiterte Großmacht. Eine Skizze des Deutschen Reiches 1871–1945*, Düsseldorf, 1980
——, *Die Zerstörung Europas. Beiträge zur Weltkriegsepoche 1914 bis 1945*, Frankfurt a. M., Berlin, 1988
Jarausch, Konrad H., 'The illusion of limited war. Chancellor Bethmann

Hollweg's calculated risk, July 1914', *Central European History*, 2, 1969, pp. 48–76

Jerussalimski, A.S., *Die Außenpolitik und die Diplomatie des deutschen Imperialismus Ende des 19. Jahrhunderts*, Berlin (GDR), 1954

Joll, J., *Europe since 1870. An International History*, London, 1973

——, 'Politicians and the Freedom to Choose. The Case of July 1914' in A. Ryan (ed.), *The Idea of Freedom. Essays in Honour of I. Berlin*, Oxford et al., 1979, pp. 99–114

——, *The Origins of the First World War*, London, New York, 1984

Kahler, M., 'Rumours of War: The 1914 Analogy', *Foreign Affairs*, 1979/80, pp. 374–96

Kantorowicz, H., *Der Geist der englischen Politik und das Gespenst der Einkreisung Deutschlands*, Berlin, 1929

Kennedy, P.M., *The Rise of the Anglo-German Antagonism 1860–1914*, London, 1980

Klein, F., *Deutschland von 1897/98 bis 1917.* (Deutschland in der Periode des Imperialismus bis zur Großen Sozialistischen Oktoberrevolution), 4th edn, Berlin (GDR), 1977

Koch, H.W. (ed.), *The Origins of the First World War. Great Power Rivalry and German War Aims*, London, 1972

Lahme, R., *Deutsche Außenpolitik 1890–1894. Von der Gleichgewichtspolitik Bismarcks zur Allianzstrategie Caprivis*, Göttingen, 1990

Lambi, I.N., *The Navy and the German Power Politics 1862–1914*, Boston, London, Sydney, 1984

Langer, W.L., *European Alliances and Alignments, 1871–1890*, 2nd edn, New York, 1962

——, *The Diplomacy of Imperialism, 1890–1902*, 2nd edn, New York, 1968

Langhorne, R., *The Collapse of the Concert of Europe: International Politics, 1890–1914*, London, Basingstoke, 1981

Lappenküper, U., *Die Mission Radowitz. Untersuchungen zur Rußlandpolitik Otto von Bismarcks 1871–1875*, Göttingen, 1990

Laqueur, W., Mosse, G.L. (eds), *Kriegsausbruch 1914*, 2nd edn, Munich, 1970

Lauren, P.G., 'Crisis Management: History and Theory in International Conflict', *The International History Review*, 1, 1979, pp. 542–56

Meinecke, F., *Geschichte des deutsch-englischen Bündnisproblems 1890–1901*, Munich, Berlin, 1927

Moses, J.A., *The War Aims of Imperial Germany: Professor Fritz Fischer and his Critics*, St Lucia, 1968

——, *The Politics of Illusion: The Fischer Controversy in German Historiography*, London, 1975

Mowat, C.L. (ed.), *The New Cambridge Modern History*, vol. 12: *The Shifting Balance of World Forces 1898–1945*, 2nd edn, Cambridge, 1968

Nichols, J.A., *Germany after Bismarck. The Caprivi Era 1890–1894*, Cambridge, MA, 1958

Oncken, E., *Panthersprung nach Agadir. Die deutsche Politik während der Zweiten Marokkokrise 1911*, Düsseldorf, 1981

Pogge von Strandmann, H., 'Germany and the Coming of War' in R.J.W. Evans, H. Pogge von Strandmann (eds), *The Coming of the First World War*, Oxford, 1988, pp. 87–123

Pommerin, R., *Der Kaiser und Amerika. Die USA in der Politik der Reichsleitung*

1890–1917, Cologne, Vienna, 1986

——, 'Seekabel und Nachrichtenbüros. Determinanten des Deutschlandbildes im Zeitalter des Imperialismus', *Vierteljahrsschrift für Sozial- und Wirtschaftsgeschichte*, 73, 1986, pp. 520–31

Rauh, M., 'Die 'deutsche Frage' vor 1914: Weltmachtstreben und Obrigkeitsstaat?' in J. Becker, A. Hillgruber (eds), *Die Deutsche Frage im 19. und 20. Jahrhundert*, Munich, 1983, pp. 109–66

Rauff, H., *Zwischen Machtpolitik und Imperialismus. Die deutsche Frankreichpolitik 1904–06*, Düsseldorf, 1976

Remak, J., *The Origins of World War I 1871–1914*, New York et al., 1967

Rich, N., *Friedrich von Holstein. Politics and Diplomacy in the Era of Bismarck and Wilhelm II*, 2 vols, Cambridge, 1965

Ritter, G., *Die Legende von der verschmähten englischen Freundschaft 1898/1901. Beleuchtet aus der neuen englischen Aktenveröffentlichung*, Freiburg, 1929

——, *Staatskunst und Kriegshandwerk. Das Problem des 'Militarismus' in Deutschland*, vols 2–4, [1890–1918], Munich, 1960–68

Schieder, T. (ed.), *Handbuch der europäischen Geschichte*, vol. 6: *Europa im Zeitalter der Nationalstaaten und der europäischen Weltpolitik bis zum Ersten Weltkrieg*, Stuttgart, 1968

——, *Staatensystem als Vormacht der Welt 1848–1918*, *Propyläen Geschichte Europas*, vol. 5, Frankfurt a. M., Berlin, Vienna, 1977

Schmidt. G., 'Der deutsch-englische Gegensatz im Zeitalter des Imperialismus' in H. Köhler (ed.), *Deutschland und der Westen. Vorträge und Diskussionsbeiträge des Symposions zu Ehren von Gordon A. Craig*, Berlin, 1984, pp. 59 ff.

——, *Der europäische Imperialismus*, Munich, 1985

Schöllgen, G., 'Richard von Kühlmann und das deutsch-englische Verhältnis 1912–1914. Bedeutung der Peripherie in der europäischen Vorkriegspolitik', *HZ*, 230, 1980, pp. 293–337

——, *Imperialismus und Gleichgewicht. Deutschland, England und die orientalische Frage 1871–1914*, Munich, 1984

——, 'Griff nach der Weltmacht? 25 Jahre Fischer-Kontroverse', *Historisches Jahrbuch*, 106, 1986, pp. 386–406

——, *Das Zeitalter des Imperialismus*, 2nd edn, Munich, 1990

Schottelius, H., Deist, W. (eds), *Marine und Marinepolitik im kaiserlichen Deutschland 1871–1914*, Düsseldorf, 1972

Schraepler, E., 'Die Forschung über den Ausbruch des Ersten Weltkrieges im Wandel des Geschichtsbildes 1919–1969', *GWU*, 23, 1972, pp. 321–38

Steinberg, J., *Yesterday's Deterrent. Tirpitz and the Birth of the German Battle Fleet*, London, 1965

Stern, F., *Bethmann Hollweg and the War. The Bounds of Responsibility*, in *idem*, *The Failure of Illiberalism. Essays on the Political Culture of Modern Germany*, Chicago, London, 1975, pp. 77–118

Stürmer, M. (ed.), *Das kaiserliche Deutschland. Politik und Gesellschaft 1870–1918*, [1970], Kronberg/Ts, 1977

——, *Das ruhelose Reich. Deutschland 1866–1918*, Berlin, 1983

——, *Die Reichsgründung. Deutscher Nationalstaat und europäisches Gleichgewicht im Zeitalter Bismarcks*, Munich, 1984

Taylor, A.J.P., *The Struggle for Mastery in Europe 1848–1918*, [1954], Oxford, 1971

Wehler, H.-U., *Bismarck und der Imperialismus*, Cologne, Berlin, 1969

Winzen, P., *Bülows Weltmachtkonzept. Untersuchungen zur Frühphase seiner Außenpolitik 1897–1901*, Boppard a. Rh., 1977

Wippich, R.-H., *Japan und die deutsche Fernostpolitik 1894–1898. Vom Ausbruch des
Chinesisch-Japanischen Krieges bis zur Besetzung der Kiautschou-Bucht. Ein Beitrag
zur Wilhelminischen Weltpolitik*, Wiesbaden, 1987

Wolter, H., *Bismarcks Außenpolitik 1871–1881. Außenpolitische Grundlinien von der
Reichsgründung bis zum Dreikaiserbündnis*, Berlin (GDR), 1983

Zechlin, E., *Krieg und Kriegsrisiko. Zur deutschen Politik im Ersten Weltkrieg.
Aufsätze*, Düsseldorf, 1979

About the Contributors

Fritz Fischer: born 1908; Professor emeritus of Modern History, University of Hamburg; D.Litt. h.c. Sussex; D.Litt. h.c. East Anglia; D.Litt. h.c. Oxford; Member, Kommission für die Geschichte des Parlamentarismus und der politischen Parteien, Bonn; Corresponding Member, British Academy, London; 1964–5 Member, The Institute for Advanced Study, Princeton; 1969–70 Visiting Professor, Oxford. Recent publications: *Griff nach der Weltmacht. Die Kriegszielpolitik des kaiserlichen Deutschland 1914/18* (3rd edn, 1964); special edition, Düsseldorf, 1967; reprint with a foreword by the author, Kronberg, 1977; *Weltmacht oder Niedergang. Deutschland im ersten Weltkrieg* (1965), 2nd edn, Frankfurt a. M., 1968; *Krieg der Illusionen. Die deutsche Politik von 1911 bis 1914* (1969), 2nd edn, Düsseldorf, 1970; reprint Kronberg, 1978; *Der Erste Weltkrieg und das deutsche Geschichtsbild. Beiträge zur Bewältigung eines historischen Tabus. Aufsätze und Vorträge aus drei Jahrzehnten*, Düsseldorf, 1977; *Bündnis der Eliten. Zur Kontinuität der Machtstrukturen in Deutschland 1871–1945* (1979), 2nd edn, Düsseldorf, 1985; *Juli 1914: Wir sind nicht hineingeschlittert. Das Staatsgeheimnis um die Riezler-Tagebücher. Eine Streitschrift*, Reinbek, 1983.

Imanuel Geiss: born 1931; Professor of Modern History, University of Bremen; 1965 Visiting Professor Oxford; 1969 Visiting Professor Tel Aviv; 1980–1 Visiting Professor Gdansk; 1983 Visiting Professor Brisbane; 1985–6 Visiting Professor Dickinson College, Carlisle, Pa; 1990 Visiting Professor Shanghai. Major publications: *July 1914*, London, 1967, New York, 1968; *The Pan-African Movement*, London, New York, 1974; *German Foreign Policy 1871–1914*, London, 1976; *Das Deutsche Reich und die Vorgeschichte des Ersten Weltkriegs*, Munich, 1983; *Das Deutsche Reich und der Erste Weltkrieg*, Munich, 1983; *Geschichte griffbereit*, 6 vols, Reinbek, 1979–83; *Geschichte im Überblick*, Reinbek, 1986; *Geschichte des Rassismus*, 2nd edn, Frankfurt a. M., 1989; *Der lange Weg in die Katastrophe. Vorgeschichte des Ersten Weltkriegs, 1815–1914*, Munich, 1990.

Willibald Gutsche: born 1926; Professor of Modern History, Central Institute of History, Academy of Sciences of the GDR, Berlin. Recent publications: *Aufstieg und Fall eines kaiserlichen Reichskanzlers. Theobald von Bethmann Hollweg*

183

1856–1921, Berlin (GDR), 1973; ed., *Herrschaftsmethoden des deutschen Imperialismus 1897/98 bis 1917*, Berlin (GDR), 1977; *Von Sarajevo nach Versailles* (in co-operation with Fritz Klein and Joachim Petzold), Berlin (GDR), 1985; *Sarajevo 1914*, Berlin (GDR), 1984; *Monopole, Staat und Expansion vor 1917. Zum Funktionsmechanismus zwischen Industriemonopolen, Großbanken und Staatsorganen in der Außenpolitik des Deutschen Reiches 1897 bis Sommer 1914*, Berlin (GDR), 1986; *Wilhelm II., der letzte deutsche Kaiser*, Berlin (GDR), 1990.

Klaus Hildebrand: born 1941; Professor of Modern History, University of Bonn; Member, Historische Kommission bei der Bayerischen Akademie der Wissenschaften, Munich; Member, Kommission für die Geschichte des Parlamentarismus und der politischen Parteien, Bonn. Recent publications (since 1980): *Deutsche Außenpolitik 1933–1945. Kalkül oder Dogma?*, 4th edn, Stuttgart et al., 1980; *Geschichte der Bundesrepublik Deutschland: Von Erhard zur Großen Koalition 1963–1969*, Stuttgart, Wiesbaden, 1984; *Das Dritte Reich*, 3rd edn, Munich, 1987; *Deutsche Außenpolitik 1871–1918*, Munich, 1989; *German Foreign Policy from Bismarck to Hitler: The Limits of Statecraft*, London, 1989; co-editor, *Internationale Beziehungen in der Weltwirtschaftskrise 1929–1933*, Munich, 1980; co-editor, *Deutschland und Frankreich 1936–1939*, Munich, 1981; co-editor, *Deutsche Frage und europäisches Gleichgewicht*, Cologne, Vienna, 1985.

Andreas Hillgruber (1925–1989): Professor of Modern History, University of Cologne; Member, Historische Kommission bei der Bayerischen Akademie der Wissenschaften, Munich; Member, Rheinisch-Westfälische Akademie der Wissenschaften, Düsseldorf. Recent publications: *Hitlers Strategie. Politik und Kriegführung 1940–1941*, 2nd edn, Munich, 1982; *Deutschlands Rolle in der Vorgeschichte der beiden Weltkriege*, 2nd edn, Düsseldorf, 1979; *Bismarcks Außenpolitik*, 2nd edn, Freiburg, 1981; *Deutsche Geschichte 1945–1982. Die 'deutsche Frage' in der Weltpolitik*, 5th edn, Stuttgart et al., 1984; *Die gescheiterte Großmacht. Eine Skizze des Deutschen Reiches 1871–1945*, 4th edn, Düsseldorf, 1984; *Der Zweite Weltkrieg 1939–1945. Kriegsziele und Strategie der großen Mächte*, 4th edn, Stuttgart et al., 1985; *Die Last der Nation. Fünf Beiträge über Deutschland und die Deutschen*, Düsseldorf, 1984; *Zweierlei Untergang. Die Zerschlagung des Deutschen Reiches und das Ende des europäischen Judentums*, Berlin, 1986; *Europa in der Weltpolitik der Nachkriegszeit 1945–1963*, 3rd edn, Munich, 1987; *Die Zerstörung Europas. Beiträge zur Weltkriegsepoche 1914 bis 1945*, Frankfurt a.M., Berlin, 1988.

Reiner Pommerin: born 1943; Professor of Modern History, University of Erlangen-Nuremberg; 1979–80 J.F. Kennedy Fellow, Harvard University. Recent publications: *Das Dritte Reich und Lateinamerika*, Düsseldorf, 1977; *Die Sterilisierung der Rheinlandbastarde. Das Schicksal einer farbigen deutschen Minderheit 1918–1937*, Düsseldorf, 1979; *Der Kaiser und Amerika. Die USA in der Politik der Reichsleitung 1890–1917*, Cologne, 1986; *Von Berlin nach Bonn. Die Alliierten, die Deutschen und die Hauptstadtfrage nach 1945*, Cologne, 1989; co-editor, *Deutsche Frage und europäisches Gleichgewicht*, Cologne, Vienna, 1985; co-editor, *Akten zur Auswärtigen Politik der Bundesrepublik Deutschland*, vols 1 and 2, Munich, 1989–90.

Gustav Schmidt: born 1938; Professor of International Politics, Ruhr-University Bochum; 1979–80 Visiting Professor Oxford; 1984 Visiting Professor Emory University; 1985–86 Visiting Professor University of Toronto. Recent publications: *England in der Krise. Grundzüge und Grundlagen der britischen Deutschlandpolitik (1930–1937)*, Wiesbaden, 1981; *Der europäische Imperialismus*, Munich, 1985; *The Politics and Economics of Appeasement. British Foreign Policy in the 1930s*, Leamington Spa, 1986; editor and contributor, *Konstellationen internationaler Politik 1924–1932*, Bochum, 1983; editor and contributor, *Großbritannien und Europa – Großbritannien in Europa. Sicherheitsbelange und Wirtschaftsfragen in der britischen Europapolitik nach dem Zweiten Weltkrieg*, Bochum, 1989.

Gregor Schöllgen: born 1952; Professor of Modern History, University of Erlangen-Nuremberg; 1987 Visiting Professor Columbia University, New York; 1988–9 Visiting Fellow St Antony's College, Oxford. Recent publications: *Handlungsfreiheit und Methodenzwang. Max Weber und die Tradition praktischer Philosophie*, Tübingen, 1984; *Imperialismus und Gleichgewicht. Deutschland, England und die orientalische Frage 1871–1914*, Munich, 1984; *Max Webers Anliegen. Rationalisierung als Forderung und Hypothek*, Darmstadt, 1985; *Das Zeitalter des Imperialismus*, 2nd edn, Munich, 1990; *Ulrich von Hassell 1881–1944. Ein Konservativer in der Opposition*, Munich, 1990.

Michael Stürmer: born 1938; Professor of Modern History, University of Erlangen-Nuremberg, now on long-term leave; since 1988 Director, Stiftung Wissenschaft und Politik, Ebenhausen; 1976–7 Research Fellow, Harvard University; 1977–8 Member, The Institute for Advanced Study, Princeton; 1982–3 and 1985–6 Professeur Associé de la Sorbonne; 1983–4 Visiting Professor, Centre for International Studies, University of Toronto; columnist *Frankfurter Allgemeine Zeitung, Wall Street Journal*. Recent publications: *Das ruhelose Reich. Deutschland 1866–1918*, Berlin, 1983; *Die Reichsgründung. Deutscher Nationalstaat und europäisches Gleichgewicht im Zeitalter Bismarcks*, Munich, 1984; *Dissonanzen des Fortschritts. Essays über Geschichte und Politik in Deutschland*, Munich, 1986; *Wägen und Wagen, Sal. Opp. jr. & Cie. Geschichte einer Bank und einer Familie* (with G. Teichmann and W. Treue), Munich, 1989.